# GLOBAL GUYANA

# Global Guyana

*Shaping Race, Gender, and*
*Environment in the*
*Caribbean and Beyond*

Oneka LaBennett

NEW YORK UNIVERSITY PRESS
New York

NEW YORK UNIVERSITY PRESS
New York www.nyupress.org

Please contact the Library of Congress for Cataloging-in-Publication data.

ISBN: 9781479826995 (hardback)
ISBN: 9781479827015 (paperback)
ISBN: 9781479827039 (library ebook)
ISBN: 9781479827022 (consumer ebook)

This book is printed on acid-free paper, and its binding materials are chosen for strength
and durability. We strive to use environmentally responsible suppliers and materials to the
greatest extent possible in publishing our books.

Manufactured in the United States of America

10 9 8 7 6 5 4 3 2 1

Also available as an ebook

# CONTENTS

# PREFACE

## A Pointer Broom Approach

This is a ole yard, okay? and this old woman is
sweeping, sweeping the sand of her yard away
from her house. Traditional early morning old
woman of Caribbean history. She's going on
like this every morning, sweeping this sand—of
all things!—away from . . . sand from sand,
seen? . . . And I say Now what's she doing?
What's this labour involve with? Why's
she labouring in this way? all this way?
all this time? Because I get the understandin
(g) that she somehow believes that if she don't
do this, the household ~ that 'poverty-stricken'
household of which she's a part—probably head
of ~ would somehow collapse
—Kamau Brathwaite, *ConVERSations with Nathanial
Mackey*

As I swept the floor in the early morning light, the dust
would just rise up and float twinkling out the windows. The
broom stroked every plank . . . sweep, sweep, sweep, stamp
the broom. Sweep, sweep, sweep, stamp, stamp. . . . The sssweep of the broom going slow, flicking at the end, before the
stamp. . . . Now all the dusty creeks joining the main river to
flow past the settee and down the steps into the dark depths
at the bottom of the front door.
—Oonya Kempadoo, *Buxton Spice*

Imagine that you are relaxing on a pristine white sand beach in Jamaica as you listen to an international chart-topping song by the Barbadian singer and global superstar, Rihanna. That Jamaica has world-renowned powdery beaches and that Rihanna has come to represent "the islands" in glossy tourist imaginings are probably not surprises to you, and if you are an outsider to the Caribbean, these facts are likely part of what attracted you to the region. If you left your hotel room early enough in the morning to secure a choice spot on the beach, you might notice broom strokes in the sand. Neat lines, etched from the dusty yard right outside your ocean-view room, all the way down to the sandy shore, left behind by a woman who had risen even earlier than you to prime the sand, creating those tidy symmetrical broom lines that make you feel as though no one has walked on this sand before you. However, had you stopped to ponder those broom strokes, you might have considered the flow from your doorstep, out to shore, and beyond, what the sweeper and the broom had cleared away—plastic straws, bottle caps, seaweed, and more sand—and what she had conjoined via those lines in the sand. If you learned that the sand on which you are reclining was most likely shipped in from Guyana and the Rihanna tune to which you are grooving is heavily influenced by the singer's Guyanese mother, you might experience a cognitive shift in terms of the way you understand your recreation on that beach.

This book makes the bold claim that we must put the small, easily overlooked South American nation of Guyana on the map if we hope to comprehend the global threat of environmental catastrophe as well as the pernicious forms of erasure that structure Caribbean women's lives. With no tourism to speak of, and previously ranked among the poorest countries in the hemisphere, Guyana is presently poised to become the world's largest oil producer per capita—offering a critical vantage point from which to parse the undercurrents of transnational race/gender formations and the extractive resources that fuel our modern world. Like ephemeral broom strokes in the morning sand, and like the tides that mimic the sweeping motion of a broom, the global flow of resources between Guyana and locations near and far coalesces people, places, and materials in ways that we do not usually consider. Interdisciplinary in its approach, this book traces the entwined histories of enslaved Africans and Indian indentured laborers, along with the contemporary crosscurrents of the Guyanese diaspora, and the broad reach of the nation's extractive industries, to reposition Guyana as constitutively interconnected with transnational gendered racializations. It explores distinct yet interrelated realms, including media representations, women's kinship ties, and the circulation of people and resources, in order to reimagine this understudied place as a cynosure that exposes the gendered and racialized nodes of global capitalism, while reshaping the geopolitics surrounding extractive industries and the very topography that has come to be emblematic of the Caribbean region—beaches and shorelines.

This book issues a call for a renewed historical and ethnographic engagement with Guyana, one that highlights the racialized and gendered dynamics of its underacknowledged global currents. It develops a powerful set of heuristics for unpacking the nation's and its people's place in the world. It does this in part by sweeping into view what I call a political economy of erasure, defined as a system for organizing and assessing interactions and exchanges that erases or obscures the interlinkages between local Guyanese social constructions and global racial capitalism. This political economy of erasure effaces Guyana in global discursive spaces and is intimately tied to the forms of ecological erosion entrenched in extractive industries.

The Bajan (Barbadian) poet Kamau Brathwaite's influential notion of *tidalectics*, which reimagines Hegel's "thesis-antithesis-synthesis" format of the dialectic as nonlinear, "like the movements of water backwards and as a kind of cyclic . . . motion," helps us to envision Guyana's global reach and flow (Mackey 1995, 14, quoted in Smyth 2014, 393).[1] *Tidalectics* "describes a nexus of historical process and landscape . . . which provides a defining image of the Caribbean and its origins" (Reckin 2003, 1). In the 1995 dialogue *ConVERSations with Nathaniel Mackey*, Brathwaite recounts that he had been writing poetry "since a born . . . on the beach in Barbados," but it is on a beach on the North Coast of Jamaica where he sees an image that provides an answer to the following question: "What is Caribbean/the Caribbean?" (Brathwaite 1999, 28–29). The answer comes in the form of an old woman sweeping sand, an image that serves as the embodiment of his theory of *tidalectics*. The old woman's sweeping seems futile ("sweeping this sand—of all things!—away from . . . sand").

So she's in fact performing a
very important ritual which I
couldn't fully understand but
which I'm tirelessly tryin to.
..
And then one morning I see her
body silhouetting against the
sparkling light that hits the
Caribbean at the early dawn
and it seems as if her feet,
which all along I thought were
walking on the sand . . . were
really . . . walking on the water . . . and she was tra
velling across that middlepass
age, constantly coming from wh
ere she had come from—in her
case Africa—to this spot in
North Coast Jamaica where she
now lives . . .
(Brathwaite 1999, 32–33)

It is only through the prism of the early dawn that Brathwaite is able to see the old woman as walking on water rather than sand. It is a visual clarification that permits the viewer to understand the woman and her labor as linked to the land and the sea, the present and the past, in ways that reposition her, not as stationary but as moving across continents and time. For Brathwaite, the Caribbean's origins as well as its present identity, including its politics and psychology, are not dialectical "but tidalectic, like our / grandmother's—our nanna's—action, like the movement of / the ocean she's walking on, coming from one continent / continuum, touching another, then receding ('reading') / from the island (s) into the perhaps creative chaos of th / e(ir) future" (Brathwaite 1999, 34). Brathwaite's metaphor of the old woman sweeping is germane to this book for multiple reasons. When he shifts from stating that he has been writing poetry all his life on the beach in Barbados to imparting the epiphany of witnessing the old woman on Jamaica's North Coast ("This is not the North Coast of the great hotels, James Bond, 'Golden Eye' and tourism"), Brathwaite emphasizes circum-Caribbean linkages—at once acknowledging but looking past the tourist gaze to imagine the back-and-forth movement that conjoins people and environment, land and water, in the region and beyond (Brathwaite 1999, 29). And even though Brathwaite writes about "islands" of the Caribbean when he articulates his notion of *tidalectics*, Guyana figures prominently in his life and work. His first wife, Doris Monica Brathwaite, the subject of his book *The Zea Mexican Diary*, was Guyanese, and his unique *videostyle* font (in which *ConVERSations* is written, a style that would be impossible to replicate here) was inspired by Guyanese Amerindian petroglyphs. For the purposes of this book, his concept of *tidalectics*, embodied in the old woman sweeping the sand (water), offers a springboard not only for underscoring circum-Caribbean exchanges and the cross-continental ebbs and flows of Guyana's reach but also for illustrating what a view-point attuned to women's lives and the natural resources within their social worlds tells us about the past, and forecasts for the future.

The pointer broom, or "pointa" broom, a handleless Guyanese yard broom traditionally homemade from the dried spines at the center of coconut leaves, then tied in a tight bundle with a small strip of cloth or twine, is an aggregating tool that generations of Guyanese girls and women have used to sweep up dust, sand, and debris in yards and Bottom Houses.[2] Those of us who have handled this broom know that over the course of days, weeks, and months, as the broom is continuously used, the dried spines truncate, rendering the tool shorter and shorter, and necessitating that the sweeper bend further and further down, getting closer and closer to the ground, and repeatedly stamping the top of the broom against a hard surface in order to realign the individual spines. In this sense, a worn broom requires more back-aching bending and additional stamping, but it can also enhance effectiveness, as the closer one bends to the ground while wielding a short broom, the more precise the sweeping. The numerous, pointy spines of the broom work in concert to extract small grains of debris while also—depending on whether the sweeper applies the broom vertically or in a horizontal swipe—operating to move larger mounds of dust and refuse. The Anglophone Caribbean saying "new broom sweep clean, but old broom know corna'" positions the broom as a metaphor for the value of experience and as a heuristic symbol for recovering the past. Also used in other parts of the Caribbean, and known as a coconut broom in Antigua, Barbados, and Trinidad, the pointer broom has origins in Asia. But, of course, brooms similar to the Guyanese pointer also hold symbolic value in African American and African traditions ranging from "jumping the broom" in the former to using brooms to "sweep away" political corruption in the latter. We can imagine the kinetic interplay between sweeper and broom as mirroring movements traceable to the African continent. The pointer broom, then, exemplifies how Guyana's material culture is inextricably connected to circum-Caribbean and global practices and processes.

Wielded in a sweeping motion, the pointer broom is an apt metaphor for this book's approach, which is both gendered labor and a historiography that susses out morsels of cultural knowledge and history that have long fallen into seemingly inaccessible cracks and crevices. In a manner akin to Brathwaite's, in her coming-of-age novel, *Buxton Spice*, the Guyanese writer Oonya Kempadoo imagines the sweep, sweep, stamp of a broom as an analogy for the ways women's daily lives are fused to the environment, to land, bodies of water, and global undulations far beyond homes and yards. While Brathwaite's sweeper is Black, and the "traditional early morning old woman of the Caribbean" who is "probably head of" her household, Kempadoo's sweeper, Lula, the narrator in *Buxton Spice*, is a young Indian girl of mixed racial ancestry, and decidedly not the head of her household. We know that Kempadoo's narrator is armed with the pointer broom because of the distinctive "sweep, sweep, sweep, stamp" method she applies. The two figures—one old, the other young—signify the ubiquity of the broom for Caribbean women and girls. Although Brathwaite ascribes a particular wisdom that comes with age to the old woman, Kempadoo imbues Lula with an ethnographic perspective—a remarkable ability to see and interpret that accompanies youth. And when Kempadoo emphasizes both the "ssssweep" and the stamp of the broom, she evokes tidal reverberations, with Lula's dust piles forming a river ("Now all the dusty creeks joining the main river to flow past the settee and down the steps into the dark depths at the bottom of the front door")—the very *tidalectics* that Brathwaite envisions as defining the Caribbean's place in the world.

Figure P.1. Aunt Gene's pointer brooms on the front porch of her house in Brooklyn, New York, 2022. Photo by the author.

This book's analytical and methodological approach echoes both Brathwaite and Kempadoo in employing the sweeping motion of the broom—the pointer broom more specifically—as an analogy that traces the global patterns of movement connecting Guyanese women to larger processes across diasporic space and time. It utilizes what I am calling a pointer broom analytic to collect discarded bits of cultural experience and social history that have been shoved into corners and swept under rugs. It sweeps what has been regarded as refuse, or not regarded at all, out into the light of the early dawn. The pointer broom approach positions Guyanese girls' and women's understandings of their own social worlds as uniquely efficacious for uncovering a more nuanced ethnographic engagement with Guyana. And the pointer broom is privileged here deliberately and in contrast to the tool that is most often taken up as a symbol of Caribbean plantation life—the cutlass. While the cutlass has been gendered as male, especially because of its dual function as a cane-cutting blade and as an implement of violence that Indian husbands brandished against their wives, the pointer broom is a woman's device that gathers rather than slashes.[3] It is an accumulating instrument that facilitates the recuperative work of assembling the disparate but related strains that conjoin global Guyana. The pointer broom analytic insists that a close-to-the-ground inquiry from Guyana's vantage point—one that utilizes varied techniques, collected together like the spines of a broom—will uncover dismissed and erased knowledge. This approach will help us disentangle the speculative but symbiotic relationship between Guyanese women's gendered labor and global racial capitalism. Just as the labor that preoccupies Brathwaite's old woman undergirds her household and spans continents, Caribbean women's sexual and reproductive labor sustained the plantation economy and continues to underpin global capitalism's extractivist processes and tourist fantasies. If, as a US State Department report on sex trafficking in Guyana notes, women and children are made victims of sex trafficking in the country's fast-growing extractive industries, then Guyana's global trade is intertwined with the most deplorable instances of gendered exploitation (US Department of State 2020, 236–37).

This book is reliant on my perspective as an anthropologist who was born in Guyana but who has lived most of my life in the United States. The chapters recenter Guyana from this positionality while sweeping together multiple contexts: Guyana's everywhereness and nowhereness in reductive representations that channel across American newspaper articles and popular television programs; an autoethnographic treatment of kinship and marriage in my own family charted from the late nineteenth century to the present day; anxieties over competition for scarce resources expressed in the Barbadian stereotype of the Guyanese woman as homewrecker set against the music and persona of Rihanna; and the persistent tropes of discovery dredged up around the extractive industries of sand and oil.

The introduction and the first two chapters unveil the forms of obliteration and effacement from mind or memory (I am drawing on the *Oxford English Dictionary* definition of "erase" here) that constitute a political economy of erasure. In this sense, a political economy of erasure operates as a calculus that situates families and individuals within colonial race/gender constructs to hide from view and memory Guyanese women's inter/cross-racial intimacies and complex gender subjectivities negotiated along the lines of kinship and marriage, and African and Indian femininities. Narratives that expunge, for example, how British colonial practices fomented ethnic conflict between Afro- and Indo-Guyanese, while assessing Guyanese social relations as defined by violent ethnic divisions and presenting the two groups as incompatible marriage partners, are components of the political economy of erasure.[4] But the book's examples recede and extend like the motion of the broom and the tides, expanding on this notion of a political economy of erasure to sweep into view a related process, *erosion*. The *Oxford English Dictionary* offers "to wear out; to eat out" and "to form by gradual wearing away" as definitions of the verb "erode." We can think about erosion both in a geological sense (as in waves eroding the sandy shores of a beach) and in the extractive sense (as in foreign companies eroding the seafloor as they drill for oil). Chapters 3 and 4 interrogate forms of erasure within popular and political narratives around gendered bodies and "ethnic conflict," while mapping the political economy of erasure vis-à-vis the ecological erosion brought about by extractive industries. Erasure and erosion go hand in hand with a contemporary neoliberal discursive apparatus that either ignores environmental devastation or places blame for it at the feet of the Guyanese government and its people. My pointer broom unsettles these processes of erasure and related forms of erosion across archives and temporalities via examples stemming from and through Guyana.

This book looks at and looks out from Guyana in consequential ways that recalibrate our summation of this nation and its place in the world. Gina Athena Ulysse's urgent call in *Why Haiti Needs New Narratives: A Post-Quake Chronicle* (2015) resonates deeply with the goals of this study. Like Ulysse, I "write back" to respond to the "damaging and restrictive" interpellation in popular understandings and international news media of an effaced but central corner of the Caribbean (Ulysse 2015, xxv). And my voice in this book is deliberately accessible; I write back not only so that fellow academics will read this text but in the hope that it translates beyond the academy and into popular consciousness.

# Introduction

*Everywhere and Nowhere: A Sweeping Vision of/from Guyana*

We can think of sand in today's world as perhaps the ultimate "everywhere and nowhere" material. The eyeglass lenses that may be assisting you in seeing these words on the screen or the printed page are most likely comprised of high-quality silica quartz, or white sand. If you are reading this book digitally, the screen you are looking at is made from sand. The university building in which you might be sitting, or the apartment building, or whatever structure you may be in, is likely made from sand—it is the primary material in concrete, glass, and asphalt. Therefore, sand resources are the foundational aggregates used to construct the road on which you traveled or will travel later today. Sand is the second-most exploited resource across the globe, behind water, and we are using it more quickly than it can be replenished (UNEP 2022). Desert sand, although plentiful, is unsuitable for construction, and our conceptualizations of deserts as vast and inhospitable to life do not account for fragile and dwindling sand ecologies (El-Hadi 2022). Grains of sand are small particles that, when combined as aggregates, form the key foundations of our modern world. But we usually only notice or recognize sand when it blankets our recreational spaces: beaches, shorelines, golf courses, sand boxes. Guyana is also small and often overlooked, but an essential player in terms of fueling modern life. And, as we will see, I am making this argument not only on the basis of extracted resources such as sand and oil but also in terms of global and regional constructions of race and gender, which are linked in more speculative ways to extractive industries.

The Caribbean woman in Kamau Brathwaite's influential notion of *tidalectics* sweeps sand away from sand on a beach in the light of the early dawn, embodying the poet's vision of the region as dependent on women's labor and linked to global processes across continents and time periods. When Brathwaite finally sees this woman as standing on water, rather than sand, the shift in perception affords him an ontological clarification. This book hopes to inspire a similar adjustment by looking anew at and from Guyana in order to alter our understandings of women, race, and resources in and beyond the Caribbean. This introductory chapter offers a sweeping vision of Guyana to demonstrate that this nation is, like sand, everywhere and nowhere in popular discourses. Like the subsequent chapters, it strokes through plain-as-day spaces and probes hidden corners, traversing regions, resources, temporalities, and representations, emulating the back-and-forth movement of the pointer broom and the flow of the tides. Here, in the introduction, I map out Guyana's everywhere- and nowhereness, an interpellation that places the country and its people in a paradoxical space in the cultural imaginary. I sweep together scattered yet connected grains—examples of how we can see Guyana everywhere and nowhere. With each stroke of the broom, I trace representations of the country: first in international press outlets such as the *New York Times*; then globally in sonic and televisual popular representations; then in academic treatments; and lastly from my own autoethnographic perspective.

## Why Guyana and Why Now?

If we are concerned with the economic, environmental, and social costs of fueling our cars and heating our homes, we need to pay attention to Guyana. Starting in 2015 and in the years since, it transformed from being consistently ranked one of the poorest nations in the hemisphere into becoming the world's fastest-growing economy due to ExxonMobil's discovery of a supergiant oilfield off its shores—one of the most valuable petroleum and natural gas findings in decades (Idrovo, Grant, and Yanoff 2022). The significance of Guyana's oil boom cannot be overstated. While that initial 2015 discovery in the country's Stabroek Block was valued at about $200 billion, the oil has kept flowing. Within seven years, ExxonMobil had made a string of additional discoveries, with the company indicating that it had found petroleum in new wells that raised Guyana's recoverable oil and gas potential to nearly eleven billion barrels—about a tenth of the world's conventional discoveries (Reuters 2022; Valle 2022). The amount of petroleum that stands to be recovered off Guyana's coast is unmatched across the globe; experts suggest it will replace Kuwait as the largest oil producer per capita (Idrovo, Grant, and Yanoff 2022). The country's transformation into an "oil hotspot" has garnered international attention from industry insiders and geopolitical observers. While Guyana's oil has made headlines, sand extraction in this country and elsewhere is causing dire environmental consequences but remains "the worldwide crisis that nobody has heard about" (Beiser 2017). As the site of both high-profile oil extraction and invisible sand mining, the nation is becoming a generative prism through which to radically reformulate the intersectional dynamics of capitalism and ecology in the Americas.

Although the country is now experiencing a dramatic reversal of economic fortunes, it has long held an incongruous global position. Guyana is a nation of approximately eight hundred thousand people, yet it has the world's highest proportion of its native-born population living abroad (Buchholz 2022). Its disproportionately large immigrant presence in the United States—Guyanese represent New York City's fifth-largest foreign-born and third-largest Caribbean-born group—is one measure of its outsized but understudied place in hemispheric American studies (New York City Department of Human Planning 2013). Within the country, the harsh lived realities that contribute to and stem from this massive outmigration surface in devastating statistics around brain drain (90 percent of Guyanese with postsecondary education live and work abroad), poverty (nearly unmatched in the hemisphere, with almost four in ten people living in poverty), suicide (it has one of the world's highest suicide rates), alcoholism, sex trafficking, and domestic violence (one study found that more than one in two women experienced some form of intimate partner violence).[1] These extraordinary statistics underscore the ways in which Guyana is central to understanding the primary challenges the Caribbean faces as a region, and Caribbean immigrants experience abroad.

Across these troubling distinctions around poverty, sex trafficking, and domestic violence, Guyanese women endure intersectional forms of economic inequality and gendered brutality. In New York's Guyanese immigrant community, women are disproportionately represented, outnumbering men at a ratio of one hundred to seventy-nine. Their larger numbers in New York are an apt indicator of their presence across the global Guyanese diaspora in which women are at once central and invisible: if we look closely, we see them as leaders in artistic production, entrepreneurship, and activism, and we witness their objectification across popular registers. This book maintains that the Guyanese woman has long embodied her nation's struggle for reconciling the interplay of race, ethnicity, gender, and resource extraction. Still, although Guyana itself is beginning to emerge as more than a blip on the radar of international geopolitical concerns, Guyanese women remain "the Other of the Other" (Wallace 2008), marginalized at home, exoticized within the region, and rendered nearly invisible beyond.[2]

Guyana is an outlier in several regards. Although culturally Caribbean, it is not an island, and it lacks the tourism industry that draws visitors to other parts of the region. It is the only country in South America whose official language is English—it borders Hispanophone Venezuela to its west, Lusophone Brazil to its south, and polyglot Suriname to its east, with close proximity to Francophone French Guiana—a geographic and linguistic singularity that positions it within but outside the Caribbean, while simultaneously placing it within but outside Latin America.[3] Its land mass is large in comparison to that of other Caribbean nations, but it is among the smallest countries in South America. And Guyana is unique among Caribbean nations demographically because it has greater numbers of South Asians than descendants of Africans, with Indians comprising its largest ethnic group. With a social landscape historically shaped around the dispossession of its Indigenous peoples, the enslavement of Africans, and the indenture of Indians, race and ethnicity have been vexed in Guyana since the dawn of the colonial period.

In the contemporary era, what little global profile the nation held before the oil discovery was usually situated around its identity as the site of the mass murder of Americans in Jim Jones's cult, often misnamed as the world's largest "mass suicide," and the origin of the expression "drinking the Kool-Aid." And although Jones and his followers were Americans, Guyana's corrupt government and remote jungles arguably facilitated the cult leader's mission to isolate and control his devotees. State corruption and ethnically divided politics have characterized Guyana's political structure since it achieved independence from the British in 1966—at that time, the country's leaders changed its name from British Guiana to Guyana.[4] Routine, large-scale election fraud perpetrated by ruthless dictator Linden Forbes Burnham pegged the country as a violent state that stifles democracy and fosters deep-seated ethnic conflicts that date back to the colonial era and continue to shape the nation today. However, Guyana's struggle for independence was marked both by an early multiethnic political coalition between Burnham, an Afro-Guyanese, and the Indo-Guyanese leader, Cheddi Jagan, and by US and British meddling that stoked ethnic divides set in place during British colonial rule and ensured Burnham's ascendence in 1964.[5]

## A Political Economy of Erasure

The distinctions outlined in the previous paragraphs have been filtered through popular, academic, and geopolitical rhetoric to either leave Guyana out of the picture in global imaginings of the Caribbean and Latin America or obscure its complex connections to the region and the world. Many published maps of the Caribbean simply end at the northern tip of South America—leaving Guyana "off the map." The pointer broom approach enables us to sweep into the light what has been erased or obfuscated: hidden dust particles of intimate relationships and small, regional, migratory ripples alongside larger global currents of resources moving in and through Guyana. This approach makes visible the correlations between circum-Caribbean and transnational understandings of people (women in particular) and resource extraction. In so doing, it can be related to Lisa Lowe's highly influential study, *The Intimacies of Four Continents*, which conceptualized intimacy beyond its conventional definition as pertaining to closeness in terms of family, friendship, and sexual partners. Instead, Lowe regards the concept "in relation to 'residual' and 'emergent' ways of construing the sense of intimacy as 'close connexion,' that is, the implied but less visible forms of alliance, affinity, and society among variously colonized peoples beyond the metropolitan national center" (Lowe 2015, 19).

Lowe theorizes the residual elements of such forms of intimacy as continuing to resonate across archives and continents, and as carrying over into the present day: "In this sense, we might consider the political, sexual, and intellectual connections and relations among slaves, peoples of indigenous descent, and colonized laborers as an emergent 'intimacies of four continents' forged out of residual processes, whose presence is often eclipsed by the more dominant Anglo-American histories of liberal subjectivity, domesticity, and household" (Lowe 2015, 19–20). While I underscore the value of complicating the definition of intimacy in order to consider it beyond the confines of individuals, families, and friendships, the pointer broom approach builds on what Lowe identifies as a "political economy of intimacies" (Lowe 2015, 18) to advance what I have termed a "political economy of erasure" calculated around gender, race, and resources. Political economy is evoked in this sense as a system of linkages and a calculus that governs global geopolitical understandings of Guyana, while also managing the stakes for racialized and gendered social constructions at the level of individuals and families.

## Everywhere

If you are always looking for Guyana, as I am, you will see it everywhere and nowhere. Even amid the massive emigration that results in a disproportionately large presence of Guyanese in America's largest city and the newfound attention stemming from ExxonMobil's oil discovery, Guyana is represented as a hinterland in global news coverage, in which analysts doubt its chances for successfully managing oil wealth. When the country surfaces in international media outlets, it suffers from reductive portrayals that distort its outlier status—its unique geographic, cultural, and linguistic situatedness—as backwardness. Considering the significant Guyanese immigrant presence in the United States, the country and its people have been inaptly disregarded in international popular and political discourses. For decades, Guyana was nowhere in American academic discussions of the Caribbean. More recently, it is everywhere—in global economic news stories fixated on the massive ExxonMobil oil discovery.

With "a cottage industry" of international newspaper articles now sharply focused on Guyanese oil, the political conflict surrounding its 2020 national election made headlines in the *New York Times*, in the *Washington Post*, and in news outlets across the globe, with some analysts even comparing the contentious 2020 US presidential contest to Guyana's recent electoral debacle (Calder 2020). The overlaps were obvious: an incumbent who lost at the polls but insisted for months that the election was rigged, a country roiled by racial conflict, and a corrupt state increasingly at odds with the international community. The difference, however, was that while this political predicament was seen as an anomaly in American democracy, reporters deemed it a pathological trait of Guyana's sociopolitical infrastructure. The fact that almost all of these articles begin by literally situating the former British colony—telling readers that it is a small country on the northern tip of South America that is culturally Caribbean and ethnically diverse—alerts us to the reality that most American audiences have no basic knowledge of the country. And, overwhelmingly, geopolitical analyses of Guyana's oil boom have represented the nation and its people as isolated, backwards, uncivilized, and ill equipped to capitalize on its newfound wealth, reproducing old colonial tropes about primitivity within a locale that has long been at the center of modern processes of capitalist extraction.

Take, for example, a front-page *New York Times* article from July of 2018, now infamous among a small but vocal group of US-based scholars focused on Guyana and among Guyanese commentators across various social media platforms. The article began with a broad description of the country before turning to an assessment of its prospects for managing oil riches: "GEORGETOWN, Guyana—Guyana is a vast, watery wilderness with only three paved highways. There are a few dirt roads between villages that sit on stilts along rivers snaking through the rain forest. Children in remote areas go to school in dugout canoes, and play naked in the muggy heat" (Krauss 2018a). The article's marred description of Guyana and its people was pointedly critiqued in academic circles (Jobson 2019; Ali 2020) and panned on Twitter.[6] The piece does not stop at framing the nation's landscape and its children as equally untamed. It also takes aim at Guyana's workers, who are represented as daft and unsophisticated, a liability for its burgeoning oil industry: "Local oil executives say one obstacle to overcome is a lackadaisical attitude toward safety among Guyanese workers, who frequently arrive at their construction and wharf jobs in flip-flops and sometimes use their hard hats as soup bowls" (Krauss 2018a). It seems that Guyanese of all ages are inappropriately outfitted. The emphasis on their vestiary lapses serves the author's revanchist mission to at once infantilize the postcolony and underscore the implausibility of a Cinderella story emerging from the boondocks.

Nowhere are international news stories about the oil boom that tackle the worldliness and cultural reach of the Guyanese. These articles mark both a shift towards increased coverage of Guyanese and an eclipsing of centuries-old transnational connections that reveal Guyana as anything but an isolated backwater. Whereas Clifford Krauss, the author of the *Times* piece quoted above, presented a disparaging portrayal of Guyanese workers, sixteen years earlier, the same paper had framed New York's Indo-Guyanese immigrants as model minorities (Kershaw 2002). In that earlier moment, the *Times* covered the efforts of Schenectady, New York's Republican mayor, Albert P. Jurczynski, who—after a small group of Guyanese relocated from New York City to his postindustrial city in eastern New York—became convinced that they were the town's greatest hope for revitalizing its struggling economy. The mayor began busing Guyanese immigrants from Queens, Brooklyn, and the Bronx up to tour Schenectady, where he wooed them with ice cream and the promise of building a cricket stadium (Kershaw 2002). With the Guyanese who relocated to Schenectady buying and fixing up dilapidated homes, "making plans for restaurants and shops, and taking jobs as construction workers and nurses' aides," the mayor's plan panned out (Kershaw 2002). By 2003 Schenectady was hosting an annual Guyana Day festival, and by 2018 a subsequent mayor was touting the immigrants' positive impact on the city (Parisi 2018).[7]

## Guyana in Global Popular Culture

While the Schenectady politicians' portrayals of Guyanese are steeped in the model-minority myth, the Guyanese enclave created in that city was, of course, not unique. There have long been Guyanese communities in global cities like Toronto, London, and New York, where the tastes and sounds of Guyanese food and music have brought the comforts of home to members of the diaspora. In the early 1980s, Eddy Grant, a Guyanese-British singer-songwriter, popularized Brixton's main thoroughfare, then the center of London's Caribbean immigrant community, with the eponymous song "Electric Avenue." As a scrappy thirteen-year-old girl traversing Brooklyn's Flatbush Avenue, I sang along with Grant, possessing an intuitive recognition of his Guyanese creole–inflected voice—the way he belted "we gonna rock down to Electric Avenue," enunciating the word "down" to sound more like "dung"—even if, at the time, I did not fully grasp his "now in the street there is violence" reference. Both an anthem for the 1981 Brixton Uprising (a boiling point when London's Black community took over the streets as they protested entrenched police brutality and social and economic disenfranchisement) and an indictment of Thatcherism, the international hit was recorded in Barbados and can be interpreted as an indicator of the stereophonic routes across which Guyanese traveled as shapers of Black Atlantic popular culture (Gilroy 1993)—from Guyana, where Grant was born, to London's Caribbean community, and then to Barbados, where he retreated in the wake of the racist policing that sparked the Brixton Uprising. Of course, when Guyana was British Guiana, Guyanese were among the Caribbean immigrants Great Britain invited to bolster its economy after World War II, and they are among the ranks of the Windrush generation, who, after living in the UK for decades, were unjustly identified as illegal immigrants.[8]

With "Electric Avenue" topping the charts as one of the biggest hits of 1983, Grant's voice seemed to be everywhere . . . until it was nowhere. He lost the Grammy Award for Best R&B song that year to Michael Jackson's "Billie Jean," and although he enjoyed some success by introducing a new genre—ringbang—to the Caribbean festival circuit, in terms of global superstardom, Grant faded into obscurity.[9] And his identity as a Guyanese did little to elevate his homeland on the world stage. Still, Guyanese continued to flock to metropoles like London in astonishingly large numbers. While Brixton and neighborhoods like it catered to Caribbean immigrants, creating spaces in which Guyanese culture was dwarfed against higher-profile contributions from Greater Antilles nations such as Jamaica, more recently urban foodie culture, stoked by gentrification in and around these enclaves, has diffused Guyanese cuisine to the online reviews and Instagram postings that fuel global food trends. From the stretch of Guyanese restaurants around Morningside, Finch, and Sheppard Avenues in Scarborough, Ontario, to Liberty Avenue's "Little Guyana" in Queens, New York, Guyanese cuisine now garners write-ups in *Toronto Life* and in the travel section of the *Washington Post* (Aksich 2019; Cavanaugh 2014).[10]

The contemporary global profile of Guyana and Guyanese has not been confined to music and food. I took note, along with other members of the diaspora, when not one but two Guyanese actresses appeared in major roles in the international blockbuster *Black Panther*. The film opened to sold-out showings in Guyana's Giftland Mall, where members of the African Cultural and Development Association turned out with "beating drums, elaborate gele (headwrap) and very colourful Afro-centric prints," declaring, "#yesweareextra" and claiming citizenship in Wakanda with tongue-in-cheek humor (*Stabroek News* 2018).[11] Wakanda, the fictional, technologically advanced African country in which the film is set, became a symbol of pan-African unity, and the Guyanese actors joined an international cast that included performers with ties to the United States, Mexico, Kenya, Trinidad, South Africa, Zimbabwe, and Uganda.[12] While Letitia Wright, who was born in Guyana and raised in England, and Shaunette Renée Wilson, also Guyana born but raised in Brooklyn, sparked pride back home and across the diaspora for starring in *Black Panther*, Guyana itself did not figure into that movie.[13] Wright went on to reprise her role as Shuri and don the Black Panther suit in the sequel, *Black Panther: Wakanda Forever*.

Guyanese homed in on these portrayals and on other, more overt representations of the country and its people. To my great surprise, at the start of the second decade of the twenty-first century, I saw Guyana and/or Guyanese, both fictitious and actual, featured on Netflix, HBO, and National Geographic. Netflix foregrounded Nadia Jagessar, an Indo-Guyanese woman, in the popular reality series *Indian Matchmaking*. Meanwhile, National Geographic's *Gordon Ramsay: Uncharted* and HBO's *Lovecraft Country* depicted Indigenous Guyanese. While female and gender-nonconforming Guyanese figure prominently in *Indian Matchmaking* and *Lovecraft Country*'s "History of Violence" episode, Indigenous Guyanese take center stage in the latter and in *Uncharted*, where they are equated with the country's natural resources. That these mediated inflection points occurred in the span of a few months and in such high-profile vehicles is noteworthy when we consider that for so long Guyana has rarely figured into Western popular consciousness.[14] I hasten to add, however, that while members of the Guyanese diaspora may take pride in witnessing the presence of fellow Guyanese within these popular-cultural spaces, my intentions here are neither to stoke nor to espouse Guyanese nationalism. Rather, I contemplate how each of these programs sketches Guyana and Guyanese as entry points into some of the centuries-old ideas about my homeland that are resurfacing with increasing frequency in twenty-first-century globalized images.

Yet, even as we sweep together the escalating protagonism of Guyanese in the televisual examples I discuss here, I am struck by the notion that Guyana may be *arriving* on the global economic stage, but Guyanese are still nowhere close to being *seen*. In all of these renditions, Guyana is everywhere and nowhere.

Even a quick gloss of Guyana's presence in contemporary global televisual representations must consider the portrayal of a Guyanese woman depicted on Netflix's *Indian Matchmaking*. The "cringe-worthy" program proved to be a huge international hit for the streaming platform, topping the charts in India and enjoying immense popularity in the United States, as audiences everywhere hunkered down in their homes in the collective attempt to curb the spread of COVID-19 (*BBC* 2020). Nadia Jagessar, an Indo-Guyanese, New Jersey–based event planner, was a fan favorite with viewers in the New York tristate area. Jagessar, the program's only representative of the Indian diaspora in Guyana, was immediately cast as an outlier whose Guyanese identity undermined her chances for connecting with an Indian suitor. Sima Taparia, the program's celebrated matchmaker, having trumpeted her adeptness at bringing countless couples together, agonizes that although "Nadia is beautiful and she has very good family values and is very good natured, she is Guyanese," and therefore, "it will be difficult for me to match her with a traditional Indian boy." The program attributes Nadia's failure to attract a suitable husband to her vices (she orders alcohol on a date, turning off a young man of Guyanese and Punjabi ancestry), and her social frivolity/independent nature (her mother wonders if the years she spent practicing Bollywood dancing distracted her from pursuing a partner).

Although the show highlights legitimate tensions between Indo-Guyanese and Indians from the subcontinent with regard to authenticity, it also transplants onto Nadia colonial-era stereotypes of the Indian indentured women who journeyed to Guyana, tropes that framed these women as dangerously independent, lacking in respectability, and headstrong in comparison to their "more respectable" Indian counterparts. These negative stereotypes pigeonholed indentured women across two continents—in India as they boarded ships to Guiana, they were, by virtue of their castes, their unmarried status, and the regions from which they came, stigmatized as sex workers, troublemakers, and rebellious women. These pernicious brands followed them to Guiana, even though, contradictorily, in the colony they were cast as more subservient than Africans. Nadia is the program's stand-in for Indo-Guyanese femininity, and although the matchmaker insists that "caste was not a problem for anybody," Nadia's failed matches reveal that she is, at best, a misfit. In the first chapter of this book, I utilize archival documents to unpack these tropes and consider how race and gender factor into the historical undercurrents of Guyanese women's precarious intimate partnerships.

On the critically acclaimed Afro-futuristic/horror drama, *Lovecraft Country*, an episode entitled "A History of Violence" portrays Yahima, an Indigenous Guyanese intersex character who is ogled in a full frontal nude shot while an African American man yells, "What are you?"[15] The same Black man slits Yahima's throat a few scenes later.[16] Between being reanimated from a mummified state in a crypt filled with the artifacts a White male explorer had pillaged from Guiana in the early 1800s, and swiftly meeting another dramatic demise at the blade of a knife, Yahima briefly speaks in Arawak as Tic, the show's African American male protagonist, translates. We are tempted to ask, "Can the subaltern shriek?" when Yahima's spatial shift from the subterranean crypt causes them to let out an ear-piercing scream, prompting Tic to silence them with a punch to the face.[17] First muted with a sock to the jaw and then murdered with a slit of the throat, the Indigenous Guyanese character meets an end that sparked criticism from commentators who denounced the well-worn images of trans or intersex characters meeting violent ends in cinematic representations, a tragic mirroring of their too-frequent fate in real life. The particular significance of Yahima saying they are "from the Land of Many Waters," as Guyana is known, landed with members of the diaspora who remarked on this shout-out on Twitter, even as online reviewers bemoaned the troubling depiction the episode offered (Brown 2020; Bethea 2020). But we come away learning that before the White explorer murdered Yahima, he had annihilated all of their people. Yahima, now twice murdered, was the last of their kind, the ghost of a now nonexistent Indigenous Guyanese past. The haunting portrayal speaks to Michel-Rolph Trouillot's analysis of how power operates to silence the past in the historical production of the postcolony (Trouillot 1995). It also resonates with anthropologist Shanya Cordis's work, which links anti-Black and anti-Indigenous gendered violence in Guyana as "tandem processes of antiblackness and dispossession" (Cordis 2019, 19).

## The Middle of Nowhere

If Guyanese are out of place in *Indian Matchmaking*, and obliterated in *Lovecraft Country*, they are exotic and hard to reach in *Gordon Ramsay: Uncharted*. In a 2020 episode of the National Geographic reality/adventure series, billed as "anthropology-through-cuisine expeditions," the British celebrity chef Gordon Ramsay journeys to my homeland. Guyana's first people, its café au lait–colored rivers, and the "threat" of dangerous but tasty piranhas are featured prominently as Ramsay treks across the country, describing it as among "the most incredible and remote locations on Earth."[18]

The episode entitled "Guyana's Wild Jungles" opens in Georgetown with a rapid-fire overview in which, echoing Krauss's *New York Times* article, Ramsay informs us that the country is made up of "thousands of miles of untamed rivers and dense rainforests," as we see a map of South America with Guyana's location highlighted. Even though cars and minivans abound in the next shot of bustling Stabroek Market, inexplicably, Ramsay rides in the back of a horse-drawn cart. From this perch, he tells us that Guyana "boasts an exciting fusion of Caribbean, Indian, and European cultures." The horse-drawn cart and reference to European cultures situate the Scottish-born chef who was raised in England as a colonial pioneer. Concomitantly, the characterization of Guyana's cultural fusion erases the country's connection to slavery because it negates its Black population, replacing "African" with "Caribbean." Why are "European cultures" named, but the nation's second-largest ethnic group, the descendants of enslaved Africans, effaced from the get-go? Even though Ramsay's local host, a remigrated Guyanese, appears to be of African descent, the program misses the boat from the outset by glossing Guyana as "Caribbean, Indian, and European." Afro-Guyanese are also erased in *Lovecraft Country* and in *Indian Matchmaking*. In *Uncharted*, the negation of Guyana's Black population assuages the chef's embodiment of the colonial era, even as, like so many European men before him, he embarks on a discovery mission in Guyana.

The ensuing depiction presents Guyana as a dense, savage frontier, brimming with an exotic but treacherous food culture. We quickly learn that cassava, a root vegetable and a Guyanese staple, in its bitter form can contain lethal cyanide. Ramsay samples pepper pot, a meat stew of

Amerindian origin, made in this instance with capybara—a large rodent known in Guyana as "*labba*." The program does not disclose that eating *labba* is no more unreasonable than eating rabbit, a common ingredient in European cuisine, with Ramsay enquiring, "Are you saying it's a rat?" The message is clear—Guyana's culinary ingredients run the gamut from life-threatening to extremely off-putting. Ramsay doubles down when his host gestures to the pepper pot they are eating and says, "This is our pride and joy right here"—to which the British chef asks incredulously, "A rat?" His host has to correct him. "No, not the rat, the pepper pot." Pepper pot is typically prepared with more readily available meats such as beef and pork, but country folk (the people from whom I came) will say, "Eat *labba* and drink creek water and you'll always return to Guyana."

Brief in duration, Ramsay's introduction to Georgetown ushers in the remainder of the episode, which takes place far from the capital city. The explorer sets out to uncover the origins of Guyanese cooking by visiting Rewa, an Amerindian village deep in the jungle. Ramsay alerts us that roads are "nonexistent" in Rewa. En route by plane, the culinary discoverer takes in a bird's eye view, remarking, "It definitely feels so uncharted. I haven't seen a house, a building, nothing!" Ostensibly to shorten a journey that would have followed the plane trip with a jeep and boat ride, Ramsay next opts to board a helicopter from which he "channels his inner Tarzan" and repels down to a beach to meet an Amerindian fishing guide. If the viewer has not already surmised that Guyana is wild and isolated, and that Ramsay is a White frontiersman bent on "conquering" the ways of the jungle, this scene drives the point home. The rest of the episode has the adventurer, under the tutelage of his Amerindian guide, catching, cooking, and eating piranhas, tarantulas, and caimans as he remarks, "It's like a jungle vending machine." Even though the episode ends with Ramsay in a position of staged deference as he prepares a meal of locally sourced ingredients for a chief of the Macushi Amerindian tribe and his family, the program's message reifies colonial tropes of discovery, replete with a frightened but intrepid outsider eager to exploit Guyana's bounty of natural resources.

Ramsay's proclaimed mission to unearth the roots of Guyanese cuisine as he celebrates the richness of Amerindian culture is a worthy goal when we consider the ways in which Guyana's Indigenous population is typically overlooked. But by literally stepping over the coastal region where the nation's vibrant, interethnic food culture thrives, he promotes a notion of Guyana as little more than rainforest and menacing, if tasty, eats, while casting Amerindians as quintessential exotic others and skilled jungle dwellers. In fact, Guyana's rainforests are increasingly threatened by deforestation, and Rewa village is the site of an eco-lodge, part of the community's strategy to rework its traditional mores centered on animal poaching to instead prioritize ecological conservation and tourism as alternative forms of livelihood. And although the actual Amerindian people in *Uncharted* do not meet the ghastly fate that befalls Indigenous Guyanese characters in *Lovecraft Country*, Ramsay's Guyana episode channels in the very tropes of erasure and exoticism we saw in the HBO program.

"I'm in the middle of nowhere," Gordon Ramsay proclaims as "Guyana's Wild Jungles" comes to a close. "I've got a boat, a helicopter, and three planes to catch before I head off to my next adventure," he adds. As the credits roll and Ramsay departs, a notation on the screen asseverates that emissions from the program "are balanced by investments in projects that benefit wildlife, air quality and local economies." Just as the program's mixed messages position Ramsay as both humble student and exploiter of the "jungle vending machine," this acknowledgment underscores the show's gross environmental footprint juxtaposed with its deference for "untouched" Amerindian life ways. Here, the erasure of modern life in Guyana comingles with the erosion of the environment. Interrogating the contradictory assertion of this emissions disclaimer amounts to taking a pointer broom to the program's unsightly corners— revealing environmental devastation and racial capitalism as twinned processes that reverberate through the political economy of erasure.

In the troubling treatment spotlighted in *Lovecraft Country*, themes of discovery abound, with African American characters rediscovering the Guyanese treasure and human remains a White male explorer hauled away in the nineteenth century. Modern-day explorer Ramsay picks up those very motifs in "real life" in *Uncharted*. These depictions share similarities with the way Africa and the Americas were limned in colonial narratives and the way the postcolony continues to be represented in global popular culture. Katherine McKittrick, a scholar of cultural geographies, notes that presumptions about Africa and the Americas as "newer" and "inferior" land masses are part of the "geographic language of racial condemnation" that "contributed to the 'old' European world-view" that the people indigenous to these "newer" lands had "unsophis-ticated and underdeveloped worldviews": "So what was geographically at stake when the European center extended itself outward, toward a space that was at once 'nowhere' and inhabited by 'no one,' yet unex-pectedly 'there' and 'inhabited,' are race and racial geographies" (McKit-trick 2013, 6). Ramsay's sign-off articulates the profound erasure and racialized hierarchy attached to the notion of being "nowhere," a condi-tion that, while not particular to Guyana, takes on specific race/gender connotations in this geographic space—connotations that I emphasize across the chapters of this book.

For too long, Guyana has been "nowhere"—nonexistent in popu-lar, political, and environmental debates. Ramsay's proclamation about being "in the middle of nowhere" unwittingly underscores a weighty double meaning; finespun portrayals of Guyana are quite literally no-where to be seen in these popular representations, while the nation is concurrently classified as a nowhere land. *Uncharted* drives home my summation that Guyana suffers from deep, multiple erasures that re-duce it to being nowhere, even while it appears everywhere. This book argues that these forms of erasure are both symbolic, as discussed here, and literal, as evidenced in the depletion of natural resources in which Guyanese oil and sand, for instance, are shipped off to fuel wealthy na-tions across the globe and replenish beaches in more high-profile Carib-bean destinations. It aims to simultaneously highlight the everywhere-/ nowhereness of Guyana while intervening in ways that add complexity to our understandings of this integral player in so many global arenas.

## Global Gendered Racializations

Although the subsequent chapters of this book do not focus on the par-ticular popular representations discussed in the preceding paragraphs, in this introduction, I sweep together the thematic elements they convey (gender, race, resources, erasure, erosion, violence, and diasporic pro-cesses) in the hopes of challenging these shallow depictions of Guyana and its people, and as a springboard for what is to come. I consider these and other "global gendered racializations," defined as transnational race/

gender constructs and labels that marked the enslaved and the indentured, and that continue to brand their descendants, who embark on
new migrations. This book asserts that as protagonists in global racial
capitalism, Guyanese women have always been at the heart of global
gendered racializations. Therefore, I take women's identities as a starting point.

While concepts such as transnationalism and diaspora are useful
for understanding Guyana's place in the world—and I use those terms
here—the book is less about the Guyanese diaspora and more about *seeing* Guyana and Guyanese women, in particular, as always-already-there
but often invisible players linked to the construction of gender and race,
globalization and resources. By outside accounts, from the moment of
New World expansion and continuing up through the present, Guyana
has been in a perpetual state of discovery. In their infamous quest for
El Dorado, colonial explorers and early global corporations exploited
fertile land and pursued gold in Guiana. In subsequent eras, Western
capitalists continued profiting from Guyana's vast industries—among
them sugar, rice, bauxite, gold, diamonds, and rum—while still operating under the rubric of "discovery." Amid all of these mediations, Guyana's identity as a site for the transfer of enslaved people from Africa and
indentured laborers from India only told part of the story. This book
sweeps us into some of the gendered undercurrents of that story.

## Academic Analyses: Past and Present

The hidden narratives of enslaved Afro-Guyanese women and men
are yet to be adequately uncovered, although the Guyanese historian
and pan-Africanist activist Walter Rodney provides critical insight in
*A History of the Guyanese Working People: 1881–1905* (1981). Brackette
Williams's erudite ethnography *Stains on My Name, War in My Veins:
Guyana and the Politics of Cultural Struggle* followed a decade later, situating Guyanese ethnic relations as a rich departure point for unpacking
salient anthropological debates about nationalism, state formation, and
ethnicity. More than thirty years elapsed before an American academic
press published another ethnographic monograph on Guyana (Sarah E.
Vaughn's *Engineering Vulnerability: In Pursuit of Climate Adaptation*),
and it has been more than forty years since Rodney's landmark historical

treatment. In recent years, scholars have put forth eye-opening studies of the harsh realities of indentureship, and of Indian women whom, after slavery was abolished, the British brought to colonial Guiana in far greater numbers than to neighboring colonies in Trinidad and Tobago and Jamaica (Shepherd 2002; Bahadur 2013).

This book arrives at a time when academic attention to Guyana is picking up steam in step with the oil boom, signaling a renaissance in the study of this country. It follows several noteworthy and daedal treatments of the nation and its people, including Natalie Hopkinson's thoughtful weaving of art, history, sugar, and colonialism in *A Mouth Is Always Muzzled: Six Dissidents, Five Continents, and the Art of Resistance* (2018); Arif Bulkan and D. Alissa Trotz's multidisciplinary analysis of Guyana's contemporary geopolitical period, *Unmasking the State: Politics, Society, and Economy in Guyana, 1992–2015* (2019); Grace Aneiza Ali's evocative, multimodal anthology, *Liminal Spaces: Migration and Women of the Guyanese Diaspora* (2020); the selected writings of the brilliant Guyanese feminist writer and activist Andaiye, *The Point Is to Change the World*, edited by Alissa Trotz (2020); *Far from Mecca: Globalizing the Muslim Caribbean*, Aliyah Khan's pioneering work on Muslims in Guyana (2020); and *Engineering Vulnerability: In Pursuit of Climate Adaptation*, Sarah E. Vaughn's rich ethnographic case study of the relationship between climate adaptation and racial inequality in the aftermath of the disastrous flood of 2005 (2022).[19] Hopkinson's and Ali's books focus on the global reach of Guyanese literary and visual artists and center women, and Trotz's edited selections of Andaiye's writings reveal her as an unsung hero of Guyana's WPA (the Working People's Alliance) and a champion of Guyanese women's rights whose influence stretched far beyond Guyana.[20] While these books are vital interventions that center Guyana, most of the scholarly attention to the Caribbean has privileged the islands of the region, leaving Guyana off the map. *Global Guyana* aims to be in dialogue with, for example, Mimi Sheller's *Island Futures: Caribbean Survival in the Anthropocene* (2020), in which she offers an exigent rethinking of Antillean geography by troubling the notion of separate or isolated islands to instead consider "the interplay of land, air, and sea space, and the infrastructural spaces for im/mobilities," especially as it pertains to the ecological vulnerability of the region (Sheller 2020, 18).

And when Guyana has been the basis of scholarly attention, some treatments have arguably fallen back on colonial-era tropes of discovery and virgin frontiers or reduced it to a perpetual backcountry. Take for example the opening of historian Marjoleine Kars's *Blood on the River: A Chronicle of Mutiny and Freedom on the Wild Coast* (2020). Kars's account is situated like Gordon Ramsay's, not only with the word "wild" appearing in both of their titles but also with an outsider, the historian in this case, arriving in Georgetown on a mission to navigate the interior. A gifted historian, Kars offers a rich analysis of over nine hundred slave narratives, unstudied until her writing, documenting the 1763 Berbice rebellion, a massive, sustained slave revolt in the then Dutch colony that should rightly be held in similar regard to slave rebellions in Haiti, Jamaica, and other parts of the Caribbean, which have received far more scholarly attention. Yet, while presenting her groundbreaking archival find, Kars positions herself as an intrepid researcher plunked down in the wild, unforgiving, potentially dangerous, and deeply disorienting landscape that is present-day Guyana:

> I had arrived in Georgetown after an all-night layover in the Trinidad airport. Bleary-eyed, I had only the vaguest idea of how to proceed. My wish had been to travel up the Berbice River to get to know the terrain. But there is no bus route or train up the Berbice, or even a direct road, and there are no hotels (Guyana's tourist industry is still developing). A month of emailing with a well-known wilderness outfit had resulted in an itinerary and price tag geared more toward a boutique "adventure" tourist than a historian on a modest grant. So on the eve of my departure, I still had no definite plan or reservations, just the assurance of a long-term Guyana resident, a Scottish woman I had contacted last minute, that she'd have a driver pick me up at the airport at five a.m. and bring me to her house. . . . For safekeeping, I left my passport and extra cash with Margaret [the Scottish woman], my acquaintance of forty-five minutes, and clambered into the cab of Alex's truck [an old friend of the woman's son]. As he wedged his rifle behind the seats my eyebrows went up. Alex explained that highway robbery isn't just a euphemism in Guyana. (Kars 2020, 2–3)

So, before we find out much of anything else about Guyana and its people, we learn that the country lacks roads and hotels, that a Scottish woman, whom the author has known for less than an hour, represents the only trustworthy guard for her passport and cash, and that a rifle is necessary for staving off imminent robbery. It is with this ominous scene that Kars commences her study and her trek into Berbice, hoping to explore a "bewildering 'jungle' that frightened Dutch soldiers" (Kars 2020, 5). But we already know that Guyana has frightened Kars, who finds just beneath the surface and literally "poking out of the jungle's soil after a rain" remnants of Dutch colonialism that seem to underscore that the country, like these relics in the mud, is stuck in the past (Kars 2020, 5). Kars's initial description reifies retrograde representations of Guyana as a terrifying, treacherous landscape that took the lives of intrepid White explorers looking to uncover its riches. To be sure, Guyana does have high rates of violent crime and kidnapping, but the common thread across Kars's academic treatment and Ramsay's reality TV/adventure documentary is that Georgetown is a hazard-ridden and antiquated stepping stone to a primordial past deep in the interior, where all of the authentic action happens.

## Mudheads Again: Dubious Distinctions

To understand why Guyana is seen as a backwater and Guyanese are rendered as unsophisticated in depictions such as Krauss's *Times* article about the oil expansion, we must look to enduring colonial epithets. The globalized tropes portrayed in *Indian Matchmaking, Lovecraft Country*, and *Gordon Ramsay: Uncharted* echo regional slurs that, since the colonial period, have equated Guyana's people with its environment. Part of my aim throughout this book is not just to critique the way Guyana is represented in contemporary global imaginings, in which American ideologies tend to be hegemonic, but also to parse how Guyana's historical place within the Caribbean intersects with those ideologies. Writing about long-standing migratory flows between Guyana and Barbados, the sociologist Linden Lewis recalls his experiences as a Guyanese boy whose family settled in Barbados in 1962. Lewis writes,

> I started to attend St. Stephen's Primary School and began to develop a network of friends both at school and in my immediate community. It was about this period that I learned I was a "mud-head." Understandably,

this was never an issue in Guyana. It was a nickname that was hurled at me often, but not so much by my peers, who were perhaps not as knowledgeable about the geography of Guyana or about the leaves and mud that made its water brown and murky. . . . The coastal plain occupies about five percent of Guyana's habitable land. It is where most of the people of Guyana live. This area is made of alluvial mud that is swept out to sea by the Amazon River. The term "mud-head" is a reference therefore to this muddy area. Unfortunately, because of the azure blue waters of the beaches of Barbados, the older boys held nothing but contempt for the murky creeks and rivers of Guyana. A story is told by a friend of seeing an advertisement in the *Barbados Observer*, a local newspaper at the time, of a man who claimed that they were selling land in Guyana at $5 a gallon! This tale is a measure of how much of a swampland Guyana is represented to people in Barbados. (Lewis 2011)

Lewis's tale of being called a "mudhead" is not only about how Guyana is seen as a swampland; it is also about how Guyanese people have long been equated with its undomesticated, muddy, and difficult-to-manipulate terrain.[21] With much of the country residing below sea level, mud and flooding have always been threats to life and crops in Guyana. These threats came to a devasting head in the catastrophic 2005 flood that Sarah Vaughn details in *Engineering Vulnerability* (2022).[22] In his foreword to Rodney's *History of the Guyanese Working People*, the Bajan novelist, poet, and essayist George Lamming emphasizes the magnitude of making Guiana's coast suitable for cane cultivation and human inhabitation. Soil and water are the star elements. "Unlike many a Caribbean island," Lamming writes, "Guyana did not offer itself easily for human settlement. . . . Every triumph of cultivation was subdued by the constant fear that overnight the ocean would advance and swallow up the achievement" (Lamming 1981, xviii). Rodney details that the combined efforts of Dutch architecture and African labor brought about the movement of at least one hundred million tons of soil.[23] "This meant that slaves moved 100 million tons of heavy water-logged clay with shovel in hand, while enduring conditions of perpetual mud and water. . . . Working people continued to make a tremendous contribution to the *humanization* of the Guyanese coastal environment. However, they were generally forced to react to circumstances, being in no position to

control the available technology or to initiate environmental intervention" (Rodney 1981, 3, italics in original).

I want to suggest that we can trace the epithet of the Guyanese mudhead not only to Guyana's muddy terrain, as Lewis does, but also to the
Sisyphean task that occupied Afro-Guyanese enslaved people as they
toiled against the land under Dutch rule. The term also materializes
as derogatory slang to connote a stupid person in writings of the era
that span the British Empire, including William Delisle Hay's *Brighter
Britain! Or Settler and Maori in Northern New Zealand* (2016/1882),
a colonial travelogue of sorts describing migrants to that region, and
Rudyard Kipling's acclaimed novel, *Kim* (2014/1901).[24] Hay was better
known for his White-supremacist fiction and Kipling was seen as the
great defender of British Empire. The mudhead label, then, extended
beyond Guiana via global articulations of White supremacy and impe-
rialism, while in the Guyanese context, it associated people with ecology
and connoted an insult. The mudhead epithet is arguably a component
of the political economy of erasure addressed throughout this book.
Lisa Lowe makes a related claim around what she terms "the political
economy of affirmation and forgetting that structures and formalizes the
archives of liberalism, and liberal ways of understanding. This economy
civilizes and develops freedoms for 'man' in modern Europe and North
America, while relegating others to geographical and temporal spaces
that are constituted as backward, uncivilized, and unfree" (Lowe 2015,
3). And this economy brews beneath the surface of the *Times* article that
framed Guyana as isolated, watery, and wild, while painting its people
as provincial, lackadaisical, and prone to eating soup out of hardhats.
It is bitterly ironic that although Rodney rightly saw the fortitude of
the working people in their ability to "humanize" the coast, enduring
stereotypes traceable to this very achievement serve to undermine the
humanity of the Guyanese people while enervating their contemporary
hopes of converting natural resources into economic gains.

Recasting "Ethnic Conflict": Afro-Asian Connections Then
and Now

Hoping to confront and interrogate inadequate treatments of my homeland, while considering the troubling reality of all that ails Guyana,

I harken to anthropologist Deborah A. Thomas's analysis of violence in Jamaica (Thomas 2011). Indeed, we might well position Guyana's distinctions under the umbrella of "exceptional violence," making the opening to Thomas's book particularly apropos: "In spite of my efforts at avoidance . . . this is a book about violence, a topic that has, in recent years, become the number one preoccupation of both Caribbean governments and citizens. The region as a whole has a murder rate higher than any other region in the world, and instances of assault throughout the Caribbean are significantly above the world's average, with kidnapping a growing phenomenon, especially in Guyana and Trinidad and Tobago" (Thomas 2011, 2). Considering that Guyana is so often overlooked even in analyses of the region, it is particularly significant that, after Jamaica, it is the second country Thomas mentions in her generative examination of violence. Thomas avers that the Caribbean is understood as "inconsequential as world regions go," while in fact it "is central to all of the processes that came to shape our understandings of modernity over the past five centuries" (Thomas 2011, 5). I am making a related claim about Guyana in particular, while arguing that we should look more closely at and from Guyana in order to better gauge those processes. Thomas follows Inderpal Grewal (2005) to posit that "Jamaica, like America, is a globally circulating entity that holds within it particular expectations and sensibilities that can be consumed without having to set foot in its actual territorial space. This is the case, on one hand, because the transnational sphere of Jamaica (its migrant communities) spans the globe, and on the other, because people's mediated experiences of Jamaica—reggae music, athletes—have been so profound" (Thomas 2011, 126–27). If we consider Thomas's point here, alongside Gina Athena Ulysse's argument that another Caribbean nation, Haiti, is often represented at worst as "invisible and at best, one-dimensional" (Ulysse 2015, xxv), we begin to see that in this sense Guyana is not exceptional—other examples of erasure in the Caribbean abound—but that like Jamaica and Haiti, it holds a particular place in global imaginings.

This book addresses this ontological crisis by resituating Guyana from being seen as *nowhere* to being understood as connected to the broader world in intricate ways. It does so by looking anew at some of the old frameworks that have dogged the country, including colonial strategies that pitted emancipated Africans against Indian indentured laborers. Guyana's early global identity was forged around Europeans transporting Africans, Indians, and Chinese to what is still today, if we are to take Ramsay and Kars seriously, a wild coast. Unfortunately, that notion of the nation as "wild" has been transplanted onto its peoples, typecasting Guyanese of all stripes as uncultivated, but depicting Africans and Indians as diametrically opposed. In the modern era, ethnic conflict between Afro- and Indo-Guyanese has perhaps become the country's most dubious distinction—it is held up as the nation's primary cultural trait. Following Walter Rodney, I insist that Africans and Indians in Guyana are not inherently at odds with one another, even though the ways in which the British colonial state depended upon casting them as enemies continue to shape both local and international diagnoses of ethnic relations there. I make this insistence with a sober acknowledgment of the brutal forms of violence that accompany national elections in Guyana. More than just a call for a new analytic around Guyana, I advocate for a grounded understanding of relationships between Afro- and Indo-Guyanese from the colonial era to the present day. This sets the stage for my broader argument—that Guyana is and has always been global and that it has something crucial to teach us about how processes around gender, race, and resources channel across multiple arenas, from the intimacy of marital ties and kinship relations to the far reaches of popular culture and global extractive industries.

But there is yet another way to delineate the scope and significance of my approach—just as we might suggest that Guyana is everywhere, we might also be so bold as to argue that we find some of the interethnic cultural exchanges and tensions present in Guyana, everywhere. Even if we take the prevalent scholarly evaluations of ethnic relations in Guyana—the notion that it is characterized by entrenched conflict between Indians and Blacks—at face value, we might suspect that Guyana has something to impart about the region and the world. Dutch, French, and British forces oversaw a massive, literal reshaping of South America's northern coast when they first exploited Amerindians, then forcibly directed enslaved African laborers to the task of moving millions of tons of mud to reshape Guiana's shoreline in order to facilitate the extraction of its vast natural resources. When slavery was abolished, the British next brought more Indian indentured laborers to Guiana than to any other country in the region. They also brought significant numbers of Chinese. But as historian Vijay Prashad has documented, African and Asian cultures were not incompatible and discrete even before the British conjoined Indians and Africans in the Caribbean (Prashad 2001). In *Everybody Was Kung-Fu Fighting: Afro-Asian Connections and the Myth of Cultural Purity*, his capacious study of Afro-Asian linkages, Prashad writes, "I have chosen to discuss the peoples who claim the heritage of the continents of Asia and Africa, not only because they are important to me, but because they have long been pitted against each other as the model versus the undesirable. I hope by looking at how these two cultural worlds are imbricated in complex and varied ways through five centuries and around the globe that I can help us rethink race, culture, and the organization of our society. This book is, if you will, a search for a new skin" (Prashad 2001, x). Prashad's "search for a new skin" can be grounded in Guyana, but it has historical and contemporary correlations in the world beyond.

Within the Caribbean region and in South Africa, where colonizers indentured Indian laborers and set them at odds with Africans, Afro-Asian cultural exchanges, as well as political tensions between the two groups, have been commonplace (Prashad 2001, 75). But the comingling of these two groups extends also to North America; in the 1800s, indentured workers were incorporated to curb the wages of emancipated Africans "from Western Canada to Southern Africa" (Prashad 2001, 75). In *Stranger Intimacy: Contesting Race, Sexuality, and the Law in the North American West*, historian Nayan Shah notes that "if we look carefully into the historical record, we find that transient migrants of varied races and classes circulated, worked, and mingled across the North American West in the first third of the twentieth century" (Shah 2011, 1). Shah details fleeting Afro-Asian interracial relationships as well as legal marriages, such as one between an Indian man and an African American woman in Yuma, Arizona, in 1916, while also underscoring how those interracial intimacies between Indians and other racialized groups, whether same-sex or heterosexual, were deemed suspicious, immoral, and illegal (Shah 2011, 1, 109). Prashad argues that across all of these locations, Black people were regarded as "undisciplined" while coolies were seen as "quiet and willing" to work (Prashad 2001, 75).[25] From both historians we deduce that people of African and Asian descent defied the notion that they were incompatible even while their intimate relationships were interpreted as threats to White supremacy.

Today, Afro-Asian individuals with Caribbean ancestry such as the hip hop superstar Nicki Minaj and the politician Kamala Harris are among the most recognizable women across the globe. In 2021, American politics faced a watershed moment in which, for the first time, Harris, a woman of Afro-Caribbean and South Asian descent, ascended to the role of vice president (and reportedly was already a front runner for president in 2024) (McArdle 2020). Leading up to the 2020 US presidential election, American political commentators grappled with categorizing Harris's Afro-Asian heritage (Chittal 2021). I make the case that because Guyana is the home of more people of African and Indian parentage, or Douglas, as we are known there, than elsewhere in the hemisphere, looking at Guyana offers a particular angle from which we can understand the kin ties that shape mixed-raced Afro-Asian figures such as Harris and Minaj, even though Harris's Caribbean father hails from Jamaica, and Minaj and her parents are from Trinidad. Guyana can afford us insight into racialized gender constructions that demystify the sociopolitical identities of these women, and other Caribbean public figures, like Rihanna, who does not identify as Dougla but does have Guyanese ancestry.

## Black Feminism and Autoethnography

My pointer broom analytic employs a number of interdisciplinary methodologies, including autoethnography, archival research, and oral history, to offer an unconventional portrayal of "the land of many waters" and its global connections. Although not all chapters are explicitly autoethnographic, my perspective as a Guyana-born anthropologist shapes the viewpoint of the book in its entirety. My reliance on autoethnography, a genre that eschews the traditional anthropological fallacy of the distanced researcher—once virtually tabooed in the discipline and increasingly utilized by scholars within and beyond the field of anthropology—enables me to place my own genealogy within a social context while destabilizing the tenacious dichotomies between insider and outsider.[26] This approach is most heavily influenced by Black feminist anthropologists, an early group of scholars identified as "elders such as Zora Neale Hurston, Katherine Dunham, and Pearl Primus [who] form the genealogical foundation of innovative approaches" (McClaurin 2001, 55).

More recently, Irma McClaurin and others (Harrison 1997; Bolles 1996; Mullings 1997) have paved a path for a new generation of scholars to situate Black feminist anthropology as a methodology that

> derives its political identity and its praxis from [an] intellectual heritage of innovation and implicit critique, from the fusion of art and politics, theory and poetics, from the interplay between identity and ethnography to produce an anthropological legacy of concrete multiplicity . . . as seen from the margins . . . [designed] to expose the falseness of the view from the top and . . . transform the margins as well as the center . . . [in which we] develop an account of the world which treats our perspectives not as subjugated or disruptive, but as primary and constitutive of a different world. (McClaurin 2001, 56, ellipses and brackets in original)

Black feminist anthropologists often speak from "'native'/community-authorized positions" in which "Self and subjectivity are never secondary but are intricately woven into the direction, content, analysis, praxis, and materiality of our scholarship" (McClaurin 2001, 51–52). Mindful of the interplay between Self and subject, content and analysis, this book draws upon previous studies of the Caribbean by Black women anthropologists who may or may not have been "native" to their field sites, whose ethnographies were not entirely or explicitly "autoethnographies," but who recognized, either within their ethnographic texts and/or in subsequent publications, that as women and as members of the African diaspora, reflecting on their positionalities was of vital importance to their studies (Bolles 1985; Harrison 1997; Simmons 2001; Slocum 2001; Ulysse 2007). For McClaurin, such work also borrows from what Lila Abu-Lughod has called "halfie" anthropologists and "require[s] us as ethnographers to continuously move back and forth between personal histories, local communities, global transactions, and ethnographic responsibilities" (McClaurin 2001, 60).

The strokes of the pointer broom mirror this continuous movement back and forth, while I unearth a political economy of erasure by tracing local social interactions, global industries, and an autoethnographic perspective. In hopes of advancing the theory and praxis tradition Mc-Claurin identifies, I build on a concept I introduced elsewhere, *auto-ethnographic kinship formation*, to situate this book's first chapter as an exercise in reconceptualizing my own kin, one that uncovers Blackness and redefines the historical race/gender projects that have structured my family's understanding of who we are (LaBennett 2018a).[27] I am defining autoethnographic kinship formation, then, as a strategy that dovetails with the innovations of Black feminist anthropologists, but uses autoethnography to (re)define my own kinship formations in ways that destabilize how colonial and global capitalist classificatory systems have categorized Afro- and Indo-Guyanese women's intimate cross-racial ties to partners and to kin. These classificatory systems have perpetuated coloniality, cultivated interethnic antagonisms, and muddled the cross-racial cleavages and affinities that developed under global capitalism. Autoethnographic kinship formation also functions as "a type of cultural mediation" for the way my own family defines itself (McClaurin 2001, 67). In so doing, it marshals the personal to reflect on the political by engaging with and troubling the summations that colonial powers have made of African- and Indian-Guyanese women, their partners, and their families.

One does not have to be an anthropologist to engage in autoethnographic kinship formation. I have theorized elsewhere that the artist Beyoncé's visual album, *Lemonade*, is an exercise of autoethnographic kinship formation, "one that employs representations of Beyoncé and her family—defined both in the conventional sense of the nuclear family and biological kin and constructed more broadly to include a sisterhood of fictive kin—to reimagine how black marriage, sexuality, and kinship are popularly understood" (LaBennett 2018a, 154). Autoethnographic kinship formation is therefore a refashioning of genealogy and of family relations in Beyoncé's case. In this book, I extend the concept to propose a more inclusive vision of how marital lines and centuries-old interethnic relations can be reconciled in the present day. We can think of auto-ethnographic kinship formation as a response to the political economy of erasure that structures and obstructs Guyanese gender and kinship formations.

In crafting a project that synthesizes personal experience, oral histories with family members, and archival exploration of my own genealogy, I negotiate nettlesome alliances and responsibilities as I make difficult choices about whose stories to elicit and include, whose names to reveal and withhold, which secrets to share and protect. I have designed this book around my notion of autoethnographic kinship formation in part as a tactic for navigating the sorts of tensions and complications around thick and thin description that John L. Jackson has theorized in his study of the African Hebrew Israelites of Jerusalem (Jackson 2013). Jackson remarks, "There is so much I do not share in this book, cannot or simply will not, a plethora of secrets kept, stories not shared, purposefully confounded, for better or worse. A different kind of thinning" (Jackson 2013, 91).[28] I have grappled with similar decisions. Still, to speak of "secrets" perhaps puts too mysterious a spin on what I elect to divulge or protect within this text. To be clear, I reference Jackson's thin description not to suggest that I am protecting or disclosing *deep, dark family secrets* but rather to emphasize that I am consciously privileging archival findings about the long-deceased. In terms of my living relatives, I only incorporate, with permission, oral histories from two individuals (my mother and my aunt), and when writing about other living relatives, I have withheld names and altered identifying characteristics. I hasten to add that we can position my handling of stories and secrets, both those revealed and those "purposefully confounded," in concert with the metaphor of the pointer broom and the sweeper laboring in the light of the early dawn. Brathwaite avers that when observing this act, in this particular glow, we see things in a unique way. Thus, in keeping with the visual uncertainty of sweeping sand on a sandy shore in the glimmer of the early dawn, the pointer broom approach advanced within this book promises to illuminate new insights but does not avow that such an endeavor will result in total clarity.

Autoethnographic kinship formation may be extended to describe the overall mission of this book, conceptualizing the vast reaches of the diaspora as kin, with all that that entails—marked differences and communal understandings. Looking first to my family, then more broadly to music, migration, and marriage in the region, and then, even more expansively, to the far-reaching social and environmental calamities surrounding mining industries makes the concept of global Guyana the parfocal lens through which to comprehend some of the most pressing issues facing the Caribbean. *Global Guyana*, then, employs an approach that redraws the contours of the African and the Indian diasporas.

## Overview of the Chapters

Chapter 1—"From Full Negro to Dougla Girl: 'All ah You in Here Is Black People!'"—uncovers the erasure of Blackness within social constructions of mixed African and Indian ancestry (categorized under the term "Dougla" in Guyana, Trinidad, and Suriname). The chapter highlights transnational race/gender formations across the experiences of five generations of female kin, beginning with my great-great-grandmother, an indentured laborer from India who had a child with an Afro-Guyanese man when such a relationship was strictly tabooed. It traces descent beginning with this remarkable union (which became a family secret) and continuing down my maternal line. The result is a woman-centered account of defining family, defying sexual taboos, and claiming ethnic identifications, chronicled from the late nineteenth century to the contemporary period. By sweeping a tattered photograph of a Guyanese couple into the morning light, I address more than what might be written off as a coverup of Blackness, the likes of which we might find in countless family records across the African diaspora. Rather, the auto-ethnographic kinship formation at play in this investigation unsettles the notion that Afro- and Indo-Guyanese identities have been incompatible from the start. Moreover, applying a pointer broom to interracial intimacies and kinship configurations from this angle disaggregates the muddled detritus of the political economy of erasure, revealing the ways in which Guyanese girls and women like my maternal kin were stereotyped as "unmarriable" and "rebellious," while also being elided from the scholarship on Indo- and Afro-Caribbean identity, when they in fact have always been central to global racial capitalism.

Chapter 2, "Rihanna's Guyanese Pattacake and the Homewrecking State in Barbados," uses a Bajan calypso sung by an Indo-Guyanese woman as a springboard for disentangling the intersections of race and gender that have long fused the two nations. Within these formations, the Guyanese woman emerges as a seductress, whose irresistible "pattacake" (the Guyanese creole term for vagina) lures husbands from their unions with respectable Bajan wives. Yet, the chapter exposes the Bajan state as the real homewrecker—blaming high emigration and infant mortality on laboring families in an earlier era, and scapegoating Guyanese immigrant women as threats to the nuclear family unit in the present day. The chapter puts gendered anti-Guyanese stereotypes in dialogue with ethnic markers and maternal knowledge delivered by Barbados's most famous musical artist, the global phenom, Rihanna. Foregrounding Rihanna's upbringing, framed around her Afro-Guyanese matriline, I complicate the picture of Guyanese women in Barbados. Juxtaposing the "Guyanese women are homewreckers" bromide alongside a reorientation of Rihanna's music and persona, the chapter takes a different look at the hypersexualization of Guyanese women (discussed in the previous chapter) as also rooted in Bajan political anxieties about competition for employment and scarce natural resources. It unveils the at-times-hidden processes of a long history of Barbadian-Guyanese migration and intermarriage, and a more recent landscape in which the state has overlooked Rihanna's Afro-Guyanese ancestry while cracking down on Guyanese immigrants as menacing foreigners.

Sand acts as a connective grain across all of the book's chapters. Swept up in yards in my family's ancestral village in the first, and blanketing beach-side tourist towns in the second, sand then surfaces as the star player in chapter 3, "Transplanted Beaches and Silica Cities: Sand, Erasure, and Erosion in the Age of the Anthropocene." This chapter brings to light the invisible crises attached to extracting Guyana's silica-quartz sand. Taking stock of the social and environmental impacts of sand mining, the chapter advances an ecofeminist analysis that uncloaks the political economy of erasure and related forms of erosion surrounding extractive industries that are deflected when we focus instead on glossy images of wet sand sticking to bikini-clad female bodies. Equating Caribbean sand with beaches and tourism obscures the ways in which this building block of modern life is being depleted far more quickly than it can be replenished. Brathwaite's old woman sweeping sand as an analogy for the Caribbean acts as a prescient forecaster of environmental catastrophe when we realize that "the world is running out of sand" (El-Hadi 2022, quoted in Ayed 2022). Although Guyana lacks the crystal blue waters and pristine white sand beaches that attract vacationers to other Caribbean centers of tourism, the nation's bounty of silica-quartz sand has been imported by the ton to replenish eroding beaches in high-profile tourist destinations and is being extracted at monumental rates to support the national development initiatives fueled by the oil discovery. The chapter sweeps into view the *tidalectic* currents of erosion that spread Guyana's sand throughout the circum-Caribbean and beyond. It issues an urgent appeal to uncover the obfuscated story of the country's sand—at once everywhere and nowhere—in hopes of calling attention to the global social and environmental pitfalls of sand mining.

In Chapter 4, "Recasting El Dorado: Representing Oil, Politics, and Ethnic Conflict," we consider how Guyana's oil cache and its chances for managing its newfound wealth have been depicted in geopolitical and global economic discourses. Sweeping together international news coverage of the oil boom, alongside that of Guyana's local press, to glean journalistic, editorial, and layperson interpretations of oil, politics, and "ethnic conflict," I argue that contemporary neoliberal narratives fail to recognize how the persistent imprints of colonialism have set Guyana up for the resource curse, thereby pigeonholing the Guyanese people as lacking in the sophistication and technological/global economic know-how needed to manage oil extraction. The chapter takes a deep dive into the debates and tensions surrounding Guyana's contested 2020 presidential elections, which made international headlines because of the country's new status as a petrostate. I frame these debates within and beyond the country and redirect the representational gaze to interrogate ExxonMobil's attitude towards ecological safeguards and the state's prioritizing of profit over people and the environment. The chapter centers local critiques of the state and links extractive violence to erased acts of violence against women and children. It also offers a critical analysis of the hemispheric environmental peril that is currently emanating from Guyana.

The coda, "The Road Ahead," brings the book full circle by using family oral histories of tragic accidents along the country's main thoroughfare as a window into the troubling environmental and gendered impacts that have accompanied Guyana's quest for global capitalist expansion. I reflect on people on the ground who express a deep sense of apprehension as they witness the frenzied transporting of resources and the relentless carving up of the landscape to produce new roads. Reiterating the volume's principal interventions and big-picture takeaways, I put forth a final rumination on the imminent sea change that new oil forebodes. Attention to the intricate interplay between Guyana's extractive industries, its marginalized status, and the social worlds of its women—the group who bears the brunt of its economic hardships—not only recasts this nation but also forecasts the global role of the region in the decades to come. Ultimately, the book advances a vision for a global ecofeminism that radiates from Guyana, one that sounds the alarm on ominous environmental catastrophes and cross-examines a political economy of erasure that concomitantly devastates fragile ecologies and endangers women and children.

## "Come-Back-fuh-Go-Back"

Many of the 56.6 percent of Guyanese citizens who were estimated to be living abroad in 2010 are "come-back-fuh-go-back" people; they return home like the tides and the currents, to visit family, tend to second homes and businesses, and pay their taxes, only to depart again (Danns 2017).[29] I, too, am in some ways a "come-back-fuh-go-back" Guyanese, although I do not hold citizenship there. I left when I was seven and a half years old, returning for long stretches almost every summer until I went to college, and going home again and again as an adult. As a child, when I did not spend summer vacations in Guyana, I spent them with relatives in a Guyanese enclave in Scarborough, Ontario, just outside of Toronto.

Since I was seven, I have known that Guyana's reach is global. At that age my brother and I left our grandmother behind and joined our mother and my father in Brooklyn, New York. Even then, I knew that our vast network of family ties extended far beyond Guyana and Brooklyn, with aunts, uncles, and cousins in Paramaribo, Suriname, and in Toronto, London, and Amsterdam. We had lived for a few years in St. Lucia—not really a memory for me, but when I looked at a color photo of my mother on the beach in a bikini, with me as a toddler wearing only bikini bottoms, and my mother boasted that we had a house on the shore there, I tried hard to remember it. And, of course, our ancestors came from Africa, India, and Portugal. As a child, I knew these global connections were not particular to my own family—almost every Guyanese person I knew, every family friend or acquaintance, had a similar story. My early understanding of this cosmopolitanism also influenced my sense of confusion and disorientation when I met people who knew nothing about Guyana. While my fellow Caribbean childhood friends, immigrants, and their children from places like Trinidad, Jamaica,

Grenada, St. Vincent, and Barbados knew of my homeland, folks I en-
countered outside of West Indian Brooklyn had either never heard of
Guyana, assumed it was a country in Africa, or only knew it as the site of
Jim Jones's mass murder. This juxtaposition perplexed me—how could
Guyana have so many global connections, how could there be so many
Guyanese spread out worldwide, and yet so few Americans knew the
first thing about our country?

Much more recently, as an anthropologist conducting research on the
African diaspora in cities from New York to Bridgetown, from Georgetown to Amsterdam, I was struck by the picture-postcard aesthetics
of the Netherlands' most visited urban locale. As I joined the parade
of cyclists peddling through Amsterdam's cobblestone streets and sat
shoulder-to-shoulder with international tourists on a boat tour of its
canals, I listened as others marveled at the beauty of Dutch architecture.
But I felt a bitter tinge as I recognized place names that also proliferate
in Guyana—"New Amsterdam," the home of my Afro-Guyanese family,
on my father's side—and saw architectural styles reminiscent of Georgetown, Guyana's capital. While Amsterdam's old buildings are either meticulously preserved or perpetually under restoration, Georgetown's
colonial structures are largely in disrepair. Still, I experienced an acute
appreciation for these ornate facades in the Dutch city when I considered that my ancestors' labor had produced the wealth that paid for this
opulence.

Today, Amsterdam's connections to Suriname (formerly Dutch Guiana) are more pronounced than its links to Guyana. Surinamese immigrants have made their mark on the city's material culture in numerous
ways, including its celebrated Surinamese restaurants, which meld tastes
and culinary traditions from Amerindians, and from Africa, Asia, and
Europe. I could tell a wider story from the perspective of all three Guianas, including Suriname and French Guiana, perhaps if I explored anti-
Black racism against the Netherlands' Afro-Surinamese diaspora, as the
anthropologist Gloria Wekker has done (Wekker 2016), or the relationship between ecological displacement and technology in French Guiana,
as in the work of another anthropologist, Peter Redfield (Redfield 2000).
Yet, looking out from all three Guianas is beyond the already vast sweep
of this book. Instead, this volume takes Guyana as its point of arrival
and departure. The presence of Guyanese and Surinamese immigrants

in Amsterdam is part of a throughline that we can trace back to Guyana's Dutch colonial rule. But recognizing Guyanese and Surinamese cultural markers and the architectural remnants of Caribbean wealth in the Dutch city also evokes more recent global crosscurrents and migrations; when one of my mother's sisters was a teenager, she migrated from Guyana to Suriname, where she raised her children, some of whom later found homes in Amsterdam. Wherever they have journeyed, whether to Paramaribo, Amsterdam, Toronto, New York, or elsewhere around the globe, the women in my family have carried new, pliable pointer brooms from Guyana—coiled and stashed in suitcases. Another aunt, Gene, keeps two now-well-worn pointer brooms on the front porch of her Brooklyn row house, where she routinely uses them to sweep up dried leaves and dirt while chatting with her Haitian and Trinidadian neighbors. My autoethnographic examples of architectural recognition in the Netherlands, and maternal kin connections across the Guyanese diaspora, then, are in keeping with the pointer broom approach of this book—it gathers, in the soft glow of the early morning light, grains that can be traced back to and through Guyana's women and its resources, scattered, but also joined by the sweep of the broom and the undulation of the tides.

1

# From Full Negro to Dougla Girl

*"All ah You in Here Is Black People!"*

If it is no longer sufficient to expose the scandal, then how
might it be possible to generate a different set of descriptions
from this archive?
—Saidiya Hartman, "Venus in Two Acts"

## Autoethnographic Kinship Formation

During my childhood, my maternal grandmother displayed a faded,
cracked, and tattered black-and-white photograph of her parents,
my great-grandparents, in her home. Although it was a framed and
treasured item, time and Guyana's humidity had not been kind to
the image. Still, the wear and tear affected mostly the edges, and the
photograph's two subjects were surprisingly well preserved. In the
picture, Robert Jaisingh, a stately Indian man with grey hair and a
full, white mustache, stands with his left hand resting on the shoulder
of his wife, Tily, an Indian woman with a thin face and a straight,
angular nose, who sits beside him. It is a posed studio photograph.
The couple is not extravagantly appointed, but their attire is neat—
save for Robert's belt, which is slightly askew at a rakish angle, and
Tily's white headwrap, which dwarfs her narrow face. Both of their
expressions are serious, perhaps even forlorn, in Tily's case. The family oral history I recalled from my childhood was that the pair came
to British Guiana from India as indentured laborers and that they
were able to purchase the small estate that became the village of Sarah
Johanna, where our family lived, because Robert worked as a land
surveyor for the government and diligently saved his earnings. But
archival research recasts the image of Robert and Tily, affording us a

more discerning look at my great-grandparents—one that uncovers Tily's hidden African ancestry.

How might we consider the archives and afterlives of slavery and indenture as interconnected? How and why does Blackness become legible or illegible, possible or impossible to "see" in a society as racially mixed as Guyana's? To address these questions, I imagine the intimate relationships of the woman in the photograph, my great-grandmother, Tily, and her mother, my second great-grandmother, Poragia, as meaningful designs for living. Although my maternal family is generally understood as Indian, Tily was the product of a union between her Indian indentured mother and an Afro-Guyanese man. This chapter recounts how I combed the archives and swept this open family secret into view. In so doing, it advances a new clutch of heuristics, a pointer broom approach—based on gathering together archival findings, oral history, and autoethnography—aimed at bringing the Guyanese woman, and the nation itself, into sharper relief. It articulates various reasons why Blackness is concealed in an Indian village at different moments, from indenture to the present day. Following Saidiya Hartman's epigraph at the start of this chapter, I *generate a different set of descriptions* from a snapshot of a couple—my great-grandparents—to illustrate the gendered racialization of the Guyanese woman vis-à-vis the erasure of Blackness along the maternal line. Applying a feminist analytic to the tattered photograph recovers Blackness in my family's genealogy, countering its cultural illegibility on my maternal side and recentering my women kin. Given that the Guyanese woman has long embodied her nation's struggle for reconciling the coalescence of race, ethnicity, sex, and land, how might such an exercise trouble the "ethnic conflict" thesis that dominates writing on Guyana? Rather than delegating the Dougla girl/woman to do such work, how might we use this work to imagine the Dougla as a complex rather than incomplete subject?[1]

This chapter explores Guyanese constructions of and interactions with global gendered racializations across the experiences of five generations of female kin, beginning with my great-great-grandmother, an indentured laborer from India, and continuing down my maternal line through my great-grandmother, grandmother, my mother and her eldest sister, and then myself. The result is a woman-centered account of race/gender formations charted from the late nineteenth century to the second decade of the twenty-first century, from India to Guyana. I center my family history in part to lay bare how my positionality shapes the project as a whole. But the chapter also foregrounds this history because fluctuating gendered racializations in my family reflect broader processes in global Guyana. Part of the story I am telling is that although ostensibly Indian, my relatives in what has been labeled as an "Indo-Guyanese village" are also Black, and their Blackness goes back several generations. This chapter is not about the incompatibility of Afro-Asian identity. Rather, it is about a group of people who mostly identify as Indo-Guyanese, but who have also been Black since the late 1800s. Although Guyanese girls and women like my maternal kin have been elided from scholarship on Indo- and Afro-Caribbean identity, they have always been central to circum-Caribbean racializations and global racial capitalism. Employing autoethnography to recenter them, I aver that we must expand the scholarly treatment of Guyana, and particularly accounts of Dougla identity—or mixed Afro- and Indo-Guyanese individuals—in order to more adequately reflect Dougla subjectivity. Like Guyana itself, the Dougla subject has long been sidelined and misunderstood, with her equivocal subjectivity and significance to Caribbean racializations underestimated.

Although autoethnography has been critiqued as navel-gazing, early interdisciplinary pioneers such as Zora Neale Hurston (1942) and contemporary researchers such as Robin Boylorn (2012) and Aisha Durham (2014) have demonstrated its utility for representing the cultural worlds of women of color while exposing the tensions of insider/outsider perspectives.[2] Elsewhere, I have argued that autoethnography opens pathways for reimagining traditional constructions of kin and relatedness (LaBennett 2018a). More than an autoethnographic approach, this chapter can be read as an act of "autoethnographic kinship formation," a term I use to describe mobilizing autoethnography as a strategy to (re)define my own kinship formations in a manner that complicates colonial and contemporary categorizations of gender and the family in Guyana and beyond. Autoethnographic kinship formation, then, rewrites my own kinship structures to oppugn the erasure of Blackness on my maternal side. Earlier, I discussed the political economy of erasure that has effaced cross-racial affinities in its calibration of Guyanese gender constructions and kinship ties. This economy of erasure informs an "ethnic conflict" scheme that maintains structures of coloniality, incites interethnic hostilities, and jumbles the cross-racial intimacies and divisions that developed under global capitalism. My use of autoethnographic kinship formation to address this type of erasure builds on Lisa Lowe's development of a "'political economy' of intimacies" (Lowe 2015, 18), which she defines as "a particular calculus governing the production, distribution, and possession of intimacy. . . . This involves considering scenes of close connection in relation to a global geography that one more often conceives in terms of vast spatial distances. It means drawing into relation with one another the abolition of slavery in the Caribbean and the development of colonial modes of biopolitical violence in Asia . . . appreciating together settler practices with the racialized laboring figures of the slave and the 'coolie'" (Lowe 2015, 18).

While Lowe enlists her notion of intimacies to do this work, the political economy that we examine here is reckoned around erasure. The pointer broom sweeps this political economy of erasure into view, and autoethnographic kinship formation is the intervention that hopes to rewrite or (re)form this obliteration in meaningful ways. Situated within Oonya Kempadoo's sssweep, sweep, stamp of the pointer broom, and Kamau Brathwaite's *tidalectics*—coming from one continent and touching another, before receding—autoethnographic kinship formation becomes an adroit flick of the broom, one that not only disinters the intimacies of geographically and conceptually distant sites and supposedly diametrically opposed peoples but also destabilizes categories of race and gender from the colonial era to the present day.

## Sarah Johanna: An Indian Village in Guyana

My maternal family hails from Sarah Johanna, a tiny village in East Bank Demerara that in 2011 had an estimated population of five hundred people. Sarah Johanna is truly *a small place*—its area is approximately 2.34 miles in length, by 990 feet in width.[3] Although less than twenty miles from Guyana's capital, Sarah Johanna feels remote, a fact underscored when Guyana's *Stabroek News* featured it in one of its "World beyond Georgetown" profiles, a series on "far-to-reach places" which "were out of sight and in several instances out of mind as well."[4] The 2011 article notes that the village consists of "people of mostly Indian descent, and most of those residing in the community belong to the Hindu faith" (Clarke 2011). According to the article, Sarah Johanna was an estate orig- inally purchased by my great-grandfather (the stately Indian man in the family photo I described at the start of this chapter), whom it misnames as "Donnie Roberts" (he was formally known in our family as Robert Ranjit Jaisingh, and had the Indian nickname, Dhoni, which means "king").[5] The newspaper story states that Robert Jaisingh bequeathed the land to his three sons, Samuel, Paul, and James. The article is fas- cinating in that it obscures as much as it reveals—Robert's wife, Tily, is absent from the narrative, as is my maternal grandmother, Victorine, who was Robert's only daughter, and Samuel, Paul, and James's sister. This is a particularly striking omission since at the time the piece was published, two of Victorine's children were living in Sarah Johanna: one, her eldest son, who inherited her house, and the other, my mother. Vic- torine was a formidable mother of seven children and a respected elder in the village. She always spoke proudly about owning her home and the land on which it stood—boastful also of the fact that her parents had once owned the entire estate.[6] By falsely positioning Robert Jaisingh's sons as the only heirs to his estate, the article promotes a narrative of patrilineal land transfer that effectively erases the maternal line from my great-grandmother through my grandmother and mother. Furthermore, the utilization of the regal nickname, Dhoni/King, rather than his legal name, Robert, implies a sovereign image of my great-grandfather that again undermines the women in his kin group. Tily was left out of the picture the article painted, and as I read it, I imagined her visage slowly vanishing from our treasured family photograph.

"The World beyond Georgetown: Sarah Johanna" presents a bucolic rendition of life in the village, with a photograph of one of my now- deceased male first cousins, once removed, relaxing in a hammock, and with accompanying shots that include a girl picking cherries, boys biking, chickens in a yard, and a fruit stand laden with fresh produce. The article briefly references three sections of the village, "the Sarah Jo- hanna squatting area which, according to residents, is called 'Somalia' because of its present condition," and "the housing scheme and the old road" (Clarke 2011).[7] One photograph, captioned "a dirt road leading to a squatting area," is the only other reference to the multiethnic settle- ment of newcomers who inhabit otherwise unused land on the outskirts of the village (Clarke 2011). The impoverished and displaced squatters who reside in derelict homes are neither seen nor heard in the piece. In this way, the article minimizes the harsh poverty on the fringes of Sarah Johanna and the vulnerable, multiethnic recent residents.

It is also important to note that many members of the village struggle to make ends meet, and contend with unreliable electricity, poor access to clean water, and the many health disparities attached to economic insecurity. Considerable poverty coexists alongside relative financial security within the village proper, with some members of my family living in dilapidated homes, and others running successful businesses. But the text presents the village in an idyllic light, and stresses its pastoral qualities: "[The] main economic activities in the community are poultry and cattle rearing, fishing and farming—mainly ground provisions." At the same time, the text contradicts this pastoral and self-sufficient slant by stating that most persons work "at the nearby Gafoors hardware store at Land of Canaan, while others seek to make their living in the mining areas in the interior" (Clarke 2011). Sarah Johanna is portrayed as a simple, peaceful place where there is little to no crime and where, although residents complained of poor roads and a lack of medical facilities, almost every home had a kitchen garden and hard-working villagers woke at the crack of dawn to commence "put[ting] their hands to work" (Clarke 2011).

Sarah Johanna *is* all that the article indicates, yet, unsurprisingly, it is far more complex than the story suggests. The town is more "out of sight" than hard to reach; it hugs the country's central thoroughfare between the airport and the capital, but it is easy to miss when one is speeding along the busy road from this international hub to most other parts of the country. Apparently, the village women are also easy to miss. The piece devotes one line to female residents ("some of [them] work from home in nail designing and hair-dressing") (Clarke 2011). It even overlooks their quotidian activities, which conform to the story's bucolic slant—on any given day in Sarah Johanna you can find girls and women handling pointer brooms as they sweep up homes and Bottom Houses, and as they tend to children and animals. And while a young Indo-Guyanese girl picking cherries is seen in one of the accompanying images, by focusing on my male cousin and his male ancestors, the piece elides the voice of the Guyanese girl/woman, so that she is fleetingly seen but not heard.[8] By glossing the village past solely through the patrilineal line, and letting male heirs stand in for Sarah Johanna's people, the article displaces the village's women. This incomplete treatment of the village as a bygone place, alongside the erasure of its women and the impoverished squatters along its outskirts, speaks to the ways in which the political economy of erasure operates between the metropolis of Georgetown, where *Stabroek News* is located, and the rural East Bank.

The newspaper story also paints with a broad stroke when it describes Sarah Johanna as a village of "mostly Indian people" who practice the Hindu faith. Like many of her relatives, Victorine Jaisingh—whom I called "Mama" and villagers respectfully deemed "Auntie Vicky"— practiced a syncretized religious belief system that incorporated elements of Hinduism and Christianity.[9] She observed the Diwali holiday (the Hindu festival of lights) and attended Jhandis (Indian thanksgiving festivities), but she also celebrated Christmas. Later in life, she became a Jehovah's Witness. Far more than through religion, Victorine articulated her Indian identity through food and kin terms. From her I acquired Hindi words like "*bowjhie*" (also spelled "*bhowgie*," a term meaning "sister-in-law," which we also used for "sister") and "*deedee*" (meaning "older sister"), an expression of respect that her younger children used in shortened form, "Dee," for their oldest sister, my Aunt Gene. In Mama's home I ate multiple versions of *chokas*, puris, and chutneys, *mohanbhog* (my favorite), and, of course, curry, from spices that she herself blended. From time to time, my grandmother also prepared dishes that can be traced back to the African continent, including *fufu*, for which she mashed plantains in a mortar with a wooden pestle. Still, our daily meals rested more heavily within Indo-Guyanese traditions. My grandmother was known for her cooking, and even in a country in which almost everyone eats curry, she asserted her Indian cultural identity and imparted my own through food.

I spent my early childhood, from 1972 to 1978 (ages one through seven)—when I immigrated to Brooklyn—in Sarah Johanna with Mama.[10] After moving to New York, I returned to spend most summers with her until I started college, also in the United States. Throughout that childhood in Guyana and Brooklyn, and in the many years since, like the reporter writing for the *Stabroek News*, I thought of my family village as the ancestral land of Indian indentured laborers brought to

Guiana to replace African enslaved labor. In fact, as a young girl, I often felt that I was the sole Jaisingh family member who was of African ancestry. I recalled a few Afro-Guyanese living in and near our village, but they were not our kinfolk. My sense of singularity stemmed from the fact that my mother had married my father, an Afro-Guyanese man— her second husband—after giving birth to my older brother, who was fathered by an Indian man—her first husband. When I was a year old my mother and father moved to Brooklyn, leaving my brother and me with Mama and her second husband. Constrained by immigration laws at the time, which dictated that adults establish employment for themselves before sponsoring their children, my mother made the difficult decision to leave us behind. So, there I was, a little Dougla girl with an Indian brother, and an Indian grandmother, living in an Indian village.

Around the age of six, I recall a family friend from a neighboring village saying that, upon seeing my brother and me waiting for the school bus on the Public Road, she wondered, "What was this Indian boy doing with this little Dougla girl?" Although I was not quite sure what it meant, her comment signaled that I was a "little Dougla girl," and that entailed being different from my Indian brother. This moment of self-recognition of my racial difference recalls foundational instances of racial self-consciousness described by Africana studies scholars like W. E. B. Du Bois and Zora Neale Hurston (Du Bois 1969/1903; Hurston 1928). But while for Du Bois and Hurston such realizations came within the context of US Black/White dichotomies, mine arrived within Guyana, known for being "the land of six peoples"—a reference to its multiethnic composition of Amerindians, Africans, Indians, Europeans, Portuguese, and Chinese (Swan 1957).[11] And as feminist readings of Du Bois's pivotal moment have shown us, such articulations of racial difference are often inextricably connected to gender constructions (Wright 2004).[12] Our family friend, an Indian woman, had pointed out not only my ethno-racial difference but also the gendered difference between my brother and me—she suggested that we were mismatched not only because he was Indian and I Dougla but also because he was a boy and I a girl. And while the seven-year age difference between my older sibling and I, coupled with my young age at the time, should have dispelled the possibility of a sexual relationship, her statement insinuated that ours was a transgressive race/gender coupling that disguised the reality of our kinship. She was only able to solve the mystery of our relatedness when she arrived to find us both under one roof at my grandmother's house.

## Can the Dougla Speak?

This autoethnographic example provides an entryway to begin parsing the social construction of Dougla in Guyana and its implications for the broader argument of this book. A commonly known term in Guyana, Trinidad and Tobago, and Suriname—Caribbean nations with significant populations of the descendants of Indian indentured laborers—"Dougla" has received some scholarly attention in Trinidad and far less critical engagement in the contexts of Guyana and Suriname. The greater attention to the term in Trinidad is indicative of Guyana's neglect in academic discourses—while Guyana is home to the largest population of Indians in the Caribbean and, I suspect, the largest number of Dougla people, the majority of the scant writings on this term is focused on Trinidad and Tobago.[13] Of course, discussions of Dougla experiences in Trinidad usefully inform my project—included in this group are treatments of "Douglarisation" as a gendered political project (Reddock 1994, 2014), theorizations on the Dougla body (England 2008), and discussions of the Dougla figure as a feature of Trinidadian national consciousness (Regis 2011).

Shalini Puri's reading of colonial law "not only for how it structured white/black and white/Indian relations, but also for how it situated Blacks and Indians with respect to one another," draws on examples from Trinidad and Guyana in ways that are meaningful to the project at hand, even though it places greater emphasis on the Trinidadian context (Puri 2004, 176). Puri's description of the Dougla as constituting what she calls a "dis-allowed identity," one that is "literally silenced" in race discussions, stems from her review of colonial law alongside postcolonial examples such as the Mighty Dougla's 1961 calypso, "Split Me in Two" (Puri 2004, 191). In another rare dual consideration of Dougla identities in Trinidad and Guyana—grounded mostly in readings of calypsos and novels—Hernández-Ramdwar briefly gestures in broad fashion to "specificities in how Dougla identities are taken up in Guyana" (Hernández-Ramdwar 1997). More useful is anthropologist Viranjini Munasinghe's ethnographic treatment of "Dougla logics," in which she notes that references to the term do not appear in Trinidad until the 1930s (Munasinghe 2006). "Dougla" has its cultural and linguistic origins in India, and Munasinghe writes, "In the 5th edition of John Platts' *Dictionary of Urdu, Classical Hindi, and English* (1930), Dogla is defined as 'Not of pure blood or breed, mean-blooded, cross-bred, hybrid, mongrel, double-faced, deceitful' (534)" (Munasinghe 2006, 212).[14]

Contrasting "Dougla" with the term "creole," which "asserts pride in mixture," Munasinghe avers that "Dougla" is a pejorative term that connotes "illegitimacy and pollution" (Munasinghe 2006, 212) and, citing Rhoda Reddock, aligns the word with two usages in India: the first invoking intercaste marriage and the second, "'bastard' meaning illegitimate/son of a prostitute" (Reddock 1994, 101, cited in Munasinghe 2006, 212). Thus, "Dougla" is a transplanted term that originally signified the progeny of transgressive intercaste marriages in India, and came to refer to people of mixed African and Indian descent in the Caribbean.[15] The New World cultural context and mutable meanings attached to "Dougla" as it traveled from India to the Caribbean should alert us not only to its global Old World/New World linkages but also to its dependency on cultural specificities that, I will argue, morph not only on the basis of place but also through time. I will also underscore that the gendered connotation in India, which, according to Munasinghe and Reddock, seems to have been decidedly male, has shifted to be more closely aligned with anxieties about female sexuality in the Caribbean.

Overlaps in the cultural meanings attached to "Dougla" in Trinidad and Guyana are numerous, including the colonial-era notion that it represented the mixture of "two alleged inferior types—the African and the Indian" (Munasinghe 2006, 207). In Trinidad, Munasinghe argues, Dougla unions did not elicit the same level of colonial anxiety as did the mixes of unequals (such as White overseers and enslaved Black people) (Munasinghe 2006, 206). In the Guyanese context, however, the planter class's struggle to pit Indians and Africans against one another as a mechanism for protecting the sugar-plantation economy (Rodney 1981) meant that the mixture of these two groups signaled a particular threat to colonial hierarchy. From Munasinghe we glean the potent assertions that the Dougla is a "rather obscure Caribbean figure" (Munasinghe 2006, 204) and that although the Dougla's voice was silent in much of Trinidad's history, "the 'dougla' constitutes a fertile symbolic space for other

Trinidadians to project their unique constellations of racial, sexual and class anxieties at different historical moments" (Munasinghe 2006, 205).

The crucial imperative to let the Guyanese Dougla speak and the projection of varying desires and initiatives onto "the figure of the dougla" surface in Gabrielle Jamela Hosein's critique of Indo-Caribbean feminist literature. While Munasinghe explores "Dougla" from an anthropological perspective and as a nationalizing political project in postindependence Trinidad, Indo-Caribbean women scholars adopted the term for a different aim. "In an attempt to celebrate blurring of Indian-African boundaries against the grain of ethnic antagonism, Indo-Caribbean feminist scholarship conceptually mobilized 'Dougla' to name Indian women's transgressive identities and politics" (Hosein 2016, 207). The Indo-Caribbean feminist movement used the term "Dougla feminists" to describe cultural and theoretical work being done by Indian women who resisted Indian notions of feminine propriety and drew on African elements around them in doing so. For these scholars, "Dougla" referred to cultural mixing—it was situated as an alternative to creolization, which centered Europeans and Africans, while marginalizing Indians (Hosein 2016, 208). These theorists rejected "Indo-Creole" because it connoted hybrid European and Caribbean identities. Instead, they marshaled "Dougla" to recenter Indo-African cultural exchanges. Yet, they were *not* ethnically Dougla and "Douglas' experiences and expressions are absented from the Dougla poetics and feminisms literature, except as background for such theorizing" (Hosein 2016, 208).[16]

Charting this precarious course of Dougla feminism, Hosein quotes Kanhai in outlining the qualities of the approach, which was meant to combine the strength of Afro- and Indocentric grassroots feminisms while eschewing patriarchal racial politics (Hosein 2016, 208). Yet, Dougla feminism was deployed without Dougla embodiment and in the absence of attention to Douglas' own gender and sexual negotiations (Hosein 2016, 210). Much of the Dougla feminism work was centered on the reading of texts—literature (Rahim 2010) and calypsos (Mehta 2004). Reflecting personally on her experience as an Indo-Caribbean mother of a Dougla daughter, and as a scholar who had previously written from the Dougla feminist perspective, Hosein considers her daughter's burgeoning subjectivity as a springboard for critiquing how Dougla feminism deployed Dougla identity without foregrounding actual Dougla voices (Hosein 2016, 209). In so doing, Hosein gestures to a critical reframing of Gayatri Spivak's pivotal query, "Can the subaltern speak?"

By privileging Dougla histories and experiences in Guyana, I aim to redirect this framing *yet again*, toward acknowledging how the Guyanese Dougla voice has been stifled both in her homeland and even in Caribbean discourses aimed at amplifying subaltern voices. Beyond merely amplifying Guyanese Dougla voices, this exercise sweeps up granular (small-scale, on-the-ground, and local Guyanese) gender constructions alongside broader circum-Caribbean and, broader still, global presumptions about Indian and African women's subjectivities to present a more nuanced understanding of both the archives and the here and now. Implicit in my reframing is a new reclamation of the pejorative term "Dougla." In this respect, my project is in dialogue with Sue Ann Barratt and Aleah N. Ranjitsingh's *Dougla in the Twenty-First Century: Adding to the Mix*, notable in the literature for its attention to actual Dougla voices in Trinidad and Tobago, and in the dual-island nation's diasporic communities in the United States (2021). Barratt and Ranjitsingh draw on scores of in-depth interviews with Dougla men and women to "interrogate the ontology of the Dougla as a mixed individual," demonstrating that "Dougla talk—narratives, descriptions, explanations" reveal shared and varied experiences that the authors bring together under a central question that surfaced among their respondents: "Am I mixed enough?" (Barratt and Ranjitsingh 2021, 30). The authors marshal this question in part to inform their aim to introduce "the Dougla as neither Black nor white, just Black, just Asian nor just other; but as *just* Dougla (to assert the position of our respondents); an individual who is well understood, taken for granted, and easily recognizable as mixed in Caribbean spaces" (Barratt and Ranjitsingh 2021, 5). This study advances new insights into Dougla subjectivity by "giv[ing] the Dougla a chance to speak their own truth as they now live it" (Barratt and Ranjitsingh 2021, 29). And these authors tread new ground, particularly in a chapter that focuses on Dougla experiences in the diaspora, even while the diaspora in question hails from Trinidad and Tobago.

## Placing the Guyanese Dougla Woman

The greater tendency to center Dougla theorizations within the Trinidadian context adds weight to the singular relevance of the Guyanese sociologist and self-identified "Dogla," Kamala Kempadoo. Kempadoo's essay "Negotiating Cultures: A 'Dogla' Perspective," from the edited volume, *Matikor: The Politics of Identity for Indo-Caribbean Women*, stands out as unique both in its grounding in the Guyanese milieu and in being based on the scholar's feminist praxis vis-à-vis her own Dougla subjectivity as a productive departure point for her scholarly thought.[17] Kempadoo maintains that although "Dougla" does not convey the same derogatory connotation the term held in India, it is still seen in many ways as a pejorative, and Douglas are held in low regard by Indo- and Afro-Guyanese alike.[18]

Mindful that Douglas are largely ignored in scholarship on Guyana, Kempadoo argues that such symbolic erasure works to vanish "people who live outside the boundaries of what we know as racial and ethnic groups" (Kempadoo 1999, 105). Her insistence on her own secure sense of self, in which she refuses to choose one identity over another, serves as a foil against her experiences in various countries where those bent on narrow or ethnocentric racial definitions saw her existence as cause for confusion (Kempadoo 1999, 105). In this way, we can read Kamala Kempadoo as writing against a body of literature that has often cast the mixed-race woman, particularly the mulatta, as a "tragic" and "confused" figure. She eschews easy categorization: "Even the self-definitions of my Guyanese grandmothers, one from a sugar plantation in a predominantly Indian community, the other from 'up-river' Berbice with African-European-Amerindian influence, are vastly different from those of many of their grandchildren who today are part of the Caribbean Diaspora in different parts of the world. In other words, the starting point for my understanding of identity is of a cultural dynamic and multi-layered complexity, defined by time and location" (Kempadoo 1999, 103–4). Time and location, Kempadoo insists, are central to the way she and her grandmothers (of different ethnicities) constructed their self-definitions. The author notes that this multilayered sense of self also goes against the grain of political analyses of Guyana that have tended to emphasize conflicts between Indians and Blacks. She credits her international upbringing, coupled with her family's progressive politics, with instilling in her the conviction for staking claims to both her Indian and her African heritage. It is worth noting that her family had ties to the Working People's Alliance and the Guyana Human Rights Committee, both of which were regarded as multiracial groups, with the former being the party of Guyanese historian and labor advocate Walter Rodney.

Kempadoo's self-reflexive snapshot of Dougla identity underscores the value of autoethnography for filling gaps in more traditional ethnographic approaches. Ethnographic approaches to ethnic identity formation in Guyana have run the gamut from Brackette Williams's brilliant landmark study, *Stains on My Name, War in My Veins: Guyana and the Politics of Cultural Struggle* (1991), to Yoshiko Shibata's far more incomplete analysis, "Intermarriage, 'Douglas,' Creolization of Indians in Contemporary Guyana: The Rocky Road of Ambiguity and Ambivalence" (2002). Williams is focused on relating "in microsociological terms" how hegemonic ideologies structure and are structured by cultural productions and identity formations that exist in present-day nation-states but are defined by past ideologies linked back to Europe. She hopes to place quotidian ethnographic dynamics of "a small community, in a small country, at the center of anthropological discourses on the relations among material inequalities, cultural productions, and the distribution of power in the formation of nation-states" (Williams 1991, xvii).

Williams's work is impactful in its attention to Guyanese ethnic relations as a window into both small-scale processes of identity formation and nation-building, and global systems of cultural meaning making. To be clear, in Williams's framework, ethnic conflict between Indo- and Afro-Guyanese is not presented as a sign of a national propensity for conflict but rather as indicative of historically rooted processes derived from European colonialism and hegemony, which parallel the politics of cultural struggle in Europe. Yet, interestingly, in their attempts to delineate intermarriage and Dougla identity in Guyana, both Williams and Shibata rely on ethnic stereotypes and the racial generalizations derived from them. It is important to note that the two anthropologists glean contradictory and conflicting emic characterizations of Douglas as being stereotyped as either inheriting the worst traits of both groups (Williams 1991, 102) or embodying the best traits of each (Shibata 2002,

212). Woefully, in Shibata's case, the anthropologist seems to have internalized the very stereotypes voiced by her "informants"—she goes so far as to state that "what [she] learned to recognize as *dougla* was the combination of certain physical features with behavioral traits" (Shibata 2002, 211). These typically Dougla behavioral traits, according to Shibata, are being reserved and diffident (Shibata 2002, 211), and "well spoken, honest, generous, thoughtful, courageous and mature" (Shibata 2002, 212). While Shibata's treatment is based on three months of fieldwork and numerous interviews with Dougla interviewees, her actual quotations from Douglas are few and far between, as she instead relies on summarizing phrases such as "the majority of my *dougla* informants displayed a deep regard for their mothers" (Shibata 2002, 213). This is a technique Williams also employs, in her case to convey how "informants" relied on racial stereotypes: "In this regard East Indian informants frequently claim that the Black man does not know how to make life, and, just as frequently, African informants say the same of East Indians. Both African and East Indian informants tend to agree that Portuguese do not know how to make a living" (Williams 1991, 56–57).

The result is that the Dougla voice is almost entirely absented in Shibata's work and only taken into account through negative stereotyping in Williams's. For example, Williams relates,

> Informants argue that despite ethnic socialization, racial/ethnic heritage "will out" (that is, manifest itself) in the long run: what is in the "blood" will sooner or later show in one's behavior. A shopkeeper, angry with her teenage son for neglecting his chores to spend the day socializing with friends, yelled at him, "You should have been born in a nigger yard! Doogla [mixed race] is wasted on you." From the standpoint of her identity preference for him, she effectively charged him with improper emphasis on sociability while reminding him that he had "grown a Doogla" because he was born into a Doogla, not an African, household. (Williams 1991, 57–58)

While I am not disagreeing with Williams on the salience of these stereotypes and on her characterization of Guyanese as seeing racial mixture as a "blood" trait that lingers only to manifest itself in the behaviors of subsequent generations, the above example does not feature the Dougla's voice but rather represents a Dougla boy through the stereotypes his mother places on him.[19]

Williams situates Dougla against earlier European/Aboriginal mixed unions and recognizes that the composition of mixed populations in Guyana has shifted and remains "largely uninvestigated" (Williams 1991, 131). She notes, like Shibata, that after 1912, terms connoting mixtures between Europeans and other ethnic groups gave way to a varied terminology for Dougla mixtures, including "'Cabbaculas' (African-Portuguese or African-Amerindian), 'Santantones' (Portuguese-African), 'Coolidooglas' (East Indian–African or other), and 'Chinnidooglas' (Chinese– and any other)" (210). Williams adds that any of these mixtures might be called "No Nations" or "Cosmopolitans"—this latter construct, I would argue, gestures to Guyana's long engagement with global racializations. Both authors point out that the proliferation of terms for racial mixture demonstrates that Guyanese society is inherently mixed and that this is articulated in the people's assertions that as Guyanese, "We'z awl wan famili" (Williams 1991, 98). Of course, this belief echoes Guyana's national motto, "One People, One Nation, One Destiny," which stands in contrast to the scholarly emphasis on ethnic conflict and the earlier labeling of Guyana as the "land of six peoples."[20] The tension between "informants" utilizing the idiom of kinship to express interracial unity and their widespread reliance on negative ethnic stereotypes signals the contradictory nature of racial constructions in Guyana and beyond. And the work of these two anthropologists gives us insight into the politicization of ethnicity and the enduring dichotomy between "Africans" and "Indians."

Ultimately, for Williams, Douglas represent the physical form of the "war in my veins" reference in the title of her book—they are the embodiment of ethnic conflict between Indo- and Afro-Guyanese. Still, Afro-Guyanese—not Douglas—are Williams's primary focus (Williams 1991, 156). The result is that when we read Williams to gain an understanding of Dougla subjectivity and cultural belonging, we get the valuable insight that Douglas perform the critical labor of informing both Afro- and Indo-Guyanese identity, but we are less clear on how they actually negotiate this terrain or how they articulate their ethno-racial consciousness beyond stereotyping. Still, the merits of Williams's study are undeniable. The fact that her field site is a bit of an outlier—unusual in that it is described as a primarily African rural Demerara village, when most Afro-Guyanese reside in the urban center of Georgetown, and most Indo-Guyanese live in the rural countryside, especially in the coastal Demerara villages—underscores the exceptions to hard and fast rules about ethnic demographics in Guyana. These contradictions come to the fore in my attention to Dougla identity in Sarah Johanna.

Both Williams's and Shibata's studies paint a picture of the Dougla as a figure largely shaped by ethno-racial clashes and racialized political violence, traits that have been marshaled in political discourse as emblematic of Guyanese society as a whole. Shibata seems to reify these understandings of Guyanese society by asserting that "Guyana has witnessed some of the worst examples of ethnic conflict over the last 50 years," making it "one of the most racially/ethnically divided countries in the Caribbean" (Shibata 2002, 193). This perspective casts the Dougla as a troublesome subject within a nation at odds with itself—a narrative that relies, in part, on characterizations of Guyana as marred by ethnic animosity.

The ethnic-conflict portrait runs against the grain of Walter Rodney's touchstone study, *A History of the Guyanese Working People, 1881–1905*, in that it characterizes the violent 1960s riots as emblematic of attitudes towards Indo-Afro Guyanese mixtures in the *longue durée*. Rodney complicates this account of ethno-racial contradictions and their engendering factors, pointing to "the sustained volume of state-aided Indian immigration, the residential separation of the two main racial groups, the mutual intelligibility of some aspects of nonmaterial culture, the slow rate of diversification of the colonial economy, and the conscious manipulation of the society by those who had state power" (Rodney 1981, 189). For Rodney, the political rivalry between Africans and Indians in the 1960s led to the politicized violence of that period—the result of "both local and international class struggle" (Rodney 1981, 189). He concludes, "The specificity of the early 1960s can scarcely be used to characterize the entire history of Guyana. On the contrary, one sides with the judgment of a Guyanese labor spokesman. H.J.M. Hubbard, who wrote (in 1969): 'It is by any standards a remarkable fact that in a competitive semi-feudal society such as British Guiana with restricted social and economic opportunities and less jobs than potential workers, very few serious physical inter-racial conflicts arose between the ethnic groups constituting the population'" (Rodney 1981, 189). We cannot discount Rodney's insistence, backed up by historical evidence, that even though colonial powers set Afro- and Indo-Guyanese at odds, the ethnic violence of the 1960s did not signal a national character.[21] Still, Rodney's decidedly Marxist efforts to organize an ethnically diverse Working People's Alliance (WPA) in Guyana in the midst of violent interethnic confrontations proved to be a lofty and unattainable goal.

If we consider Rodney's refusal to interpret ethnic conflict as emblematic of Guyanese society and his unrealized goal of multiethnic coalition building alongside the critiques and observations of another prominent voice in the WPA, that of the feminist activist Andaiye, we get an even sharper picture of the ruptures between Africans and Indians in Guyana (Andaiye with Trotz 2020). Andaiye and Alissa Trotz examine the 1961–1964 period of violence between Indians and Africans alongside the ideological differences between the two leaders who spearheaded Guyana's movement for independence, Cheddi Jagan and Forbes Burnham. With British and American forces backing Burnham, the rivalry between the two leaders became the basis for a political racial divide. Andaiye and Trotz explore the contending narratives of violence emanating from this period, highlighting how in "the narratives passed down from generation to generation, to this day people shift numbers and dates and causes and effects . . . often . . . tell[ing] only the stories of atrocities against their own race" (Andaiye with Trotz 2020, 61). Yet, even within these shifting narratives, gendered violence, rape, and women's concerns about the safety of their children emerge as common experiences for both Afro- and Indo-Guyanese women (Andaiye with Trotz 2020, 62–63). By examining violence in Guyana through a feminist analytic, Andaiye and Trotz are able to complicate both politically situated treatments such as Rodney's and ethnographic representations such as Williams's and Shibata's. Andaiye and Trotz's account stems as much from an assertion that "there is nothing unique to Guyana about the existence of two or more race groups set up in competition with each other" as it does from a clear-eyed recounting of the gendered/racialized violence of the period (Andaiye with Trotz 2020, 58).

We might consider Andaiye and Trotz's feminist reading of ethnic violence in Guyana alongside the viewpoint offered by the Jamaican writer and cultural theorist Sylvia Wynter as a way to understand what looking at and looking out from Guyana can impart to the world. In a 2001 interview with David Scott, Wynter related how being stationed in Guyana in 1971 in the wake of blatant electoral fraud and racialized violence along ethno-political lines transformed her work. On the one hand, Forbes Burnham's US-backed socialist stranglehold on the country brutalized the Indo-Guyanese population. On the other hand, Cheddi Jagan, a Marxist blacklisted by the Americans as a Soviet ally, had subjected Afro-Guyanese to economic hardship. While witnessing the riots from her position inside Jagan's Red House (the name comes from the structure's bright red color, but as Jagan's residence it evoked the antithesis of the US White House due to the Guyanese leader's communist affinities), Wynter observed a "division between the black and the Indian groups that was profound" (Scott 2000, 141). She describes how the traumatic events played out from her vantage point:

> But at this time masses of people are marching towards the Red House, and Georgetown is burning, and I am inside the Red House. I'll never forget that! . . . As I looked out the window—you see, what was traumatic for me was the stark nature of the division between black and Indian— you had a black policeman at the gate, but you had a sharp-shooting Indian from the coast with a rifle aimed at him from the upstairs window. And outside you have the masses of people streaming towards [the Red House] and Georgetown is burning . . . and riots! (Scott 2000, 140–41)

Wynter goes on to note that CIA intervention actually sparked the riots, with her own caveat that the CIA "can only act on the basis of divisions that are already there" (Scott 2000, 142). Wynter seemingly downplays the CIA's involvement while emphasizing that the divisions were already there due to influence from the British. My point in sharing her experience in Guyana is that she came away profoundly changed. "Then, coming out of my own experience in Guyana," she said, "I had become very interested in the idea of how to create a superstructure, of how you can induce a sense of solidarity, of continuity" (Scott 2000, 145). She concluded, "After leaving Guyana I realized that there is something important that cannot be explained, either in the liberal-humanist or in the Marxist paradigms" (Scott 2000, 153). Here, we have Wynter using Guyana to think through the limitations of Marxist frameworks and to assist her in conceptualizing a theory of humanness. More than refusing Marxism, Wynter is outlining the basis for her subsequent contestations of liberal humanism.[22] But her example couches the nation's fight for sovereignty within the dichotomy of the Black policeman and the Indian sharpshooter—both male arms of the state who are geographically situated—the Black policeman at the gate is understood as hailing from Georgetown while the Indian sharpshooter is "from the coast."

The Red House is now designated as the Cheddi Jagan Research Center, and present-day visitors to it might notice, as I did, the diminutive size of the building. In reality, the distance between the upstairs window from which the Indian sharpshooter pointed his rifle and the gate where the Black policeman stood is quite small. The pointer broom sweeps these two male figures closer together, both exposing their proximity to each other and calling attention to the erasure of the Guyanese woman in this dichotomy. Wynter's articulation of her experience in Guyana, no matter how foundational to her thinking, is limited (though not necessarily flawed) in accentuating men as arms of the state and as central to the ethnic-conflict narrative. From her lookout at Jagan's Red House, Guyanese women are eclipsed. Andaiye and Trotz place Guyanese women, both Indian and African, at the center of the very forms of violence Wynter witnesses (Trotz 2020). I am, therefore, following Wynter in arguing that Guyana affords a prodigious viewpoint, but I am more squarely focused on the political economy of erasure that exploits cleavages and masks affinities between Afro- and Indo-Guyanese, and on how looking at women's experiences uncovers more subtle fissures and overlaps, like broom strokes in the sand at early dawn.

## The *Tidalectics* of a Guyanese Girlhood

For my generation (born in the early 1970s), the global influence of American popular culture and cultural exchanges with Guyanese in cities like New York, London, and Toronto helped shape racial self-identifications. After my parents emigrated to New York, I became what newspaper articles from the eighties and nineties called a "Barrel Child," a youngster fostered in the Caribbean by maternal kin but supported by remittances and American products my mother shipped back from New York in large barrels.

While we lacked fresh, clean, running water, electricity, and plumbing, we had an infrequent supply of sneakers, clothes, and toys from the United States. I imagine that canned foods and other practical items were included in those shipments, but the toys reign supreme in my memory. I recall my brother receiving a skateboard—a contraption he and I knew nothing about using. So, for about a week, I sat on its plastic base, my tiny fingers gripping the sides, and my skinny legs crouched in front of me, with my knees beneath my chin. My brother squatted behind me, pushing me along our dirt road. Numerous spills ensued and I still have the scarred knees to show for it. At some point my brother must have realized that he was meant to stand on the skateboard and propel himself by pushing off with one foot. I received a bike with training wheels and a fully furnished dollhouse—some of the contents of which were a mystery. A rectangular box with a smaller rectangular inset and dials on one side confounded me. It was hollow in the back so I turned it over and used it as a trunk for doll clothes. I didn't learn that it was a television until my brother and I joined my parents in Brooklyn years later. Although we were not always clear on how to use them, our toys sent from abroad were the envy of our cousins in Sarah Johanna.[23] Therefore, this, too, positioned me as different; I was ethnically different and to an extent marked by our possession of coveted items.

My grandmother's home always had food and desirable material goods sent from New York. Still, any sense of comparative privilege evaporated when I emigrated to the United States and realized that *there* I was different because I had a mouth full of cavities (Guyana, like Jamaica and other parts of the Caribbean, lacked fresh milk),[24] and I spoke a strange dialect of English. While my American teachers and classmates were unable to fully decipher my Guyanese creole, my racial identity was clear to them—I was Black. So, I brought this racial designation back home on summers spent with my grandmother, whose only form of preparation for me when I departed Guyana was a cryptic warning that America was "very racial." When I returned home throughout my preadolescence and adolescence, I pondered my place in this Indian community, and the contradictions of hardship and abundance, and Indianness and Blackness that characterized my childhood.

Here I must add a few clear declarations regarding my racial positionality about which, no doubt, some readers will be curious: my family in Sarah Johanna never treated me like an outsider, and as I grew into adulthood my mixed heritage did not strike me as a site of confusion. As Victorine's granddaughter, I was as protected and as loved as any other girl-child in Sarah Johanna. I roamed the two dirt roads of our village as freely as any girl could, and when, after we emigrated, I returned during summers, my Indian cousins came and spent the night with me at my grandmother's house. On nights when I cried because I missed my mother, these girl cousins slept in my bed with me, keeping me company. When they could not sleep over, I slept in my grandmother's bed. Still, the more time I spent in Brooklyn, the more I came to identify as Black. There, I was surrounded by a multiethnic group of friends that included fellow West Indians, African Americans, Jews, Italian Americans, and Puerto Ricans. While I had close friends in all these groups, I identified strongly with shared experiences of racial discrimination among my African American and West Indian friends. Although I am aware that I appear to some to be racially ambiguous, most US observers recognize that I am of African descent. Indianness was far less a part of my self-identity in the United States, though it became encompassed in my broader sense of being Guyanese. Outside of Guyana, I am rarely perceived as having Indian ancestry. Personally and professionally, I have made my self-identification as Black clear, and at the point of this writing, I have spent many more years living in America than I spent as a young girl in Guyana.

## "I Knew It! Full Negro!"

On a fieldwork and archival research trip in 2016, I visited the National Archives of Guyana—now known as the Walter Rodney Archives—in hopes of learning about my great-grandparents, Tily and Robert, the Indian couple in the photograph I described at the start of this chapter. In the oral histories passed down in my family, Tily was called by her nickname, "Tent Ma." I only learned her legal name after I completed my first book, an ethnographic study of Caribbean girls—of mostly African descent—residing in Brooklyn, the publication of which prompted my mother to finally divulge that Tent Ma was "the one who brought Negro blood into our family," telling me that her full maiden name was Tily Mackania Abinsetts. That my mother's side of "our family" had "Negro blood" was news to me. I had gazed at the cracked and worn photograph of Tent Ma and Robert throughout my early years in Guyana—I would have had no reason to imagine either of them as anything other than Indian, because they appeared as such in the picture.

I went to the Walter Rodney Archives seeking clarification on my mother's disclosure, and in hopes of finding archival records on my father's family, the LaBennetts. I learned, however, that the repository only housed archival documents related to "foreign births," which for their purposes described Indian indentured laborers and not enslaved Africans and their descendants. Forced to confine my research to my maternal line, I focused on my maternal grandmother and her ancestors.[25] After a long day at the archives, my mother arrived to pick me up in the late afternoon, to find that I was still combing through the enormous tomes. My mother waited impatiently in the car, not fully understanding what I hoped to find there. Armed with Mama's birth certificate, her parents' names, and the name of the village in which they lived before Sarah Johanna, after hours of searching, I found no records for Mama's father, Robert Ranjit Jaisingh. My quest for the paternal Jaisingh line, which was so prominent in the newspaper article about Sarah Johanna, had run completely cold. But not so for Tily Mackania Abinsetts.

First, I finally located my grandmother's birth record and hurried to the archive entrance to wave my mother in from the car, exclaiming, "I found Mama!" She hustled in and, standing beside me, my mother ran her finger along the lines of the record book, which listed my grandmother's name, sex, and race, which was designated as "Calcutta." Calcutta was the port of departure for Indian indentured laborers, and immigration agents initially racialized Indians from different linguistic and cultural backgrounds according to "racial" groups such as Madras and Calcutta.[26] My mother traced the lines of the record book with her index finger—even though I whispered to her, uselessly, that she should not touch the actual pages. No white gloves were presented to us and even if they had been, how could I convince my mother that she should not try to touch this past that rightfully belonged to her?

We located a birth record number for Mama's mother, Tily Mackania Abinsetts, which opened the floodgates. The archival clerks, who until then had treated me standoffishly, seemed enlivened either by the leads we had uncovered or by my mother's presence—she possessed a local legitimacy that I obviously lacked. Additional, equally large and fraying logs were produced, and we located Tily in the Register of Births in Berbice, 1892–1896. At the top of Tily's birth records page, the heading "The Port Mourant Estate" appeared. Below it, we found a birth record number, "Name of Infant," "Sex," "Race," and "Date of Birth." Alongside this information, across a centerfold page appears "Description of Father" and "Description of Mother." Under each description appear the subcategories "Name"; "No."; "Name of Ship in which Introduced"; "Year of Arrival"; and, finally, "Remarks." These categories reduced Tily's life to dates, "facts," and labels. They are archival calculations within the political economy of intimacies and erasures about which Lowe (2015) and Hartman (2008) write.

My mother and I scanned the information pertaining to Tily Mackania Abinsetts. Her records were a deviation amid a list in which "Calcutta" appeared as the overwhelming designation for "Race." Tily's birth record appears on a page listing twenty-seven births. On this list, two infants' races are listed as "Madras" and all others, except for Tily, are racially designated as "Calcutta." There is no racial designation in the box in which Tily's race should appear; instead, there is a license record number for her marriage (a notation that was, of course, added many years after her birth), and a mysterious abbreviation: "wC." Her date of birth is indicated as "1 July, 1892." Her father's name is documented as "G. Abinsetts," and in place of the name of the ship on which he was introduced appears another anomaly on the page: logged parenthetically, the word "(Negro)" is written. My mother scrutinized the page, and stopping at G. Abinsetts's racial designation she proclaimed—her voice piercing the silence of the archives—"I knew it! *Full* Negro!" Interestingly, my mother had inserted the word "full"—it appeared nowhere on the page.

As my archival research unfolded over the remainder of the afternoon, no finding I made was as significant for my mother as was G. Abinsetts's "Negro" designation. I would later come to understand—and my mother would be very pleased by this conclusion—that she was, in many respects, right. But as I continued my search that day, I dwelled instead on Tily's mother, whose name, "Poragia," immigration number, name of the ship on which she arrived, and year of arrival were documented on the page. Finding this documentation of Poragia's arrival in

British Guiana was, for me, a monumental recovery because it put on record our ancestor who made the initial journey from India, but it was of very little consequence to my mother.

## Poragia's Passage

The harrowing separation and perilous passage that Indian indentured women experienced en route to Guiana are poignantly detailed in historian Verene A. Shepherd's *Maharani's Misery: Narratives of a Passage from India to the Caribbean* (2002) and in journalist Gaiutra Bahadur's *Coolie Woman: The Odyssey of Indenture* (2013). As I uncovered the documentation of my great-great-grandmother's journey, I saw clear parallels to the sojourn of Bahadur's great-grandmother, the subject of her book. According to Bahadur, the history of such "coolie women" is a repressed one, marked in many cases by abduction, mortal danger, and rape. Shepherd corroborates the widespread reality of rape, but complicates this historiography of indentured women by balancing accounts of Indian women's experiences of "extreme hardship, exploitation, and 'sexploitation'" against arguments that "emigration was of significant material benefit to those who left India" (Shepherd 2002, xvii).[27] Still, even in Shepherd's pointed analysis, Indian indentured women emerge as mostly young, single, and independent women and girls who could have been kidnapped or who could have made the choice to emigrate to improve their desperate economic status (Shepherd 2002, 33). Shepherd's and Bahadur's studies positioned me to imagine the multifaceted significance of Poragia's journey to and arrival in Guiana.

In a cruel twist of colonial record keeping, I learned far more about Poragia than I did about my Guiana-born ancestors, Tily and her father. Beyond her date of birth, her parents' names and races, that she married my great-grandfather at the age of sixteen, on June 1, 1908, Tent Ma remained a mystery—her racial category, one of the "definite" forms of identification included for all of the other births on her record page, was unspecified. On a subsequent archival research trip to Guyana, I surveyed the entire register of births in Berbice between 1892 and 1896, a logbook that listed about twenty-seven births per page, across 133 pages. The vast majority of infants listed in the log were racially designated as Calcutta, with a smaller group, approximately 15 percent, designated as

"Madras," and an even smaller group (about twenty-five in the entire log) designated as "China." In this entire archive of approximately 3,590 births occurring among immigrants residing in Berbice between 1892 and 1896, the overwhelming majority of the fathers are Indian men for whom the name of the ship on which they arrived appears. For a few, in place of a ship's name are the abbreviations "BR" for "Birth Register" (meaning they were born in Guiana) and "CR" for "Casual Register" (which, according to the archivist, indicated that these immigrants returned to India and were not longtime residents in Guiana).

Tily's father, G. Abinsetts, is the one and only "Negro" that I found in the *entire* log. This is to say that of the approximately 3,590 births occurring in this four-year period among indentured Indians in late 1800s Berbice, Poragia is the only Indian woman who is registered as having birthed a baby fathered by a "Negro" man. Tily's race is undesignated, and like her father, she has the distinction of being the only one of her kind among the infants registered. Her racial identity was unidentifiable, an anomaly. The record keepers either could not or would not designate her race at birth. And the "wC" notation where her racial designation should have appeared remains one of the dark corners of the archives. The letter "C" could have denoted "coloured" or "creole," as these were terms used to categorize mixed-race people at the time. It is also possible that "wC" was an abbreviation for "without caste." But the cursive flourish with which this these two letters are inscribed, with the "C" underlined, could also indicate a record keeper's initials (an abbreviated signature), suggesting that an additional official had to "sign off" on Tily's singular, unidentifiable racial status.[28]

It is clear, however, that Poragia (Tily's mother) arrived as an indentured laborer from India and in addition to the name of the ship on which she arrived, and the year, the "Remarks" section of the log indicated a record number for both her "Woman's Emigration Certificate" and her "Certificate of Exemption" (referring to the year in which she completed her indentured servitude). Poragia journeyed to Guiana on a ship called the *Lightning*, disembarking from 8, Garden Reach, Calcutta, and arriving on the 17th of March, 1881. As the capital of British India until 1911, Calcutta served as the main point of departure for indentured laborers from North India. Garden Reach was the site of three of the four colonial depots used by ten emigration agencies (Mangru 2013).

As Shepherd notes, anxieties about Indian women's sexuality were always at the core of debates around indentureship (Shepherd 2002, 9). For Poragia, this contextualization has implications not only for how we interpret the information provided on her Emigration Certificate but also for how she might have been regarded in India before she departed, and for her decision to have a child with an Afro-Guyanese man. Her departure in the late 1800s coincided with anti-emigration lobbying that suspected Indian women were being lured abroad for purposes of prostitution. Whether or not Poragia was a sex worker, her sexuality would have been stigmatized because she was a single woman boarding an indentured-laborer vessel.

In addition to her point of departure and the date and the name of the ship, Poragia's document revealed a host of other information about her. She is noted as being twenty-one years old at the time of her emigration. The convenience of this age was not lost on me. I wondered if Poragia really was twenty-one, or if that age suited the labor recruiters, who were notorious for employing nefarious methods—including widespread kidnapping—for capturing and convincing laborers to emigrate. Planters requested an age range of twenty to thirty years old for women emigrants, with younger women being acceptable if they emigrated as part of a family unit (Shepherd 2002, 10). This incentivized recruiters to misrepresent the age of women emigrants. That Poragia was listed as unmarried was also worthy of suspicion—women wishing to escape abusive husbands or having other reasons for wanting another life could have lied to meet the criteria to emigrate. With an awareness of this at the forefront of my mind, I considered the details of Poragia's certificate; she was unmarried and had no next of kin, but her father's name is indicated as Shewdesi. She hailed from the Ahir, a caste traditionally linked to cow herding and agriculture. Her "Zillah" or district is indicated as Cawnpore (now Kanpur, a large city in the northeast of India that had been a British military station from the late eighteenth century to the mid-nineteenth century) and her Pergunnah (also known as Pargana, a former administrative unit used by Muslim kingdoms in India, which under British colonialism remained meaningful as a geographic term) is indicated as Ghatumphore (Ghatampur), located in the state of Uttar Pradesh. The document states that Poragia came from the village of Situtphore, known today as Sitapur, and located in the northeast of the country, not far from the border of present-day Nepal.

How did a young, unmarried woman traveling without any kin make it from Sitapur to Calcutta, in West Bengal? The approximately 675-mile distance represents a journey that today would take twenty-three hours traveling by train. The Howrah train line, which runs from Sitapur to Calcutta, was completed by the late 1860s, well before Poragia departed from Calcutta in 1881. Therefore, it is conceivable that she made this journey by train. But on her own? It would have been forbidden for a woman to travel alone, even if she was from a lower caste, but recruiters made extra efforts to meet the quota of women because ships could not sail until quotas were met, and they were paid substantially more for recruiting females—full recruitment rates applied to girls over the age of ten (Shepherd 2002, 10). This tells us that Poragia could have been significantly younger than her documented age. Moreover, recruiters took women from their villages accompanied by *chaprasis* (messengers or orderlies), a practice that ostensibly eased the cultural anxieties of young, single women traveling alone (Shepherd 2002, 14). If Poragia did make the journey by train, what would motivate and enable her to strike out on her own for Calcutta? Was she abducted? If she was indeed twenty-one, why was she unmarried? Was she orphaned? Was she a sex worker? The emigration certificate provided no clues to aid in answering these questions. Her lower caste status does indicate, however, that she at least had an economic incentive to emigrate, and the drought and famine that struck India throughout the 1880s "provided the context in which emigration agents and recruiters lured members of the rural population to undertake the journey across the 'black water'" (Rodney 1981, 33–34).

The document also specifies that Poragia stood at four feet, nine-and-one-half inches tall, she had a scar on the inside of her right thigh, and her medical examination revealed her to be "free from all bodily and mental disease."[29] She had been vaccinated, and she was deemed "a fit subject for emigration as an agricultural labourer." Still, these medical evaluations were cursory, both because officials wanted to maintain quotas and because a close examination of women by male doctors was culturally unacceptable (Shepherd 2002, 15). Along with its declaration that Poragia was fit to travel, her Emigration Certificate indicated that "she

[had] expressed her willingness to proceed to work for hire . . . and that [the countersigned Protector of Emigrants at Calcutta and the Emigration Agent for British Guiana had] explained to her all matters concerning her duties as an Emigrant." Historical accounts such as Shepherd's tell us, however, not only that immigrants were baited into indentureship under false pretenses but also that the length of the journey and the environmental and working conditions that awaited them in Guiana were a mystery to them. The degree to which Poragia consented to her future in Guiana is suspect.

We might read some symbolic significance into the name of the ship on which Poragia traveled—the *Lightning*. A symbol of speed, energy, destruction! Lightning also conveys a sudden stroke of fortune. But Poragia's journey of over one hundred days from India to Guiana was long and fraught with danger.[30] The historical accounts presented by Shepherd, centering the rarely heard voices of Indian women aboard emigration ships, tell us that during that nearly four-month journey, Poragia would have been in constant danger of sexual assault or rape (Shepherd 2002, 23). Still, some of the conditions of her journey may have been markedly better than those aboard slave ships—the post-emancipation era brought checks and regulations for emigrant ship conditions such as size of ship and space for human cargo, food, medical treatment, and proper ventilation (Shepherd 2002, 17). Adherence to these regulations was, however, subject to great variation from one ship to another, and there were many accounts of insufficient food supplies, contaminated water, and physical punishment of emigrants by crew members—including the handcuffing and shackling of laborers (Shepherd 2002, 25).

Because British Guiana pioneered the Indian indentureship system in the Caribbean, the histories of women like Shepherd's subject, Maharani, Bahadur's great-grandmother, Sujaria, and my great-great-grandmother, Poragia, are especially significant. Guiana received 238,909 Indians between 1838 and 1917 (Shepherd 2002, 3). This represents 55.6 percent of the total of 429,623 Indians arriving in the colonial Caribbean (Shepherd 2002, 3). While, as I have mentioned, the scholarly scale tilts towards representing Indo-Caribbean and Dougla identities in Trinidad, that nation received 33.5 percent of the total number of Indian immigrants, a number considerably lower than Guiana's.

The year Poragia landed in Guiana, 1881, is the year Walter Rodney chose as the starting point of his history of the Guyanese working people. Rodney flags this year as the beginning of working people's political mobilization:

> Working people appeared as supplicants before the Poor Law Enquiry Commission which sat in 1881; but in 1905 strikes, riots, and mass public meetings shook the composure of the colonial state and detained a British warship for months afterward. . . . The tendency has been to skim over the last decades of the nineteenth century, and thus to contribute to the impression that the eventful epoch of post-Emancipation struggles was followed by a long and unrelieved "dead season." But it was in the late nineteenth century that the modern political economy of Guyana took shape. Nonindentured Indians became the largest group on the plantations, rice farming was added to coastal agriculture, gold and diamond and timber industries were promoted in the hinterland, the middle class emerged as an important entity, and the formal political arena ceased to be the exclusive concern of the planter class. (Rodney 1981, 219–20)

For Rodney, then, 1881 represented a crossroads in Guyanese history. He notes that the changing ethnic landscape coincided with other critical shifts, underscoring the ways in which burgeoning extractive and resource-related industries (diamond mining and forestry) were, from this period on, processes that shaped the shared and separate social realities of Indians and Africans in Guiana. When Poragia arrived in Guiana, her physical labor and that of other indentured women like her fueled plantation capitalism and informed Guyana's modern political economy. And Poragia's arrival, I would argue, coincided with inconstant gendered racializations—her intimate relationship with a Black man and the offspring of their union represented the formation of a new race/gender categorization.

Poragia was part of the third phase of Indian indentureship—she arrived forty-seven years after slavery was abolished in Guiana, when the balance of the plantation labor force had long turned from Afro-Guyanese domination to being comprised of 80.4 percent Indian labor (Shepherd 2002, 3). She also landed at a time when Indian men outnumbered women. Although Poragia emigrated when the gender ratios between male and female laborers had balanced out somewhat, the proportion of men to women was still much greater.[31] Men far outnumbered women immigrants in part because Indian women were reluctant to emigrate on their own and men were hesitant to travel with wives and children. Moreover, "Not all Caribbean planters were supportive of the emigration of 'lower-caste' women, categorizing them erroneously as prostitutes" (Shepherd 2002, 6). Suspicions that women were being exported for the purposes of sex work (a suspicion that influenced the anti-emigration lobby in India in the late 1800s and early 1900s) resulted in far fewer women than men boarding indenture ships to Guiana. This set in place a gender imbalance at the start of indentureship that planters and recruiters later tried to rectify when they realized that the lack of "appropriate" mates for male indentured laborers created a whole host of other problems.

## The Most Tabooed Transgression of All

Knowing that the "facts" on Poragia's Emigration Certificate were as much a colonial construct as "Calcutta" was her race, and "wC" was her daughter's race, I still regarded this document as an astonishingly significant find. It uncloaked the female ancestor whose undoubtedly arduous journey brought the Indian maternal line of my family to Guiana. But locating Poragia also left me with a profound sense of loss for having no comparable documentation for my African ancestors. The archivist's matter-of-fact declaration that the repository—now named after Walter Rodney, an Afro-Guyanese and the nation's most esteemed historian—only housed records of "immigrants"—meaning Indian indentured laborers—of course struck me as deeply ironic. Positioning only Indians as "immigrants" erroneously suggests that Africans are indigenous and, in this respect, can be read as denying Indians' legitimate claim to Guyanese identity.[32] Yet, by not housing records of Africans, the repository effectively erases Afro-Guyanese identity. When I asked why the Walter Rodney Archives housed no records on Afro-Guyanese, and inquired where I could go to find genealogical records for my Afro-Guyanese father, the archivist was completely stumped. In the midst of my day of uncovering Poragia's past, my findings seemed incomplete and bittersweet in that they ostensibly divulged nothing about the Afro-Guyanese side of my family. However, contextualized alongside the historical treatments of indentured Indo-Guyanese women, Poragia's story is unique in that she had a documented intimate relationship with an Afro-Guyanese man at a time when Indian women had their pick of Indian men and when such a union would have been rare and, by all accounts, deeply stigmatized. Considered in this light, Poragia's story is an early example of Afro-Asian intimacy and of the ways in which Guyanese women were, from the outset, crucially connected to the nation's global race/gender formations.

Still, questions about Poragia's life and about how she came to have a child with my great-great-grandfather, G. Abinsetts—about whom there were no additional records—abounded. Taking a pointer broom to the dimly lit corners in which she resides in the archives expands our understanding of global Guyanese race/gender formations in meaningful ways. D. Alissa Trotz concludes her essay "Behind the Banner of Culture? Gender, 'Race,' and Family in Guyana" with the following question: "How did racialized struggles for self-definition and self-recognition invoke other rhetorics of exclusion—of women, of others within (for instance unmarried women, women who crossed racialized divisions in their personal relationships, lesbian women) and others without (women from other racialized groups)?" (Trotz 2003, 24). As a woman who crossed racialized divisions in her most intimate personal relationship, Poragia embodied the anxieties attached to Indian women's sexuality across two continents.

My archival research determined that after her initial contract for five years of labor in Guiana, Poragia was exempted from indentured labor. Therefore, she would have been released from indentureship for six years prior to her daughter's birth in 1892. And she would have been ostensibly free to choose her employer after the initial five years of labor. But Poragia's mobility was strictly restricted by legislation that kept her bound to the plantation. She resided in Port Mourant, a coastal plantation estate east of the Berbice River. Although I found no evidence that Poragia and G. Abinsetts were legally married, their daughter, Tily, was born eleven years after Poragia arrived in Guiana. By the letter of the law, Poragia would have been at liberty not only to leave the plantation but to return to India. But at the expiration of their indenture, like Poragia, nearly two-thirds of Indian laborers remained in Guiana.[33] The timing of her daughter's birth sheds some light on how she was able to engage in an intimate relationship with a Black man at a time when such relationships were extremely rare—the expiration of Poragia's contract may have afforded her some freedom of movement and an ability to, for the second time in her life, strike out in a manner that defied the norms of her racial identity, her gender, and her social standing.

When Poragia arrived in Guiana, unindentured Indians outnumbered indentured Indians residing on plantations (Rodney 1981, 34). She would have been paid even lower wages than her unindentured peers and would have been considered to have the lowest social standing in the colony.[34] Still, some scholars have argued that because of the sex-ratio imbalance and because they were wage earners, Indian women were able to renegotiate the gender norms within the indentured community (Haniff 1999, 20; Munasinghe 2006, 216–17). Haniff also makes the case that the Indian women who emigrated to Guiana were independent minded, suggesting that, unburdened by the constraints of family and religion, they could more freely choose their partners (Haniff 1999, 20). I follow Trotz, however, in emphasizing that because there were also wage disparities by gender, Indian women earned even less than their male counterparts and could not support themselves autonomously (Trotz 2003, 17). Their impoverished status kept them tethered to the plantation in order to support themselves and their children.

Any freedom the gender imbalance afforded some women to choose their mates and to sometimes have more than one mate at a time was curtailed by extreme gendered violence against women, illustrated by the highly publicized "cutlass murders" of Indian women—the name given to the practice of using the bladed plantation tool to exercise violent patriarchal control over Indian women. "Between 1859 and 1907, eighty-seven women were reported killed on the estates, while between 1886 and 1890 alone, some thirty-five cases of women chopped with estate implements were reported" (Mangru 1987, 217, cited in Trotz 2003, 17). An Indian woman who spurned her partner for another man could be subjected to disfiguring and life-threatening violence at the hands of an Indian man. I uncovered archival newspaper articles from Tily's place and time of birth that reported numerous "cutlass murders" of Indian women by Indian men. For example, the *Daily Chronicle* from Saturday, February 4, 1893, under the headline "Murder at Port Mourant," briefly details that "a coolieman named Ponhoye was charged by Mr. Inspector Binns with having, on Friday last, killed and murdered his reputed wife at Pln. Port Mourant, by chopping her with a cutlass" (*Daily Chronicle* 1893).[35] With these gendered acts of violence in mind, this book brandishes the pointer broom in place of the cutlass as a feminist recuperative tool.

As a woman who chose a partner outside of her ethnic and racial group, Poragia would have been especially at risk for such forms of violence. Moreover, she was from a low caste in India and perhaps already suspected of being a sex worker even before she crossed the Atlantic. Negative stereotypes about Indian women's sexuality were already well established in the Indian colonial context, and these ideas traveled to Guiana. Hailing from northern India, Poragia was likely identified as being among "the greatest troublemakers" (Trotz 2003, 22) and as being "'bold, chaste and unfaithful' in contrast to the 'peaceful and law abiding' southerners" (Trotz 2003, 22, quoting Bronkhurst 1888, 144–45). Still, the interracial sexual relationships involving Indian women of the time that garnered the most attention were with White male planters or overseers. The existence of sexual abuse of Indian women by overseers was denied because they were stereotyped as seductresses against whose immorality the male overseer did not stand a chance (Trotz 2003, 19). This was considered a dangerous relationship because of the possible threat that it posed to labor production: "Given the sex-ratio disparity and the relative infrequency of interracial relations with other subordinate groups, such arrangements were bound to create disquiet within the indentured community, as Indian men's attempts to retain some degree of cultural autonomy (represented through efforts to institute control over women's sexuality) clashed with managerial assumptions of privileged access to the bodies of Indian women" (Trotz 2003, 18). This situates Poragia as a woman who had already defied gender norms and who, on the one hand, might have had her pick of Indian male partners, but, on the other, would have been subjected to sexual advances from colonial overseers. Moreover, that her partner was neither Indian nor a White overseer means that she could well have been seen as rejecting both of these groups—making her susceptible to possible violence from both. Undeniably, she was negotiating a minefield of encounters with men.

Gendered and racialized stereotypes were used to explain why unions between Indian women and Black men were extremely rare. And although I could not find evidence of a legal marriage between Poragia and G. Abinsetts, the fact that his name is listed as Tily's father indicates that he was present when the couple registered their daughter's birth—Tily's birth record is an affirmation of her parents' public union. Low intermarriage rates between Indians and Africans were marshaled as evidence of how distinct and diametrically opposed the two groups were (Trotz 2003, 22). Moreover, the tropes of the subservient Indian woman and the independent Black woman were rendered as essentializing figures and used to explain why Indian men did not marry outside their communities (Trotz 2003, 22). The proliferation of these stereotypes during the colonial period set the stage for modern-day racializations that pit Afro- and Indo-Guyanese against one another, but they also expose how Poragia and G. Abinsetts's relationship was well beyond even the imagined boundaries of interracial unions.

As Munasinghe notes regarding Trinidad, elite discourse of the early 1900s expresses concerns over the increasing intermarriage between East Indian men and European women: "The alternative scenario of miscegenation, East Indian women marrying men of African descent, appears unthinkable or inarticulable for Indo-Trinidadian elites of this period" (Munasinghe 2006, 214). Here, historical analyses of Trinidad prove useful in situating archival records in the Guyanese context: "Indeed, historian Bridget Brereton claims there is very little historical evidence of unions between Afro-Trinidadians and East Indians in Trinidad during the indenture years (1845–1917) and that sexual unions were rare until 1900. She also notes the absence of legal marriage during this period" (Munasinghe 2006, 217, citing Brereton 1979, 183). Still, understandably, the shortage of evidence confirming interracial unions is typically analyzed from the perspective of whether Indian men would engage in sexual relationships with Black women—since Indian women were scarce, why wouldn't Indian men have relationships with Black women? In Guiana, as well, early Afro-Asian intermarriage, in the rare cases in which it was documented, was decidedly between Indian men and Black women. Shibata points out that in 1841, "cases of 'shack-up' of Indian men and African women achieved notoriety in Plantation Bellevue" (Shibata 2002, 202). The same year marked the first legal marriage between an Indian man and an African woman at Plantation Wales, with two more cases occurring in 1842 at the Highbury and Waterloo plantations (Shibata 2002, 202). But G. Abinsetts's union with Poragia may be interpreted as an even more uncommon pairing since *he* was Black and *she* was Indian.

Poragia and G. Abinsetts's union was "the most tabooed transgression of all that threatened the norms of patriarchy" (Munasinghe 2006, 217). We might interject that queer unions would have been even more taboo. But among heterosexual relationships, the fact that Tily and her father are outliers in the records of "foreign births" underscores how unusual the coupling between Poragia and Abinsetts was. Still, I want to acknowledge that although the documentation of such a coupling was extremely rare, because Indian people and Black people lived in such proximity, secret sexual encounters, "shack-ups," and intimate relationships of many different brands surely took place. Such relationships have been indexed in other locations in which Indians and Blacks were seen as oppositional groups, as in Nayan Shah's study, *Stranger Intimacy: Contesting Race, Sexuality, and the Law in the North American West* (2011).

In the Guyanese context, what would have possessed a young woman already isolated and in a strange land to engage in a strictly tabooed relationship? Did the fact that she was on her own liberate Poragia to pursue a relationship based on love rather than on social acceptance? Did her exemption from her indentured contract enable her to engage in a union that plantation life would have rendered virtually impossible? Did failed unions with one or more Indian male partners predate her coupling with Abinsetts? No matter his profession, G. Abinsetts would have had a higher social standing than Poragia, and as a Black man in the vicinity of the plantation to which she was bound, he could have held a number of jobs that would have afforded him a relatively decent salary, including that of head foreman engineer, head pan boiler or pan boiler, engineer, dispenser, carpenter, blacksmith, cooper, and even cane-cutter (Rodney 1981, 148). In any of these jobs he would have earned significantly more than an Indian indentured man and would have in that respect been a desirable partner. Moreover, although it stands to reason that Abinsetts would have worked near the plantation in order to meet Poragia, the 1880s brought the trend of Black men working in the hinterland (Rodney 1981, 218–19)—he may well have divided his time between long stretches of work in the interior of the country, with a mate close to the plantation whom he saw infrequently. If Abinsetts was an intermittent figure in Poragia and their daughter's lives, a relationship of this sort could have lessened the social stigma attached to the couple's union. Still, Tily would have been the living proof of the couple's transgressive relationship, regardless of whether or not her father was present in the household. Outnumbered by Indians residing in Guiana far longer than she and as a coveted Indian woman of child-bearing years, Poragia may have been even more susceptible to male violence if her Black partner was not a daily fixture in her life.

While all my life I had thought that my mother's generation was the first to bring Afro-Indian intermarriage into her family, I learned that our first Indian maternal ancestor, the woman kin with the most definitive ties to India, had pioneered the practice against unimaginable social barriers. Poragia and G. Abinsetts's union represented a monumental divergence from the established norm. And their daughter, a Dougla girl born long before there would have even been the legal need for a term to describe the children of Afro-Asian unions, would have been the living embodiment of both colonial and Indian patriarchy's greatest anxieties. Thus, that my mother was agog, not about the details of Poragia's passage but rather about Tily's father's "Negro" designation, was remarkably astute. While scores of indentured women made the treacherous journey that Poragia endured, the historical records from her time period show that very few went on to document a union with an African man on their child's official birth record.

## "All ah You in Here Is Black People!"

My mother's proclamation—"I knew it! *Full* Negro!"—spoke to the ways in which Tily's racial identity, specifically her African ancestry, had been an open secret, suppressed yet known in my family—something that would elicit a loud outburst when confirmed in the quiet of an archive. This was knowledge that when swept out from the depths of memory would rise like dust particles that we always suspected were there but that had not yet been subjected to the light of day. Tily's mixed ancestry resonated among her descendants as a partial secret. I mean this in the sense John L. Jackson employs in *Thin Description*. Such secrets, he notes, "might even be 'public secrets,' at least within the community, inconsistencies that one could readily excavate in any social group, and the ethnographic project means determining which of these would-be inconsistencies and contradictions merit wider exposure" (Jackson 2013, 91). Most, if not all families have secrets, and mine is no different. While Jackson writes of the multiple secrets around which he had to make choices about disclosure or safe-keeping in his study of the African Hebrew Israelite Nation of Jerusalem, I would not describe my family as particularly secretive. And, by saying "*I knew it!*" my mother affirmed that Tily's racial identity was at least partially undisclosed.[36] Corrine Squire follows Derrida (1989) in noting that to name secrets even as possibilities is to shed light on them—secrets are "always in some ways partial secrets" (Squire 2015, 201).

The pointer broom approach enabled me to sweep Tily's patrilineage out from under the proverbial rug of the archives. But I did not have to dig too deeply into Sarah Johanna's contemporary landscape to find evidence of my great-grandmother's background. In the family ceme-tery—an overgrown patch of village land accessible via a narrow, muddy path that is tended to only on the occasion of a funeral—one has but to sweep away fallen leaves and dirt to find her first and middle names in-scribed on the tomb she shares with her husband. The tombstone reads, "Tily Mackania and Robert Jaisingh." And my great-grandmother's maiden name, Abinsetts, is known by several members of the family. Tily's middle name and maiden surname would of course have been clues to the fact that her father was not Indo-Guyanese. I later learned from my mother's eldest sister, the other family member whose oral history contributed to my writing of this chapter, that Abinsetts was a well-known Afro-Guyanese surname. And while I have not been able to uncover the significance of her middle name, "Mackania," in the context of Guiana, it also suggests a non-Indian origin and gestures to Africa. Although spelled differently, Makanya was the name of a chiefdom in southeastern Africa.[37] Certainly Tily's parents would have known that their daughter would be marked as African by her surname and by the unusual middle name they gave her. But Tily's name was not the only clue. In Guyana, where Indo-Guyanese skin tones range from fair to very dark, skin color does not function as a racial marker the way it does in the United States. Many Guyanese with the strongest claims to Indi-

Figure 1.1. Robert Ranjit Jaisingh and Tily Mackania Jaisingh, née Abinsetts, ca. 1940. Photo from author's family archives.

anness are far darker in skin tone than individuals designated as "mulatto" or African. Tily's skin color, although slightly darker than that of her husband, even in the black-and-white photograph my grandmother displayed in her home, would not have been the trait that outed her African ancestry. To my surprise, it was an element of her dress, one that I had long equated with her Indian ancestry, that perhaps both concealed and revealed her Blackness.

In the studio photograph that has become a treasured heirloom among some in my family (my Aunt Gene displays it prominently in her home), Robert Jaisingh stands beside his seated wife, his left hand resting protectively on her shoulder. Robert wears a light-colored cotton or linen suit, white collared shirt, and leather belt and shoes. His greying hair and completely white mustache indicate that the photograph was taken later in life, perhaps in his late sixties. Robert's features are unmistakably Indian, and the straight-haired white mustache dominates an angular face—his expression serious and his gaze directly focused at the photographer. Tily wears an ankle-length white dress, with elbow-length sleeves—her hands palms down on her lap as she grasps a large black or brown leather handbag. The boat-shaped handbag is oversized for her small frame—it spans almost the width of her body. Her wrists, ring finger, and ears are adorned with gold jewelry. The thick gold bangles she wears on each wrist are similar to ones worn by Indian women in other photographs from the time—even in the blurred photograph they appear to be bejeweled and distinct from the relatively plain gold bangles that are given as gifts to girl children and passed down from mother to daughter in my family. But her dangling earrings in particular, a floral design, are Indo-Guyanese ethnic markers. Her head is slightly tilted to the left and she wears a slight, low-spirited smile. Tily's nose is long and straight, her lips are thin, her jaw strong, and her cheekbones high. But it is her headdress upon which I, as a young girl, had always fixated. The white, apparently cotton handkerchief has a large floral pattern and covers her hair entirely—almost dwarfing her thin face. The front edge of the headwrap comes down to meet her brow line, there are dark shadows along either side where her cheekbones meet her ears, her delicate face is swimming in the oversized head cover, and her hair is not visible.

As a child I had gazed at this photograph countless times and always thought that the white handkerchief covering my great-grandmother's hair signified her authentic *Indianness*. I saw the headwrap as a signal of her respectability and perhaps, a modification of a Hindu sari shawl or a Muslim headscarf. Knowing how invested many Indo-Guyanese women are in their long, straight black hair as a marker of feminine beauty and Indian ethnicity, I could think of no other reason why Tent Ma would cover her head. My admiration of my mother's bone-straight, jet-black hair, which she wore long, past her waistline, contributed to my curiosity about my great-grandmother's hair—since my grandmother's mane was relatively short and wavy, and my own hair was comparatively curly and frizzy, I wondered about the length and texture of Tent Ma's tresses.[38]

What did her hair look like? And, how did she get her nickname? These were the two questions about Tent Ma upon which I had always focused as a child. I returned to these questions after visiting the archives and sought answers from the family oral historian—my Aunt Gene, or "Dee" to her brothers and sisters, Vicky's eldest child and Tent Ma's granddaughter: "Is I give she that name, 'Tent Ma'! Pressured with the work of being the eldest—I had no play days—there was a big tent in my grandparents' yard in front de house, and I used to want to go there to get away from my work. *Is I name her that.* I would tell mommy, 'I'm going to Tent Ma.' And so she start being called that." Aunt Gene related this story from her row house in the Midwood section of Brooklyn, a home she had purchased almost fifty years prior and that, as a single mother traveling by subway three hours daily to work as a hospital orderly in the Bronx, she had fully paid off. When I related to Aunt Gene that the archives had revealed that Tent Ma's father was a "Negro," she shared the following:

[In a loud whisper] Some of the family does skin up they nose when I tell them so. But yes, is true. Her father was a Black man. Is *she* bring Black blood into we family. I tell them [family members] that we have *Black blood.* [Speaking in a louder voice] I know from a girl because I used to ask questions. I used to ask Mommy, "Why is my uncles' [Victorine's brothers] hair so curly-curly?" Mommy had it too—the wavy hair. Mommy wasn't shame. She would tell me. But Tent Ma was a prejudice woman [even though] she was half. Is your great-grandfather who was pure Indian from Punjab. I went to India to see where he was from. But Tent Ma hair was *curly-curly*, from the root. Curly from *the root*! And she used to cover it with the handkerchief. She [would] keep she hair short and she smooth out the curls, and put the handkerchief to cover it.

Having "Black blood" was not a source of shame for Gene. While working at that Bronx hospital, she formed close friendships with other staff members, many of whom were Black women from the Caribbean. Her deep, dark brown complexion, coupled with her accent, marked Gene as a member of this group, an identity she embraced, even though she also sojourned to India to locate the origins of her grandfather, Robert Ranjit Jaising. Aunt Gene, the family storyteller, archivist (I obtained the photograph of Tily and Robert from her), and present-day matriarch, is not a woman who minces words. As the eldest of seven children, she helped raise her siblings and acquired a no-nonsense demeanor in the process. My grandmother named her "Gene," using the masculine spelling, and when she married, she took her husband's last name, "King," endowing her with a doubly masculine and powerful moniker that suited her comportment. Gene was known for being outspoken, so I was not surprised that her girlhood inquisitiveness got to the bottom of family matters usually left unsaid. Her audacity, even at a young age, to ask questions about unspoken topics impressed me. Certainly, as a little girl in Sarah Johanna, I had similar questions but did not dare raise them in a culture in which children—especially girls—are seen but not heard.

Aunt Gene never knew Tent Ma's parents, and, to her recollection, my great-grandmother never discussed them. But hidden under Tily's handkerchief and apparent in her surname were the somatic and cultural indicators of her Afro-Guyanese ancestry. And my mother's proclamation that she "knew it," suggested that Tily's secret was an open one—Aunt Gene was not the only one alerted to the truth. Still, Tily's Blackness was not publicly acknowledged—after all, I had learned the story about her and Robert coming from India as indentured laborers. (Aunt Gene echoes a variation of this tale in the above quotation, even though my archival research determined that Robert was born in Guiana.) While Aunt Gene's account indicates an intentional veiling of Tily's African features, to say that my great-grandmother was passing for Indian would be far too simplistic. The white handkerchief Tent Ma wore was a common style of dress for Indo-Guyanese women of the time—this is evidenced in the many photographs of Indian women laborers during the period of indenture and after. And since she was older in the studio photograph, it would make sense that her hair would be prudently covered.

Perhaps more compellingly, my own childhood underscored the matrifocality of childrearing in Guyana. Fathers, sons, and brothers have greater freedom to travel beyond the home, and cultural identity is largely imparted via the transfer of mother-based knowledge. And although academic theorizations of the Guyanese family have positioned matrifocal households as the almost exclusive terrain of Afro-Guyanese (Smith 1956), my grandmother was not unusual in being an Indian-identified woman who headed a household in the primarily Indian region of East Bank Demerara. Part of my broader argument here is that both scholarly and stereotypical understandings of Indo-Guyanese women as subservient housewives and of Afro-Guyanese women as independent heads of households are complicated when you look at families such as my own. Whether their home life was one in which Poragia was head of household, or whether she functioned in the homemaker role with G. Abinsetts present, it stands to reason that Poragia would have been the greatest influence on Tily's daily socialization. It is possible, indeed probable, that although it was known that her father was Black, Tily was nurtured and socialized as Indian. We could certainly criticize Tily for being "prejudice," as Aunt Gene put it—she did not call on any specific examples other than Tent Ma smoothing her curls and wrapping her hair—but any efforts to hide her Blackness may have been forged out of self-preservation in an era in which her very existence represented the defiance of both colonial and male Indian patriarchy.

As we drove back from the archives to Sarah Johanna on the afternoon of our archival recoveries, my mother was abuzz with excitement about finding proof that Tily's father was Black. "I goin' tell the whole estate!" my mother said, with a broad, mischievous grin. Then, her smile quickly faded. "But they nah ga whan believe me." To console her, I said that I could construct a family tree based on the archival findings and make as many copies as she would like—an offer I actually never made good on.[39] While my offer for creating cold, hard "proof" seemed to please her, minutes later, as my mother turned her pickup truck onto the dirt road on which she resided—one of the few roads that comprised Sarah Johanna and along which many of our cousins still lived—she was unable to contain herself. My mother rolled down her window, stuck out her head, and yelled as loudly as she could, "All ah you in here is Black people!"

The next day she goaded me into telling a neighboring cousin about our findings. I began with Poragia and the *Lightning*, the ship on which she made the arduous passage to Guiana. "No! Tell she about how Tent Ma father was full Negro!" my mother interjected. The woman to whom we were speaking was the wife of one of my mother's cousins. Her husband was a grandson of one of Vicky's brothers—so this woman's husband had some of the African ancestry that Tily passed on.[40] When I stated that Vicky's maternal grandfather was documented as a "Negro," our cousin paused for a moment, pondering my statement, and then said, "Oh, that's why she was like that." Her response seemed to entirely miss the point not only that this meant my grandmother was part Black but also that her brothers and their children, including the *woman's husband*, had Afro-Guyanese ancestry. Her statement singled out my grandmother for being "like that," without acknowledging that her brothers were also "like that." It insinuated that, as a woman, Vicky bore the greater brunt of her mother's racial heritage. Her remark about my grandmother being "like that" referred, I initially gathered, to Vicky's wavy hair, relatively broad nose, and dark skin. But considering my grandmother's reputation for being a strong-willed woman who divorced her first husband and raised seven children alone, before remarrying later in life, I also understood that referring to her as being "like that" may have also signaled the ways in which she defied gender norms of the dutiful, subservient wife.

Based on stereotypes of Indo-Guyanese and Afro-Guyanese women, my grandmother's behavior could be racialized as Black rather than Indian. And these stereotypes endure from the colonial period to the present day. Victorine's mother, Tily, and her grandparents, Poragia and G. Abinsetts, were seen as anomalies in the face of such broad characterizations of Black and Indian women, which dovetailed with proscriptions against intermarriage. Trotz quotes a Royal Commission index from 1897: "The coolie woman is respectful to her husband, and a negro woman will knock him down. A [coolie] woman waits upon him at the table, and a negress sits down with him. They are totally different people; they do not intermix. That is, of course, one of the great safeties in the colony when there has been rioting" (quoted in Trotz 2003, 23).

Although, on the surface, the Royal Commission quotation speaks to why Indian men did not marry outside their communities, it does so by setting up a dichotomy between Indian and Black women. I considered our cousin's "ah-ha" reaction of "Oh, that's why she was like that" in light of these enduring notions about what separated Indian and Black women. Her remark came somewhat as a surprise to me—never before had I heard any suggestion that my grandmother was seen as anything other than Indian, and her birth records, which clearly stated her race as "Calcutta" (even though she was born in Guiana), were proof that she was legally identified as Indian. Still, Aunt Gene's account tells us that Vicky was aware of and did not attempt to hide her mixed heritage from her inquisitive eldest daughter.

Our cousin's remark about my grandmother can be related to the forms of *misnaming* and *ungendering* about which Hortense Spillers writes in relation to African American enslaved women, whereby the racialization of Black women casts their very femininity as suspect (Spillers 1987). While, of course, Guyana's context is different from that of African American descendants of the enslaved, Spillers's broader points about how symbolic paradigms like the Moynihan Report "1) inscribe 'ethnicity' as a scene of negation and 2) confirm the human body as a metonymic figure for an entire repertoire of human and social arrangements" are relevant (Spillers 1987, 66). And Spillers's argument that such paradigms play out in racialized understandings of matrilineage and patrilineage while working to destabilize the purported integrity of the gender binary can be applied to the reading of the archive currently in question (Spillers 1987, 66). This correlation reveals how the political economy of erasure at work in Guyana resonates across the African diaspora. We catch a glimpse into the unreconcilable areas of colonial-era race/gender formations when we consider how record keepers attempted to categorize Dougla women like Tily and her daughter, Victorine.[41] At the moment of Tily's birth, record keepers would not, or could not, make sense of her racial identity. In fact, her birth record also shows that her sex was initially noted with an "M" for "male," and then crossed off and corrected with an "F" for "female."[42] Indeed, Tily's birth records indicate various degrees of uncertainty in terms of identifying her race/gender. It stands to reason that Tily and her parents, and others like them, navigated a number of unimaginable or misunderstood areas in their intimate relationships, their kin groups, and their public lives. In these opaque corners, perhaps signaled on other birth records for which no father is named, or concealed by off-the-books relationships—"shack-ups," as they were known in the colony—Afro- and Indo-Guyanese defied the prescription that they "do not intermix."

Aunt Gene's account and Tily's self-identification are knotty negotiations that traverse circum-Caribbean and Afro-Asian racial formations while being steeped in culturally specific Guyanese social processes. Efforts to enshroud Blackness and claim Indian identity over African ancestry are not unique to my family. Rather, they mirror social processes across the Caribbean, India, Latin America, and the African diaspora. Scholars have noted that Guyanese social identity constructions foreground Indian and Amerindian identities while erasing and marginalizing Blackness (Williams 1991). In my mother's family, Indian and Portuguese ancestry was always at the forefront—plain as day in surnames like "Jaisingh" and "DeFreitas," my mother's father's last name. Her father, Ivan, whose nickname was "Putagee Sonny" ("Putagee" is Guyanese creole for "Portuguese"), passed on his fair skin to my mother and some of her siblings.[43] The story of how Tent Ma hid her hair, coupled with the fact that the race of her daughter, Vicky, was listed as "Calcutta," underscores that our Blackness was neither as readily apparent nor as freely shared as our Indian and Portuguese heritage.

Deeply damaging stereotypes of Afro-Guyanese, including that they are unattractive, undisciplined, dirty, and lazy, abound in Guyana (Williams 1991, 9). In a village such as Sarah Johanna, which continues to this day to be recognized as primarily Indian, Tily could not display her hair as a marker of her Indianness. But her actions must also be understood within the time period and the social realities in which Indian indentured laborers lived. The pejorative term "coolie" connoted that Indians inhabited the lowest social strata, with other ethnic groups, including Africans, oftentimes holding power over them (Bahadur 2013, xx). Poragia and G. Abinsetts's union, then, would have been a treacherous one as it was formalized in the wake of her incorporation into Guiana as the lowest form of laborer.

Rather than dismiss her as "prejudice" and as passing, I find it more productive to ruminate on Tily's and her mother's social contexts. And although Aunt Gene described my grandmother, Vicky (Tily's daughter), as "not shame" of her own African ancestry, I recall anti-Black sentiments that Vicky exhibited during my childhood. Even though she was stern, my grandmother's love for me was undeniable. I never felt that she disapproved of my mother and father's union. However, I also never knew her to openly discuss her own African heritage. And while I felt like a lone Dougla girl in a village of Indians, there were a few Afro-Guyanese residents in our community. My grandmother treated them with a polite distance. The older Black lady who lived all the way at the end of our street was a known Obeah Woman, and Mama did not dissuade my childhood fear of her as a potentially dangerous outsider.[44] Perhaps more telling is my recollection of standing on our verandah and singing nursery rhymes across the road with the children of an Afro-Guyanese family who lived on our street. One day my grandmother caught me chiming in with these children as they sang an Afro-creole jingle that schoolchildren used to bully their East Indian peers, "Coolie water rice, pork and spice, wash ya beatie [butt] with dhal and rice!"[45] Upon hearing this, my grandmother grabbed me by the collar, dragged me into the house, and delivered a thorough thrashing. Between lashes, she warned me against ever playing with those kids and told me to never use the word "coolie" again. The maternal knowledge that she passed on to me was painfully situated in the ways Indo- and Afro-Guyanese had been positioned against each other.

If the label "coolie" evoked such a reaction in my usually mild-mannered grandmother, I can only imagine how deeply such epithets might have hurt Tily, who undoubtedly had witnessed, if not experienced, the racialized and gendered violence of plantation-bound life. Tily was born in an area surrounded by plantations in which Indians (including her mother) toiled as indentured laborers. She was only sixteen when she married. Her marriage license, noted in red ink under her birth record, named the minister who married Tily and Robert Jaisingh: Reverend J. B. Cropper, a Canadian Presbyterian missionary who spoke fluent Hindi and worked among the Indians on the Berbice plantations. The fact that J. B. Cropper officiated the couple's wedding places Tily and Robert within Indian village life—both were members of the Indian community. And Tily moved with her Indian husband to establish a village that would be inhabited by their kin. Just as Kamala Kempadoo noted in her treatment of her own self-definition and that of her grandmothers who came from vastly different communities, time and location circumscribed Tily's self-definition. As a member of an Indian village, she assumed the same race as her neighbors and her kin. But Tily's self-definition also had implications for her children, who identified as Indian. In this sense, Tily's kinship formation was constructed around and governed by her marriage to an Indian man, by her location—first in a Berbice plantation and then in an East Bank Demerara village—and by the racialized and gendered norms that perpetuated the plantation economy.

Indian settlements like Sarah Johanna sprang up along the Demerera River concomitant with the sabotaging of the African village movement.[46] Historian Rawle Farley characterizes formerly enslaved people's efforts to purchase land in Guiana's post-emancipation period as "the most spectacular village movement in the history of the people of the British Caribbean" (Farley 1954, 100). In fact, Farley notes that enslaved Africans' efforts to secure land predated emancipation; during slavery Africans applied "persistent pressure" in the form of revolts, in their pursuit of land of their own (Farley 1964, 52). Because the post-emancipation village movement threatened to destroy the plantation system, the British enacted various laws aimed at prohibiting land sales and stifling the villagers' efforts (Rodney 1981, Trotz 2003, 15). The settlement of villages throughout the country, including in East Bank Demerara, then, is part of a long, contentious history of African struggles for land ownership. The sabotaging of the village movement had considerable impacts in terms of the construction of race and gender in colonial Guiana (Trotz 2003, 17). It precipitated the out-migration of African men to mining work in the hinterland and caused African men and women to pursue work in urban centers (Trotz 2003, 17).

The attempts to squelch the village movement played out alongside the restructuring of the sugar industry, with lasting implications for indentured women, like Poragia, and for Indian family plots, like the one that Tily and Robert created. In the face of colonial anxieties over shifting forms of labor production, including the withdrawal of African women from the estates, colonial management deployed racialized stereotypes that contrasted Indians and Africans, construing African men as lazy and African women as dangerously independent matriarchs who embodied the moral inferiority of Black family units. Indian women had been pegged as wayward women when they landed in Guiana, but were newly constructed as "housewives." And Indian men were empowered as patriarchs, who, along with the estate regime, would teach Indian women "to be industrious workers and dutiful wives and mothers" (Trotz 2003, 20). As indentured laborers were released from their contracts, and as the indenture period came to an end (the Indian government abolished the indenture system in 1917), East Indian settlements were founded in coastal villages adjacent to estates. These small plots of land parceled out to formerly indentured laborers kept them dependent on the estates for employment and became essential to the continuation of the sugar industry (Trotz 2003, 20).

Within the political economy of erasure that maintained the sugar industry, the burgeoning division of labor "along racialized lines masked the specific insertion of both groups [African and Indians] in the colonial economy" (Trotz 2003, 22; Williams 1991). With Africans deemed indolent and Indians hard-working and reliable, if "volatile," settlement schemes of formerly indentured Indians were similarly reduced to racialized traits: "Small-scale peasant production was increasingly described as entirely natural for Indians and rice-growing as an ancestral skill. Again, this effaced the radically different circumstances that faced ex-slaves in the post-abolition years. Land distribution among ex-indentureds was now a method of maintaining sugar production at acceptable levels, but also a marker of racial differentiation (underpinned by the carving out of separate spaces) consciously manipulated by the state" (Trotz 2003, 22). In her numerous treatments of gender, the family, and racialized stereotypes applied to Africans and Indians during the period of colonial rule, Alissa Trotz points to various examples that we can place within the political economy of erasure outlined in this book (Trotz 2003; Peake and Trotz 1999). Peake and Trotz write, for example, that "these stereotypes erased the specificity of the colonial legacy, deflecting attention away from those women who did not 'fit' as well as from an examination of how cultural practices around kinship and the family were forged in the crucible of colonial rule and gendered and racialized subordination" (Peake and Trotz 1991, 51). Tily was, by virtue of her ambiguous racial designation, a woman who did not fit.

If the manipulation of racialized and gendered stereotypes was central to the survival of a sugar industry dependent on disenfranchising

Africans and exploiting Indians, and if land distribution became a tactic of racial differentiation aimed at preserving the plantation economy, then the settlement of villages like Sarah Johanna was entrenched within a web of colonial power. The land upon which Robert and Tily chose to build their family was a gendered and racialized quagmire of subordination and mediation. And the pointer broom becomes an apt instrument for exhuming the political economy of erasure that might have conspired to eclipse Tily's Dougla identity. This schema ensconced her within the regulated sexuality of the domesticated and dutiful Indian housewife—a figure upon whom the maintenance of Indian settlements hinged.

The literature on racial geographies is also helpful here. Katherine McKittrick situates plantations among the lands of "no one" that "were carved up to distinguish between and regulate the relations of indigenous, non-indigenous, African, and colonial communities" (McKittrick 2013, 6). Although, as McKittrick notes, "there were overlapping geographic experiences and peoples that troubled these seemingly discreet [sic] spaces," these overlaps were within "an overarching system wherein particular spaces of otherness— . . . black geographies—were designated as incongruous with humanness" (McKittrick 2013, 6). McKittrick's analysis gives us insight not only into how, for Tily and her family, both the Berbice plantation and the village of Sarah Johanna were bound as "Indian" spaces but also into why maintaining this distinction was critical for avoiding the inhumanity superimposed on Black spaces.

## Past and Future *Tidalectic* Gendered Racializations

These forces conspired to occlude Blackness in my maternal line. Sweeping into view archival "evidence" that revealed Tily's "Negro" father and ambiguous racial designation recovered Blackness from its illegibility, even though her Blackness was already known among some in the family. But as Saidiya Hartman has shown, reconstructing lives from the cold and incomplete records of the archives can never fully counteract the forms of erasure that constrict our understandings of the past (Hartman 2008). The pointer broom cannot redress the racialized violence of the plantation and the gendered brutality of the cutlass. And, while my recuperative work delighted and emboldened my mother, her reaction says as much about her personal motivations as an ostensibly Indian and Portuguese woman who defied cultural norms by marrying a Black man as it does about her adoption of American racializations. Her admonishment—"All ah you in here is Black people!"—both scolded her kin for what she saw as racial pretense and exposed her adherence to the "one drop rule," also known as the rule of hypodescent. Since Dougla exists as a separate racial category for designating mixed persons, my mother might have belted out, "All ah you in here is Dougla people!" But her statement ascribed a far more unambiguous racial marker—one that I would argue both demotes her relatives and gestures to ways in which Guyanese racializations are increasingly influenced by the globalization of American notions of race—an articulation of processes that were burgeoning even during my girlhood in Guyana.

"Stuck in time" international depictions like those unpacked in the introduction are reified, at the national level, vis-à-vis the perceived dichotomies between the metropolis of Georgetown and the country's rural areas. But even in tiny Sarah Johanna, from the colonial period to the present day, the *tidalectics* of local and global constructions of race and gender continue to circulate as nodes of global racial capitalism. Just as Afro- and Indo-Guyanese women's reproductive labor fueled the plantation economy in the colonial era and sparked the formation of novel racial categories, the intersections between present-day migratory processes and shifting extractive geographies undergird contemporary race/gender constructions. If the reporter from *Stabroek News* who wrote the piece about Sarah Johanna had returned to the village a decade later, they might have noticed even more newcomers among its most vulnerable residents. Following the collapse of Venezuela's petrostate economy and its ensuing humanitarian crisis, migrants and refugees from this neighboring country have sought refuge in Guyana in significant numbers.[47] Among these migrants, women are forced into underpaid or unpaid labor as domestics and sex workers (Solomon 2019). Venezuelan women have also coupled with local men who have long-established connections to the area. If Dougla women perform the cluttered labor of informing multiethnic race/gender constructs in Guyana, future treatments of these constructs will have to reckon with how these new migrants' presence comingles with and complicates crossracial unions and cleavages.

But more than the ethnic makeup of Sarah Johanna has changed. Today in the village, the quiet sssweep, sweep, stamp of the pointer broom—still utilized by women and girls—is more often than not drowned out by the cacophonous boom from the constant parade of large trucks hauling sand, machinery, and other extractive materials along the public road that the village flanks. White trails of silica quartz trickle from these trucks: sprinklings that track the aggregate material from the sand mines just down the road from Sarah Johanna to the infrastructure projects surging throughout the rapidly developing country. And, routinely, trucks dump large mounds of sand where the dirt roads of the village meet the thoroughfare—part of public works projects aimed at addressing climate-related erosion. Sarah Johanna's men distribute the sand with shovels and the town's women use their pointer brooms in quotidian, futile attempts to sweep up the sand that invades their yards and dwellings. Like Brathwaite's old Caribbean woman, these women's daily attempts to sweep sand away from sand connect them with *tidalectic* global Guyanese race/gender formations. I follow the tides of these formations to the shores of Barbados in the next chapter.

2

# Rihanna's Guyanese Pattacake and the Homewrecking State in Barbados

In the contemporary moment we might imagine the ripple effects of Brathwaite's old woman's broom extending across the water where the North Atlantic Ocean meets the eastern edge of the Caribbean Sea, from Guyana's muddy shores to the touristy white sand beachfronts of Barbados. And we might hear the echo of the stamping of her broom in the bass lines channeling through the soundscapes of resort towns. In 2018, while I was walking along a tourist stretch on the southern coast of Barbados, these sounds, fused with the delicious, unmistakable scent of Guyanese curry, led me into a catch-all store called "Mother's."[1] Billed in prominent signs as a mini-mart, ice cream parlor, to-go lunch counter, and sports bar, the shop inhabited a quiet corner at the end of a main drag. Inside, I found three Indo-Guyanese women: the owner, who later introduced herself as "Mother" and appeared to be in her fifties, along with her daughter, Rita, and her best friend, Rose. My mouth watering from the fragrance of my favorite comfort food, I was disappointed when the three women responded to my request for two plates of chicken curry by saying that they no longer sold food and that the dish I smelled was being cooked for their own consumption. But that initial encounter, and my unveiled deflation that there would be no curry for me that day, established our mutual bond as Guyanese women away from home, and after a short conversation, my partner and I were invited to return later that evening to share a bottle of Guyanese rum with Mother and her best friend. Late that night, after we polished off the bottle and closed up the shop, I was invited to return for Sunday lunch. I finally got to enjoy Mother's chicken curry with roti—the meal did not disappoint.

It did not take long for Mother, whose initially gruff demeanor had melted away, to reveal characteristically Guyanese quick-wittedness and a disarming sense of humor, and the other two women who worked in her store to share experiences of marginalization in Barbados. Rita said that she was not comfortable living on the island. "They don't like Guyanese here," she said. "But they make it hard for us to go home and come back. You're limited to one trip home every six months." Mother lamented that routine deportations of Guyanese were causing her business to suffer, explaining that this was why she no longer sold prepared meals. They had also been vending Guyanese eats out of a cart further down the main strip, where tourists gathered after late-night bar hopping. But with the shop's clientele of regulars now diminished, and with steep competition from restaurants that "have Guyanese dishes on the menu that are not made by Guyanese people, so the food isn't good," Mother's street-food operation also languished.

Mother's and Rita's accounts referred to the punitive nature of Bajan immigration laws, which set limits on Guyanese migrants' freedom to live and work on the island. As members of the Caribbean Community or CARICOM, the Caribbean's intergovernmental organization that forms a political and economic union of twenty countries, Guyanese had previously enjoyed relative ease of travel to reside and work in Barbados. But by 2009, the massive influx of workers from Guyana spawned immigration-law reforms and informal policies that cracked down on nonnational workers. In that year, the Barbadian prime minister, David Thompson, announced the "Barbadian First" amnesty law, whereby undocumented Caribbean nonnationals who had been living on the island prior to December 31, 1998, were required to obtain amnesty by legalizing their status of residency, or they would face the threat of deportation. Although ostensibly applying to all undocumented nonnational Caribbean immigrants, the policy was widely understood as targeting Guyanese in particular, who were blamed for "rising poverty and crime rates in Barbados" (COHA 2009). Guyanese immigrants like Mother, Rose, and Rita still felt the sting of these policies close to a decade after they were implemented, with many Guyanese on the island describing experiences of harassment from Barbadian police and immigration officials.[2] And the policies designed to limit the presence of workers from Guyana were in stark contrast to the "12-month Barbados Welcome Stamp," an act the Bajan government implemented in the wake of the COVID-19 pandemic, when, with tourism travel waning, they lured global workers to "work remotely from the beach in Barbados"—the latter policy clearly aimed at attracting a wealthy American and European workforce.

Along with Rose, who hailed from Berbice, Mother had emigrated to Barbados from West Bank, Demerara, seventeen years prior. She imparted a recognizable immigration story inflected with a crushing illustration of the magnitude of poverty in Guyana. "Back home I have five brothers and sisters," she said. "We were so poor we shared one lead pencil at school. We cut that pencil into six pieces. The lucky one got the top part with the eraser." Even in the face of such hardship, Mother exhibited a talent for business from a young age, when she began selling sugar cakes on the street after school. With this entrepreneurial spirit luring her to Barbados, for a time her store enjoyed great success, but that was now waning. Over the course of our far-reaching conversation, Mother's husband, a Black Bajan man, came into the store to replenish a backpack stocked with sundries—batteries, pens, chewing gum—which he peddled on the street. When she introduced her spouse and I attempted to lightheartedly discuss a notion I had heard repeatedly around the island, that Bajan men like Guyanese women, Mother and Rose demurred. Clearly, the stereotype about Bajan men preferring Guyanese women struck a nerve. Later they shared that upon arriving in Barbados they had worked as domestics and live-in cooks for affluent Bajan families. "But the women them fire we because our food was better than how they cook and because them husbands start to look at us."

This chapter examines the tensions undergirding Rose's, Rita's, and Mother's experiences in Barbados. I use a popular Barbadian calypso sung by an Indo-Guyanese woman, "GT Advice," as a springboard for investigating the tangled gendered racializations that have entwined the two nations. The Guyanese woman emerges as a seductress and a homewrecker in "GT Advice," but blends in as a legitimate generator of national pride in the persona of Barbados's most famous performer, the world-renowned cosmetics and fashion mogul, Rihanna. The chapter puts "GT Advice" in dialogue with Guyanese ethnic markers and maternal knowledge delivered by Rihanna, whose mother is Afro-Guyanese. Unpacking the politics of Rihanna's overlooked Guyanese ancestry, I posit that from the post-emancipation period to the present, the Bajan state has operated as homewrecker while scapegoating the Guyanese woman as a threat to the nuclear family unit. More broadly, this chapter connects a throughline from the previous one by taking up themes of kinship and marriage, and erasure and visibility. The previous chapter

outlined how esoteric global race/gender constructs and Guyanese kinship formations conspired to blot out my great-grandmother's African
ancestry. In this chapter, the political economy of erasure that channels
across global Guyana manifests in the ways in which Rihanna's Afro-
Guyanese ancestry remains shrouded, only surfacing at key moments
when the singer chooses to assert her Guyaneseness.

## "Just a Little Advice from a Guyanese Girl"

"GT Advice" was released in Barbados in 2009 and became a massive hit
after it was performed that year at the Crop Over festival, a historically
situated summer festival commemorating enslaved Africans' celebration
and public resistance upon the completion of the sugar cane harvest.[3]
Nalini Sukhram, an Indo-Guyanese woman, recorded the single, but a
Black Bajan man, Eric Lewis, produced, wrote, and arranged the track
under the auspices of Madd, a Barbadian entertainment group and com-
edy production company. Madd, which began in 1983, with Lewis joining
as songwriter in 1985, produces a satirical album to accompany each
annual Crop Over festival. The production company's songs are known
for humorous lyrics mixed with biting political commentary and social
critique. In addition to producing satirical music, Madd also creates
characters such as Ali Singh, a stereotypical Indo-Guyanese salesman
perpetually focused on selling subpar wares to Bajans while complaining about his circumstances. Another character, Ali Singh's son, John
Muhameed, is portrayed in "brownface" and a clown suit while waving
Guyanese flags.

The song's byline, "Madd, featuring Guyanese Girl," tells us that the
tune is a Bajan production with a satirical spin. However, by crediting
Nalini Sukhram under the moniker "Guyanese Girl," the production
company reduces the singer to an unnamed archetype, signaling that
her role is to represent all that has come to mean Guyanese femininity
in Bajan society. Considering Madd's well-known performances, which
lampoon the Indo-Guyanese presence in Barbados, we are informed,
from the start, that Lewis is the ventriloquist behind Sukhram's vocals.

For her part, Nalini Sukhram said that she was in Barbados on a
work permit and employed as a painter in the construction sector when
her friend, Lewis, heard her singing "and said there was an issue which

needed to be addressed." She went on to tell the *Guyana Chronicle*, "We discussed the matter about the frequent claims by Barbadian women that Guyanese women are coming to Barbados and getting more attention from the men than themselves. It was also said that while the men were in Guyana, they were falling for Guyanese women" (*Guyana Chronicle* 2009).

Unsurprisingly, Sukhram's gloss of how the collaboration unfolded only scratches the surface of the song's broader social and historical context. As Guyana's *Stabroek News* notes, the songwriter, Eric Lewis, links the single's creation to the contentious atmosphere surrounding documented and undocumented Guyanese residents. The release of "GT Advice" coincided with the introduction of a series of state policies aimed at controlling migration within the region and removing CARICOM nationals from Barbados. The legislation gave the thousands of undocumented CARICOM nationals residing in Barbados an ultimatum: turn themselves in to immigration authorities and begin the process of "regularizing their immigration status" or risk deportation (Sutherland 2009). Thus, "GT Advice" emerges amid both governmental and social backlash against the presence of immigrants from Guyana. The song grounds this backlash within the sexual and culinary foreignness of the Guyanese woman, evoking Mother, Rose, and Rita's grievance that Guyanese women's ability to earn a living was curtailed just as their sexualities were rendered suspect.

Taking a pointer broom to "GT Advice"—decluttering its lyrical grooves and riffs—provides us with a rich entry point into the complexities of how Guyanese women are understood within the *tidalectic* flows across the Caribbean. The title of the hit Eric Lewis penned refers to Guyana's capital, Georgetown. Rivalry between the two nations is sometimes flagged as "GT vs. BT," with "BT" being an abbreviation for Barbados's capital, Bridgetown. And Guyanese in the diaspora often evoke camaraderie by calling each other "GT." The track begins with a frenetic calypso beat and a spoken dialogue between a Bajan man and woman; the man beckons to the woman, his domestic partner, "Come, come! I got something on the radio I want you to hear. A Guyanese girl singing." "GT Advice" unfolds with the female partner hurriedly setting aside her household work, as she rushes to hear the song her husband or live-in boyfriend so urgently wants to share. From there, Nalini Sukhram takes to the mic with a spoken voiceover, "To all you Bajan girls out there, no disrespect. Just a little advice from a Guyanese girl."

The subsequent verses of the song (only partially quoted here) are worth analyzing in detail, as they articulate the stereotyping of Guyanese femininity in Barbados, while hinting at how these gendered constructions are linked to labor and resources. In a second, suspense-building preamble to the first verse, Sukhram sings, "Oh lawdy," followed by the nonlexical vocables, "di da die," as the Bajan man eggs her on: "Sing de song, girl. Sing de song!" The man's wife or girlfriend responds, "Man, hush, nah. Lemme hear what the girl sayin." From there, the first verse establishes Bajan women as frequently complaining about Guyanese women stealing their men:

> . . . . Bajan gal stop it right now, stop all de finger pointing
> How we Guyanese gals thiefing all yuh husband and all yuh men
> . . . . If yuh wanta keep yuh man, darling, take my good advice
> Some o' yuh Bajan gal mus learn to treat a man nice.

This advances the song's ironic cautionary tale to Bajan women who have made the mistake of "finger pointing" at Guyanese homewreckers, when in fact it is Bajan women who are in need of advice. By citing natural occurrences such as "bees does find honey and ants does run to sugar," the tune portrays Bajan men's penchant for Guyanese women as a "natural" phenomenon, while also likening Guyanese women to one of both nations' natural resources, sugar. Here, sugar, like sand in tourist imaginations, stands in for Guyanese beauty and sexual desirability. Tellingly, the sugar metaphor also implicitly references Guyanese women as an imported commodity, one that jeopardizes Bajan women's chances at successfully maintaining heterosexual domestic relationships. In this way, the track reproduces the discourse surrounding Guyanese immigration to Barbados, casting the immigrants against Bajans, from whom they are presumably stealing jobs. Men come to symbolize Bajan labor—the Guyanese women are stealing the men themselves, thus staking a claim to the vitality and strength of the Bajan workforce while jeopardizing the island's nuclear unit. The final line of the verse signals the song's next task, that of critiquing Bajan women's approach to heterosexual courtship and domestic life.

The chorus follows, with a tongue-in-cheek how-to for Bajan women to reform their approach: "So yuh must learn to wine, like de Guyanese / Learn to grind like de Guyanese." Here, the Guyanese girl's power resides in being willing and able to please men sexually, both with her "wine" (a reference to a Caribbean dance reliant on circular hip movement) and her "grind," or sexual abilities. The Guyanese girl is fetishized as a masterful sex partner focused on pleasuring her mate to the point of making his hair curl.

The next verse outlines negative gendered stereotypes that position Bajan women as prudish, unattractive, and unwise in the ways of sexual seduction, evidenced by the way they slather themselves at night with sexual turnoffs such as "Benje's balsam, citronella, candle grease and Alcolada" and "sleep in a church dress, petticoat, and two brassiere." The Bajan woman literally repels her man's sexual advances by dousing herself in home remedies known for emitting strong and decidedly unsexy odors.[4] Moreover, she is pegged as a fuddy-duddy who eschews sexy lingerie for old-fashioned, figure-obscuring sleepwear. As if swaddling herself under layers of matronly clothing and engulfing her body in a fog of pungent home remedies were not enough, the verse also portrays the Bajan woman as a snapping alligator who fends off sexual advances in the name of resting for work in the morning. The verse concludes with a zinger that contrasts all of the above with the Guyanese girl's sexual prowess: "But when he find a Guyanese girl to give him movementation / Yuh get she deport, yuh run and call immigration." The only recourse the Bajan woman has in the face of Guyanese competition is to call immigration officials and have the Guyanese deported. Thus, the nationalist sentiments that position Barbados as a place of extremely limited resources being sacked by an influx of thieving Guyanese find resonance. Bent on resting in preparation for work, the Bajan woman embodies the national identity of a workforce whose livelihood is endangered by foreign laborers from Guyana. And the sexless marriage of the Bajan couple is analogous to the island nation's perceived inability to reap the benefits of its own natural resources, which subsequently become fodder for foreigners wise enough to exploit them.

The name of the singer, Nalini Sukhram, along with the ostensibly improvised lilt of the nonlexical vocables she employs between verses when she sings "di da die," signal that she is Indo-Guyanese. And in the final verse we learn that Indian ethnicity is integral to her ability to "thief" the Bajan man from his wife or girlfriend: "De man wuk hard a whole day, stirring concrete and lifting bricks / Come home looking for a hot meal, you gi de man sardine and biscuits / Meanwhile at Rajeena she got roti and *dhal puri*." In the verse, canned sardines and crackers ("biscuits") represent an unsatisfying no-cook meal that cannot possibly nourish a weary, hard-working man. And the reference to a Hindu/Muslim name, "Rajeena," and to freshly made, labor-intensive Indo-Guyanese flat-breads classify the Guyanese as a superior cook and a more dedicated homemaker, recalling Mother and Rose's story about being fired from their jobs as cooks and domestics. These Guyanese culinary delights are contrasted with another canned item, corned beef, and a processed food, macaroni—a reference to Bajan macaroni pie. Like Mother and Rose, Indo-Guyanese have found success as food vendors and restaurateurs in Barbados, where their culinary contributions, including roti, *dhal puri*, and curry, are popular additions to the local cuisine. The song acknowl-edges these examples of Guyana's culinary influence on the island, while juxtaposing them with a representation of a Bajan woman whose marital bickering embarrasses her husband in front of his friends: "And when de man he wid he friends, yuh quarreling and keeping noise . . . mek him shame in front ah de boys." These lines convey the gendered tropes of respectability and reputation long interpreted as mainstays of Caribbean gender constructions. The "church dress–wearing" wife signifies respect-ability and religious piety, while her husband is more concerned with his reputation vis-à-vis male peers (Wilson 1973).[5]

Amid the verses I have summarized here, "GT Advice" performs a complex intertextual act; the Bajan couple's voices reemerge in the mid-dle of the song, situating the text within the nuclear unit and demon-strating that the "Guyanese Girl" has infiltrated the private confines of the home. This collapsing of the public (a song heard on the radio) and the private (the family unit in their home) reveals that the Guyanese presence in Barbados is intimate and ingrained. Finally, when the Bajan woman cannot take anymore, we hear her beseeching her male partner to "turn off that radio." And throughout, the husband/boyfriend's laugh-ter signals that he is really enjoying this "advice," and relishes bringing it to his partner. The intertextual dialogue that frames "GT Advice" as diegetic sound *within the home* evinces that the Guyanese presence is fundamentally interwoven with Bajan society. The song vocalizes a male fantasy, one that sets his loyal domestic companion against a mythic Guyanese seductress whose only mission is to please him. Still, it also gives a throw-away line to the Bajan woman's interests when Sukhram offers, "Bajan men, you have to treat your woman right too," to which the Bajan woman responds, "Now I hope you hear that!"

According to an interview published in *Stabroek News*, Lewis reflected on choosing Sukhram to voice the lyrics. "He recalled that at first they thought of getting a man to sing about why Bajan men seem to find favour with Guyanese women, but they decided it would be even better to get a woman to do the song, since they are constantly accused of stealing the men" (Sutherland 2009). This back story puts an illuminating spin on the fact that Sukhram performs a track written by a Bajan man. Ostensibly, Lewis ventriloquizes his voice through her. The lyrics support this reading: the song's overt representation is a male fantasy around reforming his prudish wife (based on the well-worn idea of a sexless marriage caused by a wife who perpetually has a headache) with the threat of her replacement by an always already sexually available and submissive Guyanese woman, who is both a freak in the bedroom and adept in the kitchen. Yet, coverage in Guyanese newspapers promotes Sukhram not as a ventriloquist's dummy but as an agent with a complicated stake in the discourses surrounding the song. For example, the Guyanese press reported that although Sukhram is the mother of twin boys and "grew up in a culture which taught her to 'treat her menfolk good,'" the singer's primary employment as a painter was "an occupation traditionally reserved for men" (*Guyana Chronicle* 2009).

The tune struck negative chords with Bajans—among whom women in particular took issue—but garnered mixed reviews among Guyanese.[6] Although the calypso reinforces stereotypes of Guyanese as outsiders who pillage Barbados's limited resources, it also situates Guyana, and more specifically Georgetown, as a place from which Bajans might learn something, while lauding the attractiveness of Guyanese women. And in Guyana, the "uproar" that the song sparked in Barbados, coupled with the notion that Bajan men are "sweet on Guyanese women," was a source of pride and humor (Sutherland 2009).

Competitive ribbing aside, "GT Advice" underscores the ways in which Guyanese femininity, in particular, and Guyanese identity, in general, are otherized in Barbados. The stereotypical "Guyanese Girl" sets Bajan and Guyanese women at odds and sows dissension against Guyanese more broadly (after all, the refrain urges, "learn to wine, like de Guyanese," a non-gender-specific identification). Guyanese women, then, are stand-ins for the nation as a whole, whose people are essentialized as lascivious and decadent in their consumption of food and sex. This stands in stark contrast to the Bajan woman, who is portrayed as matronly and pragmatic, along with her partner, who is represented as hard-working, if fickle. Actually, home remedies very similar to the ones the song applies to Bajan women abound in Guyana. And it is mothers and grandmothers who pass on homeopathic treatments such as rubbing oneself at night with Vicks VapoRub for colds, splashing on mentholated rubs like Limacol to reduce fever, and ingesting foul-tasting remedies like senna and castor oil to cleanse the body.[7] Therefore, the picture "GT Advice" paints—of a Bajan woman whose nighttime regimens make her sexually undesirable—smacks directly of what Guyanese women practice in their own homes.

## Historicizing "GT Advice": "Going to Guyana to Get a Wife"

In Barbados, stereotypes voiced in "GT Advice" about Guyanese women's desirableness, their penchant for sexual experimentation, and their adeptness at pleasing a man through superior cooking skills and adherence to patriarchal domestic norms have accompanied the fraught presence of Guyanese immigrants on the island. Conversations with Bajans reveal the prevalence of these presumptions, while historical research grounds them in competition for employment and racialized notions of beauty traceable to the colonial era. When I mentioned being Guyanese to a Bajan cab driver one afternoon as he drove me around the neighborhood in which Rihanna grew up, the driver was quick to disclose his own Guyanese ancestry. "Oh! My mother is Guyanese! All the men in my family marry Guyanese women! My father's mother is Guyanese too! It's true—Bajan men love Guyanese women. Going *way* back the men in my family used to go to Guyana to get a wife," he said.

The taxi driver's account that "going way back the men in my family used to go to Guyana to get a wife" prompted me to track the historical processes of Barbadian migration to Guyana. While Guyanese migra-

tion to Barbados has been a contemporary hot-button issue, during the
colonial era, Guiana was the receiving site of emigrants from Barbados
and other parts of the Caribbean. In the post-emancipation period, Guiana was characterized by a surplus of land and agriculture but an Afro-
Guyanese labor force that refused to be exploited.[8] This, of course, led
to the British introducing indentured laborers from Asia, but there were
regional migratory processes at play as well, particularly from Barbados. In fact, in her article "Confined Spaces, Constrained Bodies: Land,
Labour, and the 1836 Emigration Act of Barbados," Dawn Harris writes,
"In post-emancipation Barbados, imperial and colonial legislators were
presented with a set of problems that were virtually unheard of in other
parts of the British West Indies. Whereas, for instance, reports of insufficient labour and crippled plantations were heard in places like British
Guiana, Trinidad and, to a lesser extent, Jamaica, Barbados experienced
a glut of labour and dearth of land" (Harris 2010, 238).

Outmigration of Barbadian laborers was significant enough to war-
rant an act designed to prohibit post-emancipation laborers from seeking work in Guiana, which promised employment opportunities and
higher wages (Harris 2010, 241). Harris examines the arguably unique
case of Barbados: "The 1836 Emigration Act represented one of the more
notable instances where law, land and labour were manipulated in tandem to constrain the bodies of labourers in the post-slavery period"
(Harris 2010, 241). During this period, Barbados's relatively high ratio
of inhabitants to land—as Harris notes, between 1841 and 1844 it had
the region's highest population—meant that the island nation could not
support the development of peasantries (Harris 2010, 239–40). Debates
about Barbadian emigration were, from the start, centered neither on
individuals' rights to move nor on the nation's labor shortage but rather
on the state's mission to ensure that the laboring class did not neglect
their family responsibilities (Harris 2010, 242). Potential migrants had
to prove that their "dependents" (defined as "legitimate" and "illegiti-
mate" children, parents, and grandparents) would be taken care of in
their absence (Harris 2010, 242). In this way and in others, including
such horrendous tactics as falsely linking migration to infant mortality,
the state construed Barbadian labor-class migration as a threat to the
family (Harris 2010, 244–45). Effectively, from this early period, the state
situated Barbadian migration to Guiana within the realm of jeopardiz-

ing the domestic kin group. Tellingly, Harris cites anti-emigration state discourse around attempting to curtail "the creation of a class of 'impotent families' and 'helpless infants'" (Harris 2010, 242).

While an exact recounting of each of the related post-emancipation acts the colonial state deployed to curb the freedoms of Barbadian laborers is beyond the scope of this work, suffice it to say that colonial officials struggled to keep their stronghold on Black laborers upon whose cheap labor the plantation economy depended. Laborers continued to be lured away by the promise of greater autonomy and higher wages in British Guiana. Although Harris does not focus on the gendered breakdown of emigration from Barbados, her study indicates that more men than women emigrated, and that women outnumbered men in Barbados—at the time of emancipation, her data places the female population at 20,500 and males at 16,000.⁹ This breakdown—a reversal of the Guyanese gender disparity between male and female indentured laborers detailed earlier (in which Indian indentured men outnumbered their female counterparts)—has implications for the intersection of gender and Barbadian emigration. Within the dictates of heterosexual courtship, Bajan women were already competing for a small pool of eligible men, and the men left the island in greater numbers than women. Harris's research paints a picture of a Black laboring class for whom restrictions on the freedom to travel for work were couched in a narrative fostering a fear of "impotent families," within a social context in which wages and labor were not far removed from the oppressive structures of slavery. Of course, the oppressive dictates of the post-emancipation era created the dire circumstances that motivated laborers to migrate, but Harris's study suggests that from this period on, the colonial state helped to construct an image of British Guiana as enticing able-bodied, marriageable men to abandon their kinship responsibilities in Barbados.

The years 1863 to 1886 marked "the most intense period" of Barbadian emigration to Guiana (Lewis 2011). But Barbadian emigration continued in the 1920s and 1930s, and as late as the 1960s, when, in the post-independence era, Guyana was regarded as the "bread basket of the Caribbean" due to its significant successes in agriculture, including the proliferation of major crops like sugar and rice (*Guyana Chronicle* 2011). If we consider that most of the Barbadian laborers who migrated to Guyana were male cane cutters (Lewis 2011), we can see the origins of contemporary cultural notions that Bajan men went to Guyana to "get a wife." Sociologist Linden Lewis writes, "The genealogies of Guyanese and Barbadians are so intertwined that it is not uncommon to learn of Guyanese who have grandparents from Barbados, and vice versa. There are deep families [sic] ties in which, in one family half of the children could be born in Guyana and the other half in Barbados. My own extended family embodied this split national profile. The familial ties are enduring, but the vicissitudes of development have been more favorable to Barbados, while the fortunes of Guyana have rendered the country less attractive by comparison in the contemporary period" (Lewis 2011).

Lewis goes on to recount that his Barbadian grandparents traveled to Guiana, where they lived and worked as missionaries and where their son (his father) was born. While his grandparents' missionary posting eventually brought them back to Barbados, Lewis's father returned to Guiana in 1942, where he met and married Lewis's mother. The Lewis family story situates the notion of going to Guyana "to get a wife" within the actual migratory, labor, and familial processes that fostered close genealogical ties between the two nations. And those family ties surface in the marital bond between the Barbadian poet Kamau Brathwaite and his first wife and collaborator, Doris Monica Brathwaite, who was Guyanese. After learning that she was terminally ill, Brathwaite chronicled the six months between that diagnosis and the tragic death of Doris (whom he had nicknamed his "Mexican," "in honor of her part-Amerindian ancestry") in his book, *The Zea Mexican Diary, 7 Sept 1926–7 Sept 1986* (Walmsley 1994, 747). Brathwaite's searing portrayal of love and loss, like Lewis's account of shared genealogies, unveils the intimacies behind the popular trope of the Bajan husband and the Guyanese wife.[10] The poet describes gazing lovingly at his wife as her life comes to an end:

> . . . . her naked body stretched there on
> the bed was as beautiful & as desirable as ever.
> i cd have made love to her that Sunday morning
> felt that accustomed leap of love the golden warm
> & copper colour skin the plump & curves that I
> have so long known & loved my darling Mexican.
> (Brathwaite 1993, 68–69)

Although I have not attempted to replicate Brathwaite's signature font in the above quotation, as previously noted, the poet's unique typeset, what he referred to as his "video-style," was inspired by Guyanese Amerindian petroglyphs. In *The Zea Mexican Diary*, Brathwaite acknowledges Doris's profound influence on his development as a poet; she typed his work, proofread his poetry, debated its meaning with him, assisted him in publishing a literary journal, and mastered the desktop computer when it was a nascent technology—leading to the creation of his video-style (Sharpe 2020, 135).[11] Accounts of how Doris's generous devotion and her own brilliance fostered Brathwaite's career abound in *The Zea Mexican Diary*. It should come as no surprise that the intimacies Brathwaite describes are in contrast to the coarse representation of the seductive Guyanese woman that channels in popular discourses like "GT Advice." In the face of losing his collaborator and companion, he poignantly conveys love and corporal desire within the sanctity of a Sunday morning and the brutal certainty of the deathbed.

## Rihanna as Guyanese Girl

The realities of love and marriage between Bajan men and Guyanese women are rooted not in inherently sexualized qualities Guyanese women embody but in the very *tidalectic* undercurrents of love and loss, and in the migratory processes through which Caribbean women symbolically and literally traverse diasporic spaces. Putting the Bajan state's history of regulating labor-class migration and the Guyanese woman as homewrecker stereotype in conversation with Lewis's and Brathwaite's accounts reveals the intersecting registers along which the political economy of erasure operates. My pointer broom sweeps together these historical currents of international migratory labor, cultural exchange, and intimate partnerships, elucidating profound familial processes and kinship ties that undermine the economy of erasure. As we have seen, migratory flows between Guyana and Barbados informed shifting gender and kinship constructions that initially rendered the Bajan family impotent by outmigration to Guyana, and during the twenty-first century represent Guyanese women as threats to the Bajan heterosexual nuclear unit. Amid Barbadian popular and political discourses pigeonholing Guyanese women as sexually dangerous foreigners, the national pride bestowed on Rihanna begs unpacking.

I first confronted the degree to which Rihanna's Guyanese ancestry remains invisible outside the two nations in question, and the wide-reaching roots of the objectification of Guyanese women, when I brought up Rihanna's Guyanese ancestry with a Black male academic working in the United States. Baffled, the male colleague, who was not from the Caribbean but had traveled extensively in the region, responded with an attempt to make sense of this remarkable news: "Rihanna's mother is Guyanese?!? No wonder! That makes sense, I mean all of the cricket players take White wives because Bajan women are ugly!" I was aston-ished at the audacious racialized misogyny in this statement. Arguably, the speaker felt he was not only praising Rihanna's beauty but also com-plimenting me, since he knew I was Guyanese. His linking of Rihanna's Guyanese ancestry with a rejection of Bajan women, and with the al-leged practice of professional cricket players taking White wives, placed Rihanna as phenotypically closer to White and thus more in line with European standards of beauty. Furthermore, he was tracing what he saw as Rihanna's European traits—she has green eyes and is comparatively light-skinned—to her Guyanese rather than her Bajan ancestry. This disparagement of Bajan women and objectification of their Guyanese counterparts strikes at the heart of the raced/gendered notions of beauty and sexuality from which the shibboleth springs. It also illustrates that stereotypes reinforce false logic; Rihanna's mother, Monica Braithwaite, is a comparatively deep brown–skinned Afro-Guyanese woman, while her father, Ronald Fenty, is a light-skinned Barbadian of mixed African and Irish ancestry. Of course, the high percentage of Indians in Guyana (alongside smaller percentages of other ethnic groups, including Portu-guese, Chinese, and Indigenous Guyanese) suggests that Rihanna may very well also have mixed-race ancestry on her Guyanese side. But the ways in which my male colleague connected Rihanna's "beauty" with her Guyanese ancestry signaled a misreading of her mother's racial identity that equated "Guyanese beauty" with the embodiment of features that are decidedly non-African, while perpetuating the global degradation of Black women's looks.

While my colleague's assessment of Rihanna, and of Barbadian and Guyanese women alike, was woefully shortsighted and deeply misogynous, it prompts us to question why, in light of the sorts of cultural tensions revealed in relation to the song "GT Advice," Rihanna is not read as Guyanese and has enjoyed exemption from the stereotype of the Guyanese woman as foreign threat. Rihanna represents a particularly fruitful site for exploring the tensions and contradictions around simultaneously marking Guyanese femininity as dangerous and rendering it illegible. The most commercially successful Caribbean musical artist in history and the world's wealthiest female musician (with a fortune estimated at $1.7 billion in 2021), Robyn Rihanna Fenty, popularly known as Rihanna and RiRi, has been the subject of global controversies—in the popular realm she has been a lightning rod—critiqued both for her hypersexual "rude girl" image and for briefly reconciling with her domestic abuser and former boyfriend, the African American singer Chris Brown.[12] Scholars of the Caribbean have held her up for her "uncompromising articulations of national belonging coupled with her unprecedented transnational success" (Beckles and Russell 2015, 2). In their introduction to the edited volume *Rihanna: Barbados World-Gurl in Global Popular Culture*, Hilary McD. Beckles and Heather D. Russell position Rihanna's relationship to Barbadian society this way: "The essays in this collection trouble the long-standing mythology surrounding Barbados which simplistically reads Bajan culture as socially conservative, the 'Little England,' as it were, of the Caribbean. In other words, as Hilary Beckles points out in this volume, RiRi is not a Barbadian anomaly . . . ; her unequivocal affirmation of black women's right to unfettered sexual mobility and expressivity, her highly publicized challenges to global racism and her radical nonconformity all mark her as 100 per cent Bajan" (Beckles and Russell 2015, 5).

In the above passage, Beckles and Russell could well have been articulating characteristics ascribed to Afro-Guyanese women. Although passing references in two of the volume's essays acknowledge Rihanna's Guyanese ancestry, these are fleeting but significant cracks in the representational veneer that frames RiRi as "100 per cent Bajan." Still, these scholars offer thoughtful and generative deconstructions of Rihanna's persona as quintessentially Bajan, to the point where in 2008 she received national recognition in the form of being named "honorary youth and cultural ambassador" by the then prime minister, and concurrently as the subject of relentless criticism for embodying a sexual permissiveness that is interpreted as a corruptive influence on her young fans.[13] For our purposes, it is important to note that although Rihanna has been besieged in Bajan social media and in other regional public commentary for the explicit sexual content in her lyrics, music, and videos, and for cultivating a persona that celebrates female sexual liberation (Jones 2015), these criticisms have generally not traced her "slackness" to her Guyanese ancestry. In this respect, Beckles and Russell are on point; in the Barbados popular context, Rihanna is read as "100 per cent Bajan" and is ostensibly, at least, not subject to the xenophobic, gendered bromide that Guyanese women are a menace to Bajan marriages and the nuclear family unit.

The anti-Guyanese sentiments considered at the start of this chapter are specifically grounded in gendered (female) and racially marked (Indian) ways—reflected in the song "GT Advice" through examples such as Sukhram's eagerness to do what Bajan women allegedly will not and in references to Indo-Guyanese food. It begs exploring why Rihanna has not been saddled with the Guyanese-woman-as-foreign-threat label. Although her Guyanese ancestry has been largely under the radar in US discourses around the performer, Rihanna has made no secret of it. Reportedly estranged from a father who struggled with addiction and physically abused her mother, Rihanna has placed credit for her upbringing squarely with her mother and grandmother. Her mother raised her, and in a globally televised ceremony, presented Rihanna with the AMA (American Music Awards) Icon Award in 2013. And the singer has publicly professed her devotion to her Guyanese grandmother, Clara Braithwaite, whom she lovingly called "Gran Gran Dolly." Rihanna's tight bond with Gran Gran Dolly, a mainstay of her Instagram posts, was depicted in an "Oprah's Next Chapter" interview in which the performer reflected on her late grandmother's life and shared lessons learned from her. As a child, she spent summers with her grandparents in the Flatbush section of Brooklyn, where she would have mingled with New York City's oversized Guyanese immigrant community. Rihanna founded a nonprofit, the Clara Lionel Foundation, in the name of her grandparents, focused on educational and emergency-response programs in several countries, including Guyana.

Rihanna's immense wealth has supported her considerable philanthropy. She amassed a global business empire, comprised of her astronomically successful makeup line, Fenty Beauty (valued at $2.8 billion in 2022), her lingerie line, Savage X Fenty (valued at $3 billion in 2022), and her couture fashion label, Fenty Maison (she is the first Black woman to create an original brand with the prestigious LVMH corporation).[14] And she is increasingly recognized not only for her business acumen but for injecting her capitalist endeavors with the very forms of rebellion and contestation of hegemonic gender norms/beauty standards for which she was both adored and maligned in her private life (LaBennett 2021). So, for example, Rihanna's Savage X Fenty lingerie fashion shows feature diverse models and performers, including a model with vitiligo, pregnant models, and trans performers. In 2022, after Rihanna announced that she was pregnant, the singer redirected global coverage of her pregnancy so that it focused less on the fact that she and her boyfriend, the American rapper A$AP Rocky, were not married, and more on her efforts to redefine the norms of maternity fashion by exposing her growing belly (Nnadi 2022). Across all of these maneuvers, the singer/mogul evokes her mother's influence. She has said that watching her mother put on makeup when she was a child inspired Fenty Beauty (Hirsch 2020). In 2019, she told *Essence* magazine, "I'm a Black woman. I came from a Black woman, who came from a Black woman. It's a no-brainer. That's who I am. It's the core of who I am in spirit and DNA. My mother is an incredible example of how to fight through obstacles in life. I'm sure her mom taught her that and that's how I'm going to be. We are impeccable, we're special and the world is going to have to deal with that" (quoted in Scott 2020).

The emphasis Rihanna places on both her mother's and her grandmother's influence underscores that her Guyanese cultural heritage was formative in her upbringing and continues to inspire both her art and her global business ventures (and in the above quotation, her philosophy on motherhood). Yet, within the political economy of erasure that operates across global Guyana, Rihanna's accentuation of her Guyanese matriline goes largely unnoticed. Local contradictions surrounding this effacement point both to Bajan national anxieties about claiming the superstar as their own and to the ways in which Afro-Guyanese gender identity is rendered illegible, while Indo-Guyanese femininity, as portrayed in popular culture, comes to represent an essentialized Guyanese woman. Rihanna's Afro-Guyanese ancestry may in some respects shield the performer from the sorts of racialized and gendered otherness that Sukhram embodies, and that Mother, Rita, and Rose voiced.[15] Yet, while Rihanna's Blackness may have facilitated her absorption as a symbol of Bajan nationalism, her Guyaneseness has positioned her as an insider/ outsider in Bajan society.

Deconstructing key moments in which Rihanna has publicly outlined her family tree demonstrates how her genealogy follows the trajectory parsed earlier, echoing the *tidalectic* processes under which Bajan men went to Guyana to "get a wife." On Instagram in 2013 Rihanna celebrated her grandfather's birthday with this post: "Happy Birthday Grandfadda Bravo!!! You are so special to all of us!!! If it wasn't for you buying out the whole tray of mangoes from gran gran Dolly that one day off your ship in Guyana, and charmed her with that smile laced with a gold cap, NONE of us would be here!! So I'm saying a special thanks to you for having a heart of a lion. . . . They will never know what it took for you to get us here!! I love you way past unconditional!!! You're true az steel BRAVO!!!!" (quoted in *Caribbean Media Network* 2013). Here, Rihanna indicates that her grandfather, only temporarily docked in Guyana on a ship from Barbados, forever changed the national and cultural makeup of the family by choosing and "charming" a Guyanese woman. Taken alongside more recent comments Rihanna has made about the treatment of Guyanese in Barbados, the line, "They will never know what it took for you to get us here!!" is significant. The message, posted during a birthday celebration in Barbados, positions the family as "us" and Barbados as "here." The "us" and "them" dichotomy Rihanna sets up separates her Guyanese family from Bajans. Rihanna lauds her grandfather for making a crucial decision, using his day off the ship to court "gran gran Dolly," resulting in starting a family in Guyana. Yet, while the post illustrates RiRi's unconditional love for her grandfather, it is the Guyanese women in her family—her mother and grandmother—to whom she points in terms of shaping her worldview.

## "I's a Guyanese, Bai, Eh-eh!"

Rihanna has publicly identified as Guyanese in mediated, yet under-the-radar-moments that have been celebrated in Guyanese social media spaces but ignored by global media outlets. When, in 2012, she tweeted,

"Big up to my Guyanese people!!!" it was retweeted over two thousand times (Rihanna 2012). One key moment occurred in 2014: YouTube video footage captures the performer chatting with an Indo-Guyanese man who approaches her as she arrives at New York's John F. Kennedy Airport. Rihanna is walking through the airport, accompanied by a bodyguard, but graciously greeting fans and pausing to pose for selfies with them. In the thick of flashing camera lights and numerous fans and paparazzi calling out to RiRi as she exits the terminal, an Indo-Guyanese man is almost undetectable in the video. He walks up beside Rihanna and quietly asks, "You is from Guyana?" The pop star responds enthusiastically, speaking in Guyanese creole, "Guyana! I's a Guyanese, bai, eh-eh!" She then asks the man, "Is where you from?" After he replies, "I's from Georgetown!" Rihanna adds, "Is Georgetown you from? Me family is from Berbice and Georgetown." The pair exchange additional inaudible words before Rihanna parts ways with him as he calls after her, "It's good to hear yah voice!" She responds, "Ah-right!" This interaction, in which Rihanna seamlessly code switches from her usual Bajan-inflected accent to speak in Guyanese creole, marks her as Guyanese. Tellingly, the subtle encounter with the Guyanese man takes the back seat in the video because the dominant voice on the footage is a loud-talking paparazzo speculating that Rihanna will be cast as the next "Bond Girl" in a then upcoming James Bond film. That the declaration of her Guyaneseness occurs while she is fielding fans who recognize her as an international performer and at least one industry person, the paparazzo, reflects on her commercial viability as an actress in the Bond franchise is a testament to Rihanna's malleable persona as an international symbol of Bajan culture, as a marketable genre-crossing icon, and, in the least legible sense, as a Guyanese girl.

As we might expect, Guyanese social media commentators had mixed interpretations of the YouTube video footage—with some seeing it as undeniable proof that Rihanna *is* Guyanese and others insisting that her Bajan paternity means she is only half-Guyanese—but the majority of the comments the video received on Facebook reveled in RiRi's Guyanese creole. Rihanna has unveiled her Guyanese ancestry beyond these siloed conversations, within the pages of the high-fashion magazines that trade in her persona as a global trendsetter; in a 2017 *Elle Magazine* interview, in which "twenty of her friends and fans" asked her questions, she answers the query, "What food do you cook when you want a little comfort?" by saying, "Bajan macaroni pie, which is our version of baked mac 'n' cheese" (Long 2017). However, for the very next question, another interviewer asks Rihanna, "What's your secret family recipe?" She responds, "It's a secret! LOL. But they make a mean 'cook-up' and pepper pot. Both are Guyanese recipes" (Long 2017). It is telling that Rihanna positions Bajan macaroni, the very meal the song "GT Advice" disparages as inferior to Indo-Guyanese home cooking, as a dish she herself prepares, while offering cook-up and pepper pot as secret recipes. The typical meaning attached to a "secret family recipe" takes on a double entendre in that her Guyanese heritage is not readily legible.

These instances suggest that Rihanna's Guyaneseness is always just beneath the surface and only apparent when she decides to make it visible, or when reporters find it newsworthy. We might discern that Rihanna's Guyanese identity is always already there but rendered illegible by a public that either prefers not to acknowledge it—as may be the case with Bajan nationalist interests—or that is unable to read the markers of Guyanese ethnicity—as is the case with observers outside the Caribbean. Beckles and Russell make a related case in their volume, namely, that although Rihanna is subject to various readings by global audiences, it is useful to destabilize the potent Euro-American gaze if we wish to understand the artist from a Caribbean postcolonial perspective (Beckles and Russell 2015, 4). I expand Beckles and Russell's call to push back against the Euro-American viewpoint by demonstrating that Rihanna has been read from multiple perspectives, but rarely, if ever, from a Guyanese standpoint. This is a critical oversight for an artist who routinely credits her Guyanese maternal line for her weltanschauung and is part and parcel of the political economy of erasure that this book tackles.

By 2020, with Guyana increasingly more within the sights of international press coverage—albeit for oil, not beauty, fashion, and music—Rihanna's Guyanese ancestry made it into the published version of a story about the performer/businesswoman when she appeared on the cover of *British Vogue* (Hirsch 2020). Arguing that "Rihanna's connections are more personal and complex than they are often portrayed," interviewer Afua Hirsch turns to her Guyanese background.

It is well documented that the star was born and raised in Barbados, but her mother, Monica, was an immigrant to the Caribbean island from Guyana. . . . Rihanna tells me that Guyanese immigrants were unpopular in Barbados when she was growing up. "The Guyanese are like the Mexicans of Barbados," she says. "So I identify—and that's why I really relate and empathize with Mexican people and Latino people, who are discriminated against in America. I know what it feels like to have the immigration come into your home in the middle of the night and drag people out." (Hirsch 2020)

Hirsch quotes Rihanna as quick to note that Monica Braithwaite was a legal immigrant in Barbados. But the star links her mother's immigrant community with a passionate plea for appreciating the cruel realities that immigrant children face in the United States: "My mother was legal . . . but let's just say that I know what that fight looks like. I've witnessed it. I've been in it. I was probably, what, eight-years-old when I experienced that in the middle of the night. So I know how disheartening it is for a child—and if that was my parent that was getting dragged out of my house, I can guarantee you that my life would have been a shambles" (quoted in Hirsch 2020). Here we see Rihanna speaking directly to the forms of state-sanctioned violence Guyanese immigrants and their children face in Barbados. And although she is currently celebrated as the "quintessentially Bajan girl," by her own account, as a child she felt the sting of an outsider status akin to that of Mexicans in the United States. The continued presence of this threat is illustrated in the superstar's readiness to emphasize that her mother "was legal"; suggesting otherwise could well open Monica up to criticism at best and state violence at worst. Rihanna is not alone in relating the treatment of Guyanese in Barbados to that of Mexicans in the United States—a *Guyana Chronicle* editorial from 2006, entitled "Other Mexicans," makes the same case.[16]

How might we reflect meaningfully on Rihanna's insistence that "Guyanese are like the Mexicans of Barbados," while also recalling that Kamau Brathwaite referred to his wife, Doris, as his "darling Mexican"? The poet explained that he affectionately called Doris "Dearest Mexican" in a nod to her part-Amerindian ancestry (she was also Afro-Guyanese). Although the Warao people from whom Doris descended inhabit multiple territories, including Guyana, Venezuela, Suriname, and Trinidad and Tobago (their name translates as "boat people"), calling Doris a "Mexican" arguably conflates indigeneity across distinct locations— South America and the Caribbean, and Mexico. Still, scholars focused on indigeneity and Afro-Latino identity have underscored the blurred lines of these distinctions. Paul Joseph López Oro draws on John D. Márquez (2013), pointing to the "centrality of the imperial construct of the US-Mexico border as a symbolic demarcation [and] as a racialized geography" that opens up discussions of "the corporeality of brownness in Latinidad" (López Oro 2016, 72). The evocation of "Mexican" in Rihanna's and Brathwaite's instances, then, gestures speculatively both to the "othering" of Guyanese women within the region and to the parallels between the malignment and marginalization of Guyanese in Barbados and Mexicans in the United States. Thus, we might understand a global Guyana perspective as one that acknowledges relational ties, blurred racial geographies, and political economies of erasure that channel across the aquatic borders between Guyana and Barbados, while also mirroring the very land-border racializations so intensely debated in the United States. Brathwaite supports such an interpretation when he describes the Caribbean woman as walking on sand *and* on water, as she traverses vast bodies of water and continents.

## Trafficking in Guyanese Girls' Sexuality

Rihanna's childhood fear that as the daughter of a Guyanese immigrant, she could potentially be separated from her mother by government officials, puts the artist's ambivalence about being a poster girl for the Bajan state in a stark light. As Esther Jones has noted, RiRi has both leaned into deploying her image and persona as a vehicle for the Bajan tourism industry—appearing in video and print advertising as a "pretty little Bajan girl" with just the right amount of respectable sexuality to entice tourists—and rebelled against a Bajan public that harshly criticizes the expression of her sexual liberation (Jones 2015, 106–7). Just as Jones has argued that the performer's artistic evolution and concomitant maturation to womanhood have at the same time rested on taking control of her image and sexuality and on managing the ups and downs of a Bajan public that alternately adores her and bashes her as sexually inappropriate, I want to suggest that RiRi's maturity has hinged on becoming more and more bold about confronting the ways in which the state's co-opting of her image has denied her Guyaneseness, evidenced in the above quotation in *British Vogue*. Jones sets us in this direction, albeit without deconstructing the significance of Rihanna's Guyanese background, by averring that "Rihanna's authenticity as a true Bajan native" is wrapped up in "invok[ing] the communal, national identity that she represents in a manner that is both gendered and sexualized. . . . This trading upon Rihanna's sexuality, while simultaneously attempting to contain that sexuality beneath a youthful veneer of innocence, ironically enters into the discourse of an ostensibly less desirable commodity that the Caribbean region struggles to contain as well: the sex tourism industry" (Jones 2015, 103). By focusing on the "sex tourism industry," Jones alludes to one of the key vectors within which Guyanese women are demonized as illegal elements in the Bajan nation-state: sex trafficking. Concerns abound in Barbados that "an alarming number of Guyanese women are prostituting" (Fernandes 2018). But behind headlines such as "Traffickers Paying Guyanese Girls Airline Tickets to Come to Barbados" are references not to tourism but rather to local Bajan men manipulating the insidious trafficking network between the two countries, which puts undocumented and documented Guyanese women and children at high risk (Fernandes 2018).[17]

## Learn to Wine, like a Guyanese: Rihanna's Pattacake

Considering Rihanna's assertions that her Guyanese mother and grandmother influenced both her fashion/beauty empire and her social consciousness, it is perhaps unsurprising that we would find the imprints of Guyanese maternal mores in Rihanna's musical performances as well. Released in 2011 and performed on *Saturday Night Live* (SNL) in 2012, and subsequently throughout her Diamonds World Tour, the song "Birthday Cake" is one example that locates Rihanna's oeuvre within Guyanese cultural knowledge. The star's SNL performance of "Birthday Cake" received scholarly attention because the singer, not widely known for her dancing, incorporated a Caribbean wine, a dance based on rotating the waist and hips in a circular motion (Jones 2016; Jones, LaBennett, and Lindsey 2016). Although Adanna Jones's attention to Rihanna's wining performance thoughtfully situates it within the context of Barbados (Jones 2016), as my consideration of Sukhram's "GT Advice" demonstrated, around the same time, Bajan women were being instructed to "learn to wine, like a Guyanese." In the SNL performance and in subsequent live performances of "Birthday Cake," Rihanna stuck with a choreographed routine in which she wined and slapped her groin repeatedly throughout the song. "Birthday Cake," and the moves Rihanna employs when she performs the tune, can be understood vis-à-vis the sexually explicit performance styles emanating from the Crop Over festival, at which Rihanna has been a regular participant, and as indicative of the resistant body politics of dancehall. Although the latter is based in Jamaica, its influence on artistic and public expressions across the Caribbean region is clear (Jones 2016). However, I want to make a different case, one for reading Rihanna's "Birthday Cake" from the standpoint of intergenerational Guyanese maternal knowledge.[18]

"Birthday Cake" begins with the sounds of a school bell ringing and hands clapping—with the hand claps repeated throughout the track. At first blush, the song's repetitive lyrics read as a rather simplistic, bold-faced sexual analogy:

> Come and put your name on it
> Put your name on it. . . .
> It's not even my birthday
> But he want to lick the icing off
> I know you want it in the worst way
> Can't wait to blow my candles out
> He want that cake, cake,
> Cake, cake, cake, cake, cake
> Cake, cake, cake, cake, cake
> Cake, cake, cake . . .

Considered alongside live performances of the tune, in which Rihanna wines and gestures to her vagina in both a patting motion and with a chopping action, the song is simultaneously an acknowledgment of a male partner's sexual desire, an invitation to sex, and a dominating warning of the singer's power of consent: in the final verse she states, "I'mma make you my bitch." These lyrics, for which the singer has a songwriting credit, coupled with Rihanna featuring her ex-boyfriend

Chris Brown on a remix of the tune, led to it being read as steeped in the very controversies of consent, domestic violence, and "bad girl" sexuality that had for so long dogged the star.[19] Although Rihanna's wining moves and transgressive sexuality fit neatly into the interpretive framework that has permeated the scholarship of the diva, "Birthday Cake" also draws from decidedly Guyanese cultural markers, not only in the use of the wine—which is as much a mainstay of Guyanese dancing as it is in neighboring Barbados and Trinidad and Tobago—but also in the lyrics, instrumentation, and production of the song.

The aforementioned school bell and hand claps situate the track within the cultural space of childhood, with the children's birthday party ritual of blowing out candles on a cake now brazenly co-opted as part of the sex act. And while the birthday cake and school bell can be read as global markers of childhood, the lyrics, coupled with Rihanna's movements, signal that she is not just a child of Barbados and a borderless offspring of the Caribbean, but rather, explicitly a daughter of Guyana. I base this reading in the equating of birthday cake with patting the singer's sexual organ—a reference that conjures the Guyanese creole term for vagina, "pattacake." "Pattacake" is the term that Guyanese mothers employ when teaching girl children about their bodies. It is significant that the song does not rely on other, more broadly recognizable island-specific terms for vagina such as "nuk nuk" (Barbados) or "punani" (Jamaica)—its reliance on the repetition of "cake, cake, cake, cake" and on Rihanna's patting of her own "cake," evokes the Guyanese moniker for the singer's sex organ. If we consider the Guyanese maternal transfer of knowledge in teaching a young daughter to call her vagina her "pattacake"—a term Rihanna would have learned from both her mother and her grandmother, if not from her time spent among the Guyanese diaspora in Flatbush and/or Barbados—we can see Rihanna's usage of birthday cake as a marker of her Guyanese matrilineage, as well as an indicator of the global intertextuality of the song. My point here is not to index the identity politics at play in "Birthday Cake" but rather to emphasize how a reading of its origins allows us to see some of the circuits of global Guyana.

Rihanna's "Birthday Cake" is a clear nod to the British nursery rhyme from which the term "pattacake" is likely derived:

Pat-a-cake, pat-a-cake, baker's man
Bake me a cake as fast as you can.
Pat it, prick it, and mark it with "B"
Put it in the oven for baby and me.

Imagined as a comforting lullaby conveyed from mother to baby, but of course rendered beyond the nursery as a sidewalk, Bottom House, and schoolyard hand-clapping game practiced by young girls, the rhyme asks the listener to "pat it, prick it, and mark it with 'B.'" The "B" is traditionally replaced with the baby's name or initial, but when Rihanna implores her male sex partner to "put your name on it" she sexualizes both a global childhood ritual (enjoying a birthday cake and blowing out the candles) and a Guyana-specific term that is steeped in the maternal transfer of knowledge. Under Rihanna's control, "pattacake" morphs from a girlhood euphemism to an adult sign of sexual defiance. Rihanna both teases her male partner to "put his name on it" *and* denies him access; he is presented as "wanting it in the worst way" but the song never confirms that he obtains it. The tune's circum-Caribbean elements and global cultural references—spanning Guyana, Barbados, England, and New York—speak to the oral-kinetic practices of Black girls' play-songs that ethnomusicologist Kyra Gaunt has argued embody the mainstays of Black music making across the diaspora (Gaunt 2006). That RiRi never says "pattacake" in the song, but signals the Guyanese term by patting her own cake and by referencing the nursery rhyme situates "Birthday Cake" as a hidden transcript with embedded Guyanese maternal knowledge that is only accessible to a listener who is in the know.

"Birthday Cake" is not one of Rihanna's most well-known mega hits, yet the remix of the song was certified as platinum twice. And the tune's reverberations, which are stereophonic, multilingual, and transnational in the sense articulated by Paul Gilroy (1993), continued to channel in pre–COVID-19 New York City long after its release and the SNL performance. If you happened to celebrate your birthday at either of the two New York locations of a wildly popular and fashionable Caribbean restaurant called Miss Lily's Favorite Cakes, you would find that as the wait staff dims the lights and brings out your slice of coconut cake topped with a lit sparkler, the constant soundtrack of reggae and dancehall hits is temporarily silenced and instead of gathering to sing "Happy Birthday to You," the DJ blasts Rihanna's "Birthday Cake," as everyone—staff, birthday revelers, and other diners—claps along and chants, "Cake, cake, cake, cake, cake!"[20] In this way, Rihanna's "Birthday Cake" and Guyanese cultural knowledge play a starring role in the New York establishment, where Guyanese chow mein is regularly a menu item, even if its more overt musical references are to Jamaican artists, such as Grace Jones, whose iconic portrait with cigarette dangling from mouth and steely side-eye glance adorns a focal point. "Birthday Cake's" reincarnation as a birthday ritual at Miss Lily's speaks to Rihanna's currency not only as a Bajan and as a daughter of Guyana but as a wide-reaching voice of the Anglophone Caribbean and its global diaspora, in which she shares sonic space with the likes of Grace Jones.

## Big Up to My Guyanese Mother

The massive cruise ships constantly docked in Bridgetown's port cast looming shadows over Westbury, the hard-knocks neighborhood in which Rihanna grew up, where she was bred with "badness, slackness and boldness" (Beckles 2015, 19).[21] These luxury liners and Bridgetown's upmarket jewelry stores—to which day trippers from the boats flock to buy duty-free diamonds from Cartier and other high-end dealers—are a stone's throw from the modest Westbury bungalow in which the diva was raised. Rihanna's estranged father no longer lives there, but the singer reportedly purchased him a million-dollar home after the house was beset by photo-hungry tourists. As of 2018, the house appeared to be freshly painted in bright lime-green and orange tones. A yellow sun along with the word "Rihanna" and a Bajan trident are stenciled on the cement pavement in front of the house. The street on which it sits has been renamed "Rihanna Drive," and the overflow of national pride for the superstar is illustrated in a plaque mounted at the end of the road, identifying Rihanna as "Our Diamond," a nod to her 2012 global megahit, "Diamonds." That this Bajan/Guyanese diamond lived so humbly and so close to the Cartier gems she can now so easily afford rings with as much paradox as the pride the Bajan state evokes in naming her "Cultural Ambassador" on the plaque.

Just as it has attempted to mute her sexuality, the Bajan state has had to ignore or deny Rihanna's Guyaneseness in order to lionize her. If, as Rihanna herself notes, Guyanese are the Mexicans of Barbados, then the state cannot beam with pride as it upholds her as a national hero *and* acknowledge Rihanna's Guyanese roots. Just as the singer situates her understanding of this bitter truth within childhood experiences, it is childhood maternal knowledge that positions "Birthday Cake" as a performance of Guyanese femininity. This performance recalls Jamaica Kincaid's choreo-poem "Girl," in which a Caribbean mother both admonishes her daughter for lapses in respectability and simultaneously instructs her in how to please a man (Kincaid 1978). And if we can hear Monica and Clara Braithwaite's Guyanese creole in their daughter/granddaughter's ear as Rihanna chants "Cake, cake, cake, cake, cake" while patting her pattacake, then perhaps we can also imagine the song as a defiant message against the intimate partner violence that both Monica and Rihanna experienced, as well as a clap back against the state violence that Guyanese femininity garners in Barbados.

With the multigenerational presence of Guyanese wives and mothers in so many Bajan genealogies, Guyanese femininity is intimately connected to Bajan family life and sonically embodied in both Nalini Sukhram's "GT Advice" and Rihanna's "Birthday Cake." In the former, however, Guyanese femininity represents a menace to the marital bond; the Indo-Guyanese woman's wanton sexuality signifies that she cannot be naturalized by the Bajan state. But in Rihanna's case, Afro-Guyanese ancestry, coupled with a Westbury upbringing, perhaps facilitates a more convenient incorporation as "100 percent Bajan." Still, if Sukhram personifies foreign threat, then Rihanna straddles the blurred lines between Guyana and Barbados. Her family history is a testament to the truism that Guyanese and Bajan families share inseparable kinship ties.

Rihanna's prominent role as a poster girl for Barbados tourism destabilizes the myth of the Guyanese woman as a dangerous, husband-stealing outsider, but only if you are in the know. And, as I have argued, much as Guyana's political system is characterized by a flawed but hard separation between Indo- and Afro-Guyanese, Barbados's immigration policies and popular discourses are framed around the hollow notion that Guyanese are "foreigners" on the island. In accepting state roles such as Youth and Cultural Ambassador, and as of 2021, "National

Hero," while acknowledging that as a child, she felt the sting of state violence against Guyanese immigrants, Rihanna walks a tightrope between representing Barbados and understanding that even her own national membership is fraught. Whether in relation to the oppressive dictates of the post-emancipation era or the contemporary practice of deporting Guyanese workers, the Bajan state has acted as homewrecker while shifting the blame for broken families either onto the families themselves or onto the Guyanese woman. In the first instance, the colonial-era denial of living wages forced Bajan men to leave their families to pursue work in British Guiana. In the second, the contemporary state disregards CARICOM norms and deports Guyanese laborers, leading to the home wreckage Rihanna laments. The constant across both eras is that the Guyanese woman is the scapegoat for the state's homewrecking practices, a labeling that Barbados's most celebrated and rebellious daughter belies by "big upping" her Guyanese maternal line.

This chapter brooms across temporalities, from the release of "GT Advice" in 2009, and the concomitant government policing of Guyanese immigrants in Barbados, back to the colonial era in which Bajans flocked to Guyana looking for jobs, and perhaps wives. The broom mirrors the *tidalectics* of Caribbean migration, which swell and recede, drawing waves of migrants to alternating shores—with Guyana now enjoying a petroleum windfall, the tides are turning again. The broom mimics this reversal of fortune, sweeping us into the twenty-first century, in which Rihanna has risen to the ranks of world's wealthiest female musician and has unabashedly proclaimed her Guyanese ancestry. Rihanna's Guyanese matriline has been an erased but meaning-laden throughline for tracing the Caribbean's musical routes. In the next chapter, imaginings of Rihanna surface again, in the hidden ecological circuits of Guyana's sand.

# 3

## Transplanted Beaches and Silica Cities

### *Sand, Erasure, and Erosion in the Age of the Anthropocene*

In my formation, our
history starts far far
beyond [before] Columbus.
Far even beyond the West
African sources we supp-
ose to come from. Becau-
se I'm concern with Afri
cans *themselves* nigratin
out of the heart of our
continent, out of the de
serts of the Sahara, Sa-
heel and far far farward
into the Nile and Nubia, and
being transferred into
the similar—no—*famil
iar*—forests and desert
(s) and valleys—of Sri
Lanka, South-East Asia,
Fiji, Papua New Guinea,
the Australasias, the Am
ericas and the Caribbean
– our *nanna* brooming the
sand with her dawn and
walking on the water
—Kamau Brathwaite, *ConVERSations with Nathanial
Mackey* (spelling in original)

Kamau Brathwaite employs his metaphor of the Caribbean nanna brooming the sand in order to juxtapose vast reaches of time, space, and territory. His *tidalectic* vision of the region is one in which the old woman walking on the water, as she manipulates the sand beneath her feet, evokes the temporal, geographic, and environmental divides that Africans have navigated ("nigratin"), bringing them into contact with Asia, the South Pacific, and the Americas. The above passage is as much about the movement of peoples as it is about "similar—no—familiar" ecologies. For our purposes, the poet's constant evocation of land and water, and sand in particular, opens us up to witness and survey, to *see*, that is, how a fluid resource like sand can be reshaped in the local context ("our nanna brooming the sand") while on the global scale it signifies a visionary interfusing of territories previously imagined as distanced and separate. The previous chapters of this book have explored answers to some of Brathwaite's questions—"How do we come from? Where do we come from? And why are we as we are?" (Brathwaite 1999, 34)—in the stories of nannas—great-grandmothers, grandmothers, mothers, and daughters. Taking a pointer broom to archives and oral histories, song lyrics, and historical discourses centers women's lived realities, exposing the political economy of erasure that formulates race and gender, and kinship and intimacies in global Guyana.

In this chapter, I am brooming again, and because my tool is made from natural materials fashioned to manipulate the environment, it is particularly efficacious for moving sand. The individual coconut spines of the pointer broom, especially when the broom is broken in—reduced to shorter, stiff spikes—enables the sweeper to pinpoint and extract the finest grains. Attention to the minuscule example of singular grains is critical because this chapter sifts through the particularities of a political economy of erasure and its related forms of erosion. This deployment of the broom and the sweeper, to gather and inspect resources emanating from Guyana, sets my approach apart from, while putting it in conversation with, those of other theorists who utilize Brathwaite. For example, my reliance on the poet's articulation of *tidalectics* dovetails with Tiffany Lethabo King's conceptualization in her book *The Black Shoals: Offshore Formations of Black and Native Studies*. King argues for the shoal as a metaphor that "cannot be reduced to the ocean, the shore, or an island" (King 2019, 8). Her deeply generative theorization of the Black shoal "opens up analytical possibilities for thinking about Blackness as exceeding the metaphors and analytics of water and for thinking of Indigeneity as exceeding the symbol and the analytic of land" (King 2019, 4).

Here, I apply Brathwaite's notion of *tidalectics* not only to destabilize the dialectic that would consider sea and land as separate, and that would interpellate the Caribbean from a Euro-American perspective, but also to reflect on the interstices in which Caribbean resources move within the region and across the globe. The pointer broom remains my privileged device because, as we see in the way Brathwaite's Caribbean nanna wields it, the sweeper conjoins land and water, human and environment, women and resources. Of this Caribbean grandmother, Brathwaite writes, "She walk on water *and* in light, the sand between her toes, the ritual discourse of her morning broom" (Brathwaite 1999, 35, emphasis in original). Because sand is both solid and fluid, the prism of the morning light enables the poet to see the old woman as walking on water rather than sand. And the sand between her toes, which she has been sweeping, becomes the organizing knowledge, the "ritual discourse" of her broom strokes. The sweeping motion of the broom serves as a metaphor, then, for centering a feminist culling of sorts that recalls the intimately intertwined histories and geographies Brathwaite evokes.

Although Brathwaite's brooming nanna is our springboard, in this chapter, our analysis extends this metaphor as we trace Guyanese sand extraction, contextualizing its ecological and social impacts alongside other forms of mining. Extractive industries pollute rivers and contaminate food sources. They create hazardous health and nutrition impacts and are responsible for half of the world's carbon emissions (Watts 2019). I sweep together environmental concerns, geographic situatedness, and feminist analysis, enabling us to witness the colossal movements of sand that are, in the contemporary period, literally eroding territories under our feet, and in the process, shaping and reshaping imaginings of the Caribbean that depend on globalized images of the region as replete with sandy beaches and sexually available women. Brooming the hidden cracks and crevices of Guyana's extractive industries illuminates processes that plunder the region's natural resources, grossly destabilizing its ecologies and exploiting women, not only as the embodiment of the Caribbean beach fantasy but also via the sex trafficking that goes hand in hand with mining industries. Sand signifies both erasure and erosion, as the extraction of this taken-for-granted material erodes the very ground upon which nanna brooms.

## Finding Sand in Guyana

In 2014, I received a direct message on a social media platform that changed the way I understand my birthplace. The message, from a Brazilian businessman, Mr. B., contained a link to a forty-minute film he produced entitled "Guyana Exploits International Businessman."[1] I surmised that Mr. B. had targeted me because I self-identify on social media as "From Guyana and Brooklyn." "Guyana Exploits International Businessman" tells the story of how Mr. B. embarked on a business venture with Mr. R., a North American of South Asian descent (and at the time, a Guyanese national), that ended with the Brazilian accusing Mr. R. of absconding with a sand mining company in Guyana, which Mr. B. claimed to own. In the video, Mr. B. alleges that the Guyanese businessman employed corrupt state institutions, bribing police and members of the judiciary to swindle four billion Guyanese dollars from the Brazilian. In response, Mr. B. enlisted Guyanese Presidential Guards to launch a late-night raid to dismantle the conveyor mechanism on the sand mining facility on the East Bank of Guyana's Demerara River, resulting in his arrest and imprisonment, and years of legal entanglements between the two men.

Mr. B.'s tale of government-sanctioned fraud and his representation of Guyana as a place where foreigners could become endangered smacked of colonial renderings of the country's "wild coast" that continue to surface in international press coverage that sketches the nation as ill equipped to handle its newfound oil wealth. The Guyanese national, Mr. R., later presented documents that resulted in a court win for him. The documents included proof that while Mr. B. claimed sole ownership, initially both men were equal partners in the company and now Mr. R. owned the sand conveyor mechanism. The Guyanese businessman lamented that even though he had largely discredited Mr. B., the story would defame both his and Guyana's international business profile. But the legal disputes and charges of fraud between the two men, steeped in "he said" accusations and contradictory claims of ownership, resemble examples of corruption that accompany various forms of mining around the globe. And the controversy between the two businessmen sheds light on how individual players become embroiled in the state's political and economic vision of progress, which exploits Guyana's resources in order to succeed in global capitalist processes. Yet, the video shocked me for another reason. I was stunned when I realized that the sand mining company in question was located on the East Bank of the Demerara River, just a few miles down the road from Sarah Johanna, my childhood home. My most vivid memories of Guyanese ground beneath my feet always centered on mud, not sand. Guyana is called the "land of many waters," as portions of it are situated from 19.7 to 39.4 inches below sea level and, especially during the rainy season, the mud can get so thick that it sucks the shoes right off your feet. Earlier, I contextualized the monumental labor of enslaved Africans whom the Dutch tasked with moving millions of tons of mud to reshape the colony's coastline and delineated how that work fed the transnational label of the "Guyanese mudhead," a racialized epithet.

Guyana lacks the clear blue waters and coastal white sand beaches that have come to characterize the Caribbean region in popular tourist imaginings—we are known for our mud rather than our beaches. Sand does not appear in Guyana's visual landscape as it does in other parts of the Caribbean. The web of controversy and corruption in which Mr. B. and Mr. R. were enmeshed is part of the back story of Guyana extracting its bounty of silica-quartz sand to replenish beaches in other countries and to support the post–oil discovery push for development. I had never given our sand a second thought. In fact, a white sand belt, largely coated in trees and scrubs, and south of the coastal plain, covers 14 percent of the country. My own failure to recognize Guyana's sand as a vital part of its landscape underscores a global imagining of the Caribbean that erases Guyana's presence in environmental and tourism discourses.

## Sand Mining: An Unseen Global Environmental Crisis

Geologists, geographers, environmentalists, journalists, and observers of international trade are increasingly sounding alarms about the "staggering" global reliance on sand—by volume, we use only one resource more, and that is water (Fritts 2019). Headlines such as "Sand Mining:

The Global Environmental Crisis You've Never Heard Of" (Beiser 2017) and "The World Needs to Get Serious about Managing Sand, U.N. Report Says" (Fritts 2019) spotlight the growing demand for sand and the grave environmental consequences of its extraction, while acknowledging the invisibility of this crisis. Sand is a major constitutive element in a myriad of constructions; everything—from skyscrapers, asphalt roads, apartment buildings, malls, hospitals, and schools to glass, computer screens, and cell phones—is made of sand. This means that with increasing worldwide urbanization, countries across the globe must extract or import more and more sand to feed an insatiable drive for urban growth and technological advancement. Journalists use adjectives like "mind-boggling" to describe the amount of sand being extracted, and "catastrophic" to convey the environmental destruction left in the wake (Beiser 2017). "All around the world," Vince Beiser writes, "riverbeds and beaches are being stripped bare, and farmlands and forests torn up to get at the precious sand grains. It's the worldwide crisis that nobody has heard about" (Beiser 2017).

China and Singapore are leading importers of sand, relying on the resource for the construction of sprawling cities and, in Singapore's case, for both vertical and horizontal expansion (Chua 2020). From the start of the twenty-first century, Singapore has been the world's largest importer of sand, and its horizonal expansion has been immense, the city-state having imported a reported 517 million tons of the material to increase its territory by about 24 percent (Chua 2020, 240). Global studies scholar Charmaine Chua has foregrounded both the environmental toll of Singapore's sand extraction and its implications for territorial jurisdiction. Singapore's demand for sand has resulted in "the erasure of at least twenty-four Indonesian islands since 2005" (Chua 2020, 240). In territorial terms, "large-scale movements of sand throw into question the legality of practices of terraforming under international law, as they exacerbate geopolitical conflict by encroaching on territorial jurisdiction with neighboring countries" (Chua 2020, 241). Harkening back to earlier, more perceptible forms of expansion such as colonialism and military conquest, terraforming is "shadowy" work that relies on "concomitant acts of extraction, erasure, and dispossession" (Chua 2020, 242). And across the globe, the story of sand extraction and exportation is one that is also mired in violent forms of theft, with the emergence of "sand mafias" who illegally exploit sand resources in places like India and Jamaica (Fritts 2019).

Pascal Peduzzi, a researcher with the United Nations Environment Programme, illustrates how such activities impact people's lives in Jamaica: "We went to a small fishing village, and the villagers told us that one night some people came with trucks, armed with guns, and they stole their beach away" (quoted in Fritts 2019). Surveying this crisis at the global scale reveals common themes of erasure, environmental devastation, exploitation of poorer nations by wealthier territories determined to build ever-more-sprawling global cities, and local/international actors like Mr. R. and Mr. B., who become implicated in the illegal practices surrounding sand mining. The world over, where there is silica extraction, there are murky business dealings and contradictory assertions of ownership, if not downright violent theft, played out on the unsettled ground of sand. A global perspective also uncovers that not all sand is equal—desert sand is too smooth for construction, so although Dubai is located on the edge of an enormous desert, it imports sand from Australia (Beiser 2017).

Just as not all sand is the same, the forms of environmental impact attached to sand mining vary depending on the method and volume of extraction. According to journalist Vince Beiser, "In some places locals dig out riverbanks with shovels and haul it away in pickup trucks or donkeys; in others multinational companies dredge it up with machinery. Everywhere, the process impacts its surroundings in ways that range from cosmetic to catastrophic" (Beiser 2017). In California, industrial-scale sand mining has killed off wildlife (Beiser 2017); marine mining dramatically impairs seabed flora and fauna in the western Baltic Sea (Peduzzi 2014); in Botswana aggregate mining supported the building of an extensive system of roads—a sign of that country's "successful development" and urbanization—but also deteriorated river ecosystems and created new runoff channels, depriving dams and contributing to water shortages (Livingston 2019, 105); and in the Caribbean, where rising sea levels and coastal erosion are among the region's biggest environmental challenges, coastal erosion occurs mainly from the direct removal of sand from beaches.

The scientist, economist/practicing industrial engineer, sand mining company owners, and sand machinery entrepreneurs with whom

I spoke paint a picture of sand deposits and sand extraction within Guyana that converges with but also differs in key ways from the global overview I have just provided.[2] Guyana and Suriname have large, pristine, inland sand belts that are unique in the region. While the beach sand that blankets the coasts of many Caribbean islands has been exposed to the ongoing actions of the seas and to external forces from contact with humans and various pollutants, Guyana's inland sand deposits have been protected for centuries by a top layer of plants and trees. This means that the nation's untouched sand deposits remained unaltered and remarkably pure, until the onset of large-scale sand mining. Ulric (Neville) Trotz, a chemist and former director of the Institute of Applied Science and Technology (a Guyana-based research organization aimed at developing and commercializing the use of the country's natural resources), told me that due to sand's dryness, the ecologies surrounding these sand deposits are low in nutrients and very fragile (Trotz 2022b). Hence, in this geological setting, one of the impacts of sand mining is the clearing of vegetation and the disturbance of delicate ecologies that have been millions of years in the making. Guyana is also environmentally remarkable in that its forests and vegetation-covered sand deposits have acted as enormous "carbon sinks" absorbing carbon dioxide from the atmosphere. Trotz lamented, "Clearing vegetation is certainly not favored by anybody who is thinking about carbon sequestration. . . . There has been talk of replanting but it's very difficult due to the very fragile ecosystem" (Trotz 2022b).[3] In short, mining sand in large quantities in Guyana increases humans' "carbon footprint," thus counteracting global efforts to address climate change.

When beaches in other parts of the Caribbean experience erosion, there are visible environmental changes that politicians, resort owners, tourists, and locals can see with the naked eye. However, the extraction of Guyana's pristine deposits does not evoke the same response as that engendered by a disappearing beach. Rather, local experts told me that sand mining in the country has progressed largely unchecked and that the areas in which sand deposits are located are viewed as "wastelands" housing "limitless supplies" of a profitable resource. In the first and second decades of the twenty-first century, Guyana's mining industry morphed from exporting the material to replenish beaches in nations

Figure 3.1. A sand deposit dug up by a mining company near the Soesdyke-Linden Highway, East Bank Demerara, 2016. Photo by the author.

with larger tourism economies to extracting silica quartz in large quantities to support the country's drive to modernize its infrastructure. While in the first instance, Guyana deployed its sand to coat the eroded coasts of other Caribbean nations, in the current moment the nation appears to be emulating Botswana by using sand extraction to support urbanization and ambitious infrastructure projects at home. What does the use of Guyanese sand to replenish "beach destinations" say about transnational destination branding, the country's marginalized status in terms of Caribbean tourism, and its place in the global environmental crises that stem from urbanization? While tourists from the Global North do not flock to Guyana, they unwittingly enjoy the nation's sand. How does a beach experience in Jamaica or St. Vincent and the Grenadines exploit Guyana's landscape while contributing to the erasure of its presence in global imaginings? Sand mining has been studied from an ecological perspective but has received far less attention from the transnational, socio-ecological angle I employ here.

My approach builds on the work of anthropologists Vanessa Agard-Jones (2012) and Julie Livingston (2019), and global studies scholar Charmaine Chua (2020). Agard-Jones offers a thoughtful analysis of the composition of the region's sand, a historical contextualization of French colonialism and sexual politics in Martinique, and a generative theorization of sand as a metaphor for understanding same-sex desire and gender transgression (Agard-Jones 2012, 340). Her work provides a rich jumping-off point for my own treatment, especially in terms of our overlapping attention to what she eloquently deems "the rapport between tropes of invisibility and the physical landscapes" (Agard-Jones 2012, 326), even while our approaches to sand differ in that here I am concerned with how extraction and sand exportation not only shape those tropes but also result in negative social and environmental impacts. Livingston depicts Botswana as representing a planetary parable for "self-devouring growth," a term she uses to "refer to the ways that the super-organism of human beings is consuming itself" (Livingston 2019, 1). She reveals how that country's successes in diamond mining have resulted in the building of schools, roads, hospitals, and telecommunications—solidifying its identity as a "paradigmatically successful" upper-middle-income nation, while also positioning it as a stark example of the convergence of multiple forms of climate and environmental catastrophes, from record-breaking temperatures to sinking water levels and disappearing wildlife (Livingston 2019, 3).[4] Livingston's work foreshadows a frightening future for Guyana, one characterized by the paradox of progress and environmental failure. This chapter sounds the alarm in hopes that increased attention to the hazards of sand mining will help us dodge catastrophe in Guyana.

## Missing Grains: Extracting Guyana's Sand

Unlike bauxite and gold extraction, large-scale sand mining is a relatively new player in Guyana's extractive industries. Andre Mann, an economist and practicing industrial engineer who was head of the Institute of Applied Science and Technology's (IAST) Industrial Extension Unit, told me that under Neville Trotz's leadership, the organization conducted pioneering research detailing the nature and quality of Guyana's sand (Mann 2022).[5] When the IAST began that research in the

1980s, the quality of the country's sand was largely unrecognized, the possibilities for commercializing it were unexplored, and it was thought to be an inexhaustible resource. In that early era, the IAST hypothesized that due to its superior quality, Guyanese sand had potential value in the ceramics and glass industries. These researchers never imagined the scope and scale of sand extraction that would develop in the present day.

According to Mann's recollection, by the mid-1990s, Guyana's sand was being exported in small quantities for construction and as a glass plant material (Mann 2022). But by the start of the twenty-first century, more rapidly eroding coastlines and increasing urbanization and infrastructure development drove up the demand for sand from Guyana. By 2009, multiple large-scale sand mining companies were established. These companies characterize Guyana's sand as "fresh water, almost pure silica-quartz sand, formed by ancient rivers which deposited the fluvio-lacustrine sands as extensive deposits along the coast of Guyana" (Guyana Silica-Sand 2019). Just as Tripadvisor and *U.S. News and World Report* portray a curated image of bountiful soft, white sand pillowing the coastlines of their top-ranked Caribbean vacation spots, Guyana's sand mining industry constructs a lofty narrative about its global reach—albeit on less glossy and visually stunning websites. Guyana Sand Inc. described itself thus in its online business profile: "Our company is a complete Silica Sand Export Business located in Guyana. We have the best white Silica Sand in the Caribbean for beaches, construction, glass, plastering, concrete, golf courses and other general uses. We have a private wharf, mining areas and the complete logistic facilities to export our sand from Guyana to the world market. Our operational capacity is over 100,000 metric tons per month. We deliver our product in your country in the port of your choice" (Guyana Silica-Sand 2019). Other sand mining companies make similar claims.

In addition to private investors, the Guyana Geology and Mines Commission (GGMC) also owns sand pits for which it sells "agricultural leases" that can be converted for mining purposes—a route that I believe Mr. R. pursued after his troubled venture with Mr. B. ended. While Guyana's sand mining companies make big claims about shipping sand to "the world market," it has been difficult to pinpoint who imports Guyanese sand. In addition to Jamaica and St. Vincent and the Grenadines, I found online business dialogues and newspaper reports indicating that Guyana's sand is shipped to St. Lucia, Antigua and Barbuda, Guadeloupe, Grenada, and Tortola, with few numbers in terms of tons shipped and dollars spent. But the industry experts I spoke with estimated that mining companies extract between one and two hundred thousand tons of sand per month. My investigation has turned up a spotty trail, I believe, because it is not in the interest of importers' reputations to admit that the sugar-white sand that attracts tourists comes from the poorer stepchild of the Caribbean, a South American nation whose global image is decidedly less romantic than that of its higher-profile Caribbean neighbors.

When import nations do publicly admit to purchasing sand from Guyana, their admissions are encompassed in concerns about what the ecological devastation brought on by illegal sand mining on their own shores means for their expenditures. This was the case in a 2016 story in the Jamaica *Gleaner*, in which Daryl Vaz, the Opposition Spokesman on Land and Environment, appealed to Jamaican government ministers to create guidelines and policies to prevent illegal sand mining. Vaz bemoaned, "Millions of dollars in foreign exchange, which the country can scarcely afford, are being spent each year to import beach sand from our Caribbean neighbours, Guyana, the Bahamas, and Turks and Caicos Islands for beach replenishment" (*The Gleaner* 2016). If, this minister suggests, environmental damage is not a compelling deterrent against illegal mining, loss of millions of dollars should be. His comments underscore the GDP construct's ignorance of ecological notions of value (Mies and Shiva 2014). Left completely out of the equation is the reality that importing Guyanese sand only shifts the environmental crisis to Guyana, which at the time was a more vulnerable neighbor. And while in other Caribbean nations the discourse has foregrounded how using sand in constructing hotels and other buildings has led to beach erosion and related ecological imbalances, these environmental consequences have taken a back seat in Guyana. For much of the timespan of the industry's growth, domestic debates over Guyanese sand mining have centered on ownership disputes, and allegations of fraud and government corruption (as in the case between Mr. B. and Mr. R.); on competition for space and resources; on worker safety; on governmental enforcement of regulations; and on the payment of royalties. Government officials have noted disparities between sand mining activities and the data the Minister of

Natural Resources has gathered on such activities: "The inability to carry out proper monitoring results in the State and the citizens of Guyana being denied the royalty of $15 per tonne, especially when in the end consumers pay as much as $18,000 per truck load of sand" (*Kaieteur News* 2014).

Guyanese are losing more than their minuscule cut of the fifteen-Guyanese-dollars-per-ton royalty due to them (less than a US cent at the time of my writing). Obscured sand exportation erases Guyana's role in literally reshaping the landscape of the Caribbean and further marginalizes the nation in global popular imaginings of the beauty and splendor of the region. And, in its quest to be competitive in global capitalism, the state prioritizes profit over social and environmental impacts. Relatedly, Julie Livingston notes how a primary impetus of self-devouring growth is the drive to catch up with "modern development" by consuming and/or exporting enormous quantities of aggregate (Livingston 2019, 103). "It turns out that sand and gravel, or aggregate, as they are called in construction, are also finite resources [in addition to petroleum and water]; humans are using them faster than they can replenish. We are all living in sand castles now. Aggregate, the principal element in concrete, is the material substance from which urban development grows" (Livingston 2019, 103). Sand is, of course, also the principal substance of beaches and shorelines, and the primary building material of the hotels that hug the Caribbean's shores.

## Sand and Women in Caribbean Destination Imaginings

Calculations of the gains or losses attached to sand extraction in relation to beach tourism must also consider women's labor. Sand and women's labor must be swept together as foundational elements of the tourism industry. In *Women and Tourist Work in Jamaica: Seven Miles of Sandy Beach*, anthropologist A. Lynn Bolles notes that travel to Jamaica is driven by tourism imagery that promises sand, sea, sun, and sex, and that these are basic components of the global beach (Bolles 2022, 36, 72). In Bolles's estimation, the success of Jamaica's tourism industry is dependent on "a primarily female workforce whose service, hospitality, and professionalism produce this 'product' called 'tourism'" (Bolles 2022, 128). In his study of globalization and sex tourism in the Dominican

Republic, anthropologist Steven Gregory underscores that the Caribbean's tourism economy puts women at the bottom rungs of the global division of labor, employing them in the lowest-wage positions in tourist resorts and often relegating them to pursuing sex work as they struggle to support themselves and their children (Gregory 2014, 165). Being central in global imaginings of the Caribbean would arguably only increase these forms of "real and imagined subjection" for Guyanese women (Gregory 2014, 165).

Still, we know that the lure of soft, white sand translates into higher GDPs for countries like Jamaica, St. Vincent, and Barbados. With no beach tourism to speak of, Guyana strove to carve out a niche in ecotourism in hopes of drawing tourists with its biodiversity, sprawling rainforests, and majestic waterfalls—yet sadly its new push for progress threatens these natural assets. And mainland Guyana is literally off the map even in academic discourses of Caribbean environmentalisms and tourism: for example, Sherrie Baver and Barbara Deutsch Lynch's study, *Beyond Sun and Sand: Caribbean Environmentalisms*, repeatedly characterizes the region as "island landscapes" (Baver and Lynch 2006, 3–4). Therefore, I contend that Guyana would have to first hold a place in popular imaginings of the Caribbean for state officials, researchers, and global environmentalists to confront what happens to its sand.

The intersecting dynamics of resource extraction, environmental destruction, global capitalism, and violence against women and children amount to the ecological and human toll engendered in the political economy of erasure and erosion. We must trace the early imperatives of the sand mining industry that positioned Mr. B. and Mr. R. against each other if we hope to sweep together these seemingly disparate and ensconced forms of erasure and erosion. These imperatives were, at the outset of the industry, framed around sand extraction for beach replenishment. Global North tourist conceptions of the Caribbean often start with the commodification of the region's beaches and its women, refracted through the imperial lens of the Internet.[6] Google searches with the subject headings "world's best beaches" and "best beaches in the Caribbean" show us how travel sites like Tripadvisor and *U.S. News* construct global imaginings of Caribbean destinations. On Tripadvisor, beach rankings and their accompanying traveler reviews serve as emic depictions of how tourists interpret coastal geographies, even if we keep in mind that such commentary is curated by the companies themselves. Privileging traveler accounts, Tripadvisor's "Top 10 Travelers' Choice Beaches in the World" offers the following description of its number one choice in 2016, Grace Bay beach in Turks and Caicos: "Unbelievably clear, clean water with hundreds of shades of blues and greens and white sugar sand beaches—ahhhhh!" (Tripadvisor 2016). Here, sugar, the export Sidney Mintz theorized as inextricably linking enslaved Africans in the Caribbean to British laborers, is used as an adjective to describe sand (Mintz 1985). The beach is thus rendered as a consumable resource for which color, together with texture, elicits the "ahhhhh" effect for tourists seeking idyllic landscapes conducive to banishing their "real-world" cares.

While the beach destination that is ranked number one shifts from year to year on these travel sites, sandy stretches of Caribbean beaches routinely take spots in the top ten, as in the case of St. Vincent and the Grenadines (SVG): "Why go: Comprising 32 islands, St. Vincent & the Grenadines is not wanting for shoreline. You've probably seen some of it already—SVG's sands were featured in the film *Pirates of the Caribbean*. But you'll probably fork over a lot of loot to see these beaches in person" (*U.S. News & World Report* 2017). John Urry's notion of the "tourist gaze" accounts for the fixation on sand and water (2002). More pointedly, Jamaica Kincaid brings to light how tourists, awestruck by the beauty of the Caribbean's environment, are blind to the poverty and ecological crises that also mark the landscape: "No real sand on any real shore is that fine or that white (in some places) or that pink (in other places) . . . No real earth is that colour brown; no real grass is that particular shade of dilapidated, run down green (not enough rain)" (Kincaid 2000, 78). For citizens of the region and for scholars attuned to the sociopolitical challenges the Caribbean faces, the tourist gaze erases poverty, environmental devastation and pollution, racialized gender inequalities, and health crises. This gaze, even when it is fixed on sand, a material often interpreted as both ubiquitous and distinctive, does not fully comprehend what it sees. *U.S. News* re-presents what the film *Pirates of the Caribbean* has already represented for the blockbuster audiences who consumed it.

Clearly, sand—white, soft, and plentiful—features prominently in the way tourists, tourist companies, and Hollywood films envision the Caribbean. But domestic and international monitoring of beach erosion reveals that St. Vincent and the Grenadines *are* wanting for shorelines.[7] And, unsurprisingly, the *U.S. News* ranking does not tell us what a 2011 article in Trinidad's *Daily Express* discloses: "The beaches of St. Vincent, because of the ever present volcano, La Soufriere, has only black sand and while beautiful white sand beaches are available a short boat ride away [in the Grenadines], Harlequin Hotels and Resorts imported tonnes of white sand from Guyana in order to give tourists the white sand beach fantasy expected of a Caribbean island" (*Daily Express* 2011). In this quotation, contrasting black sand with "beautiful white sand" connotes an ecological black/white dichotomy while situating Guyana's role as that of invisible handmaid who makes the tourist fantasy possible. I propose that importing Guyana's sand is a dirty little secret that is hidden from the tourist gaze, and if fully revealed, could disrupt constructions of authentic experiences not only for the tourists who enjoy these beaches but also for the travel conglomerates, resort owners, and Global North media outlets that promote notions of the Caribbean as "a series of uniformly breezy landscapes of sun and sand designed for loafing, sailing, diving, and perhaps for gambling and sex" (Baver and Lynch 2006, 3).

Geologist Michael Welland begins his book *Sand: The Never-Ending Story* with a quotation from another Hollywood film, *Eternal Sunshine of the Spotless Mind*: "Sand is over-rated—it's just tiny little rocks" (quoted in Welland 2009, xiii). Of course, Welland "hope[s] to convince the reader [that] sand is anything but 'just tiny little rocks'": "Sand is one of our planet's most ubiquitous and fundamental materials and is both a medium and a tool for nature's gigantic and ever-changing sculptures. Because, as William Blake recognized—'To see a world in a grain of sand'—every sand grain has a story to tell, of the present and the past. Because without it, our world, both on a global scale and on the scale of our everyday lives, would be dramatically different" (Welland 2009, xiii). And sand is a material that, because of its size, as Welland tells us, is "born to be transported by gravity, rivers, waves, ocean currents, and winds, shape-shifting into ever-changing landscapes" (Welland 2009, 77). Humans transport sand, both intentionally, on a large scale, and unintentionally, on much smaller scales—we all know that after a beach vacation we unpack our suitcases to find that grains of sand have invaded the most intimate crevices of our clothes and our bodies. It is this tendency of sand "sticking to our bodies' folds and fissures," in part, that propelled Agard-Jones to utilize sand as a metaphor "to track fleeting references to same-sex desire and gender transgression in Martinique" (Agard-Jones 2012, 326). Each grain of sand not only carries a geological lineage but also links gendered bodies to geographically, temporally, and culturally situated places. Although the use of Guyanese sand to replenish beaches in Jamaica and SVG occurs on the scale of hundreds of tons, I argue that any amount of sand, whether a ton or a single grain, forever reconstitutes both the sending and the receiving locations in ways that are intimate and ultimately gendered.

## Erasure and Erosion: Mining and Gendered Violence

Maria Mies and Vandana Shiva's influential theorization of ecofeminism foregrounds interconnections between the material resourcing of women and nature within capitalist patriarchal systems (Mies and Shiva 2014). Caribbean state officials' tunnel vision, fixated on what sand extraction and importation means for national GDPs, erases the ways in which sand mining exacerbates the global inequalities that have accompanied the destructive Anthropocene age. Scholars and activists from various fields contend that in ecologically and economically precarious Global South regions, the frenzied drive for participation in the global economy supports a perfect storm of climate catastrophe, environmental devastation, and violence against women and children (Mies and Shiva 2014; Colchester and La Rose 2010; Cordis 2019; Sheller 2020). In her preface to the second edition of *Ecofeminism*, Ariel Salleh writes, "First, the economic model focusing myopically on 'growth' begins with violence against women by discounting their contribution to the economy. . . . The transformation of value into disvalue, labour into non-labour and knowledge into non-knowledge is achieved by the most powerful number that rules our lives: the patriarchal construct of GDP, gross domestic product, which commentators have started to call the 'gross domestic problem'" (Salleh 2014, xv). Guyana has sought to compete with nations bent on increasing their "gross domestic problem." From its location at the margins of Caribbean tourism, sand extraction for beach replenishment rendered it as an erased but foundational shaper of the region's shorelines. Although Guyana may never appear on a list of "the best beaches," its sand has facilitated the existence of such vacation hotspots, and in the current moment, its development dreams are built on sand. This chapter grapples with issues of material loss and geographic erasure, brooming through dwindling mounds of sand to uncover a more nuanced understanding of Guyana's advancement dreams and the social and environmental tolls of resource extraction.

Sand extraction, like other forms of mining across the globe, results not only in environmental destruction but also in menacing social ramifications. Accounts of the environmental and social impacts of medium- and large-scale sand mining in Guyana are hard to come by because the industry is relatively young, the material was thought of as limitless, and the state has been reluctant to recognize sand deposits as critical ecologies.[8] But we can look to analyses of higher-profile mining industries for insight into what sand extraction augurs. A "buoyant market in mineral prices worldwide" resulted in a steady increase in Guyana's mining sector in the first decade of the twenty-first century (Colchester and La Rose 2010, 12). Rising gold prices (there was a 400 percent increase in the price of gold between 2000 and 2010) alongside increasing diamond prices sparked a Guyanese mining boom.

In a report stemming from a collaboration between the Amerindian Peoples Association (APA) and environmental researchers in the United Kingdom and in Canada, Marcus Colchester and Jean La Rose sum up the trajectory of the mining industry: "As a result of the high world prices, small- and medium-scale operators . . . increased [their] investment in mining equipment, including more sophisticated metal detectors, excavators, new types of dredges, crushers and heavy earth-moving equipment" (Colchester and La Rose 2010, 12). They underscore that the expanded use of advanced technologies employed by the mining industry resulted in "greater impacts on the environment and a wider footprint" that is steadily encroaching on Amerindian ancestral territories (Colchester and La Rose 2010, 12). The environmental repercussions included "impacts on forest loss, polluted waterways . . . mercury contamination," and riverbank erosion, siltation, and increased river turbidity (Colchester and La Rose 2010, ii, 18). Amerindians experienced considerable health and nutrition problems because of polluted waterways, including contaminated food supplies, skin rashes, diarrhea,

and vomiting. Beyond the health and nutrition hazards, the social ramifications are devastating examples of how cruelly persistent "plantation
futures" conspire with Indigenous dispossession in present-day mining
to produce gendered violence (McKittrick 2013). The Colchester and La
Rose report, "Our Land, Our Future," lists "criminality, drug abuse, sexual exploitation, and abuse of very young Amerindian girls" among the
key outcomes of Guyana's mining industries (Colchester and La Rose
2010, ii).

In Guyana, state environmental and economic initiatives ostensibly
aimed at advancing a "green economy" have, in actuality, placed Indigenous peoples "within spaces of *corporeal-spatial precarity*" by advancing mining and logging into Amerindian territories (Cordis 2019, 22,
emphasis in original). The anthropologist Shanya Cordis notes that Indigenous organizations like the APA and the Guyanese Organization
of Indigenous Peoples (GOIP) have spent decades doggedly advocat-
ing on behalf of the rights of Guyana's Indigenous communities, while
documenting the environmental and social consequences of mining
(Cordis 2019, 23). Akin to the analyses offered by scholars focused on
global industries and nation-building initiatives throughout Africa and
the Global South, Colchester and La Rose impart that mining fosters
sex trafficking and violence against women. Their Indigenous interviewees testified to gendered impacts such as "abusive relations with Amerindian women in mining camps, prostitution of Amerindian women,
trafficking in young girls, increased levels of violence. . . . [and] miners
'marrying' Amerindian women demand[ing] residence in Amerindian
villages" (Colchester and La Rose 2010, 18). Colchester and La Rose list
these complaints without providing ethnographic thick description or
direct quotations. But as with survivors of rape and gendered violence
everywhere, fear and silence can erase first-person accounts and render
"data collecting" difficult, to say the least. In the Guyanese context, this
can be attributed at least in part to the ways in which gendered violence
operates within the coexisting forces of a political economy of erasure
and erosion—the erasure of Amerindian women's gendered oppression
and the erosion of the riverbanks that provide their food.

Amerindian women, locally labeled with the raced-gendered epithet
"buck women" (a term Cordis traces to the colonial era in which the
Dutch word "*bok*" loosely translated to mean "male deer"), have been

relegated to "geographic domination" that imagines them as "less-than-human subject[s] brimming with excess sexual nature (read: availability)" (Cordis 2019, 24, 26). Cordis argues that the state has responded to pressures from the United States to address sex trafficking with a "mobilization of indigenous territories and bodies as political devices for redemption" (Cordis 2019, 27). The anthropologist avers that although sex trafficking affects interior-dwelling Amerindian women in devastating ways, it also routes "coastlander" women into the hinterland (Cordis 2019, 27). But the trafficking of Amerindian and Afro-Guyanese women from the coast is erased from state initiatives around trafficking. Instead, "the hinterland—and the gendered Amerindian body in particular—emerged within the scope of the state as the primary site of trafficking and the quintessential 'victim,' respectively" (Cordis 2019, 27). In this way, the state's development push, dependent on extractive industries, and the concomitant gendered violence against Amerindian women, underscores this book's accentuation of the speculative but ingrained manners in which global racial capitalism circumscribes Guyanese women's lives. Put plainly, the story of Guyana's long history as an unequal but central participant in global capitalism, and its present-day drive for development, cannot be starkly told without sweeping the racialized sexual exploitation of marginalized women and children out from under the rug.

Cordis's attention to the misleading distinction between "coastland" and "hinterland" as it pertains to extractive industries and sexual violence can be applied to the everywhere and nowhere paradox with which this book began. The state's focus on Indigenous women and on Amerindian territories as "political devices for redemption" belies gendered violence against and trafficking of coastlander women (Cordis 2019, 27), just as it misrepresents Guyana's mining industries as exclusively confined to the hinterland. In effect, the state's response to both the environmental destruction that stems from resource extraction and the gendered violence that permeates Guyanese society (as previously noted, one study found that more than one in two women experienced some form of intimate partner violence) is to situate both catastrophes in the "nowhere land," deep in the country's interior. Facile distinctions between coastal Georgetown and the Amerindian territories, between "cosmopolitan capital" and "wild hinterland," between "town" and "village," and between "everywhere" and "nowhere" come to a head when we consider that one of the nation's burgeoning extractive industries, sand mining, is largely located not in the hinterland but on the East Bank close to the Demerara River, less than twenty-five miles from the capital.

## Silica City: Development Dreams and Local Nightmares

While gold and diamond mining are typically conducted deep in Guyana's interior regions, sand mines sprawl along the Soesdyke-Linden Highway like apocalyptic moon craters. With vast plots ranging from 24 to 283 acres, these mines are a stone's throw from Cheddi Jagan International Airport and just off the country's main artery, the East Bank Public Road (EBPR), which leads past my family's ancestral village of Sarah Johanna, and on to Georgetown. My initial 2016 fieldwork in Guyana revealed some of the consequences of the silica extraction industry. At that time, the sand pits in East Bank Demerara were undergoing a dramatic transformation. In this part of the country, trees and other vegetation shield the sand from the naked eye, exposing sand dunes only after miners have carved out stark cavities. The contrast between the dense greenery pushed to the parameters of enormous sand pits and the trash-strewn craters left in the wake of extraction foreshadows the ecological crisis that will metastasize if sand mining continues unabated. Guyana is literally being dug up and carted off—the fragile ecological systems of which sand are a part disrupted if not completely erased. There are a few small homes near the sand pits I observed—some teetering precariously on the precipice of hollowed-out cavities—where women hung laundry on clotheslines and children and dogs played in sandy yards.

By 2022, the EBPR was besieged by traffic as trucks hauled sand and heavy machinery from the mines, en route to Georgetown. In May of that year, one of the country's primary newspapers, *Stabroek News*, ran an editorial under the one-word headline "Sand" (*Stabroek News* 2022a). The piece summarized the urgent crisis that the United Nations Environment Programme had outlined in a report entitled "Sand and Sustainability: 10 Strategic Recommendations to Avert a Crisis." Among its recommendations were banning beach extraction, reducing the use

Figure 3.2. Paths leading to a sand mine off East Bank Demerara's Soesdyke-Linden Highway, with trucks hauling silica-quartz, 2022. Photo by the author.

of sand, and prioritizing a place-based approach that accounted for the voices of people impacted by sand extraction (UNEP 2022). The report linked the world's massive overconsumption of sand to growing demands for urbanization. The *Stabroek News* editorial noted that "not much is known" about efforts to protect Guyana's sand resources "save for the regular notifications by the Environmental Protection Agency (EPA) about the approvals of applications for sand mining" (*Stabroek News* 2022a). It also surmised that it was "unclear" whether the Guyana Geology and Mines Commission (GGMC) was making decisions about conserving the resource.

The editorial can be situated both as a response to the UN's "Sand and Sustainability" report and as a reaction to the state's development initiatives in general, and President Irfaan Ali's vision of building a new "Silica City" in particular. Flush with oil wealth, Ali set his sights on constructing a new metropolis, described in the government-run *Guyana Chronicle* as "the country's first sub-urban Smart City located on the

Linden-Soesdyke Highway which links the capital City with that of the mining town of Linden and eventually with Lethem and the neighboring country of Brazil" (*Guyana Chronicle* 2022). The appellation Ali chose, "Silica City," was meant to evoke Silicon Valley, and hence, connote Guyana's dreams of being a site of innovation, technological advancement, and global commerce (*Guyana Chronicle* 2022). But its name forebodes the monumental volume of sand that will be extracted to realize the project. Ali's administration promotes Silica City as a "smart city" and as "modern, sustainable, and environmentally friendly" (*Guyana Times* 2022). However, the first-stage plans for Silica City involve clearing about three thousand acres of land—a stripping of the environment that would have a significant carbon impact. And while in the second decade of the twenty-first century the plan to displace Georgetown with its decaying wooden colonial buildings and instead relocate commerce and government to a new-fangled city of quartz remains a sand castle in the sky that harkens back to Julie Livingston's planetary parable of self-devouring growth, Guyana's people lament the more immediate consequences of extraction and the push for modernization.

Residents bemoan that the sand mines are increasingly being dug too close to the highway, and that the "excessive weight from vehicular traffic and mining of sand" are "main contributing factors to the soil erosion along the road" forming large depressions throughout the route (Papannah 2020). This in turn slows traffic on the EBPR, stymieing daily commutes to and from the capital. People also complain about increasing vehicular fatalities on the EBPR, a narrow, potholed, and overrun street along which vulnerable pedestrians, including school children and women vending food, compete with cars and massive trucks heading to and from the capital. Local coverage of the traffic nightmare and its resultant forms of vehicular violence and noise pollution was acutely attuned to how the country's development push centered on the sites of political power and global finances in Georgetown (and in the future, Silica City), while marginalizing the East Bank Demerara villages as a nowhere land, figuratively if not literally bulldozed in the name of advancement.

## Beautiful/Ugly

In *Poetics of Relation*, Édouard Glissant engages topographical imaginings of beaches and shores to reflect on Caribbean ecology, dispossession, and opacity in ways that converge with Brathwaite's notion of *tidalectics*. For Glissant, the ever-changing beach has the potentiality to serve as a metaphor for a more agile attitude towards Caribbean economic strategies: "I wondered whether, in little countries such as ours ('I believe in the future of little countries'), economic prospects (their inspiration) ought not be more like the beach at Le Diamant: cyclical, changeable, mutating, running through an economy or disorder whose detail would be meticulously calculated but whose comprehensive view would change rapidly depending on different circumstances" (Glissant 1997, 125). Yet, Glissant is cognizant of how such economic goals must resist what Livingston refers to as the impulse for self-devouring growth. In this chapter, I have sought to move beyond the beach as a metaphor for economic prospects, to consider the political economy of (sand) erosion as a calculation that (literally) erases Guyana's place in the world. In a subsequent passage, Glissant brings forth some of the forms of erasure at work in this political economy: "Beneath the conventional image, the kind one sees developed—or summarized—in publicity films in the United States or Japan, the luxuriously fatal image for selling a country ('The Antilles cheap'), beneath this insipid façade, we rediscover the ardor of a land. I see the mockery of the image, and I do not see it. I catch the quivering of this beach by surprise, this beach where visitors exclaim how beautiful! how typical! and I see that it is burning" (Glissant 1997, 205).

Seeing Guyana's sand, then, means seeing that "the beach" is burning both at the site of extraction and at the site of importation. The Guyanese scientist Neville Trotz is painfully aware of the tension between modernization and safeguarding the environment. "In the final analysis," he said, "the question of the environment is tied up with the welfare of the people. We need ecosystem services to maintain a particular quality of life. But on the other hand, without development there is abject poverty" (Trotz 2022b). For his part, and expressing a vision akin to Glissant's, Trotz published an op-ed in which he advocated for utilizing Guyana's pure sand deposits for producing photovoltaic cells for the solar energy industry (Trotz 2022a). He also proposed more energy-conscious construction alternatives to sand, including converting discarded rice husks as an extender for cement (Trotz 2022a). Other experts told me that such alternatives, including recycling cement, are technologically more complicated and slower than digging up sand. Still, if we take the UN warning seriously, pursuing alternatives such as those Trotz recommends is a worthy endeavor. It is yet to be seen whether calls for a more sustainable utilization of sand will influence Guyana's government.

For now, constructing buildings, roads, hospitals, and cities is dependent on sand extraction. The sand pits on the East Bank have multiplied exponentially. Heavy machinery and male workers toil in an endless loop of digging up sand and loading it onto barges and trucks, with the material now in high demand as the country scrambles to realize President Ali's vision for the future. Men are the overt shareholders in Guyana's mining industries—at the level of corporation owner, government official, and machine operator. Women, children, plants, and animals are largely invisible in local representations of the sand industry. It is for this reason that the role Mrs. R. played in media constructions of the controversy between her husband and Mr. B. has significance. Mr. R. responded to Mr. B.'s film with a press conference in which he, his wife, and their attorney told their side of the story. A local TV news outlet broadcast parts of the press conference. Presenting documents to legitimize his claims of owning the sand mining company, Mr. R. countered that the Brazilian slandered him and, in turn, the Guyanese government, jeopardizing the nation's international business profile. Himself a naturalized Guyanese citizen, Mr. R. stakes his credibility and his claim to Guyanese national identity on having spent decades in the country and on his union with his Indo-Guyanese wife—Mr. R.'s Guyaneseness is at least in part predicated on his marriage to a Guyanese woman. At the press conference, Mr. R.'s pushback noted emotional pain and suffering, but centered largely on quantifiable losses—money, productivity, and time: "Now [Mr. B.] attack me through the Internet, through the video. He was terrorizing me, my family and my business past two years. Okay, it cost me a lot of pain, lot of sleepless night, lose money, my business is not functioning effectively. And more than anything, I lose my productivity. I like to work. I like to build. I don't like to engage my time and money in these kind of things." Visibly exasperated, Mr. R. continued, saying that had he not been distracted by Mr. B.'s allegations, he would have segued into the lucrative industry of gold mining.

We can contrast this with how, in the very same press conference, Mrs. R. assessed the damages resulting from Mr. B.'s video: "I felt very betrayed and hurt by the video . . . which [Mr. B.] has been broadcasting. He has stooped so low to fabricate these lies and the most ugly photos of me and my husband he has exhibited, while showing himself as this well-dressed, beautiful businessman. And it goes to show he was planning this—this thing against us." Mrs. R. focuses on her feelings of hurt and betrayal, and on how Mr. B. shared unflattering photographs of her and her spouse, a stark contrast to his carefully curated self-representation in the video in which he appears in well-tailored suits and ties, and fashionable sunglasses. Apparently edited for brevity, the clip that the TV news program selected of Mrs. R. does not tell us that she worked as the company's accountant during the partnership between the two men— wouldn't she be qualified to enumerate monetary losses? The framing of her account around sartorial concerns connects her to conventionally feminine experiential and socio-material constructs. Her rendition of injuries suffered, at least as the news report recaps it, emphasizes intangible damages, "the most ugly photos of me and my husband he has exhibited." Mrs. R. bewails being captured as comparatively underdressed, embodying an unprofessional ugliness alongside a "well-dressed, beautiful businessman." The original video, which was subsequently taken down from YouTube, depicted a disheveled and barefoot Mr. and Mrs. R. If we recall that the New York Times coverage of Guyana's chances for managing its oil boom rendered the nation's children as naked, and its workers as unprofessional and lackadaisical—showing up to wharf jobs in flip-flops and eating soup out of hardhats—we can situate Mrs. R. as being preoccupied with salient, demeaning "underdevelopment" stereotypes of Guyanese that circulate globally.

The Caribbean tourism economy has been inextricably linked to women's labor and racialized conceptions of beauty (Freeman 2000; Brennan 2004; Gregory 2014). Mrs. R.'s beautiful/ugly critique centers on transnational understandings of Guyana that traffic well beyond the controversy in which she and her husband were steeped. Paradoxically, these representations at once construct Guyana and Guyanese as "ugly," which Mrs. R. highlights, and as sexually desirable, as we saw earlier in

our exploration of the gendered meanings attached to Guyanese immigrants in Barbados and deconstruction of the global superstar Rihanna's
Guyanese heritage as a relatively unknown but fundamental component
of her persona. I want to conclude the present chapter by linking Mrs.
R's beautiful/ugly dichotomy to the way the Barbados Tourism Authority
juxtaposes its most beautiful "export," Rihanna, with its sandy beaches.

In 2011, the Barbados Tourism Authority signed a multiyear marketing agreement with Rihanna, enlisting her in boosting the nation's tourism economy. One of the resulting ads, a one minute and twenty-seven
second commercial video, begins with the heading "Rihanna & Barbados present," framed by a bright blue sky canopied by palm trees. From
there, Rihanna's hit song, "Diamonds," provides nondiegetic sound as
the singer frolics on the shore and kneels on a white sand beach, wearing
first a Barbados t-shirt with a bikini bottom, and later a coral-colored
bikini. The less-than-subtle message is that the "vision of ecstasy" about
which Rihanna sings is both the singer and her island home. Here, as
wet sand clings to Rihanna's bent knees, we understand that she embodies the beauty of Bajan beaches. Rihanna's symbolic role eclipses as
much as it reveals. Like the pristine sand that blankets beaches in Jamaica and SVG, Rihanna's origins can be traced back to Guyana, where
her mother, Monica Braithwaite, was born. Earlier we saw that Guyanese maternal knowledge informs Rihanna's music and her global business empire. But like Guyanese sand, Rihanna's connections to Guyana
only surface after some digging. Mrs. R's insightful use of the beautiful/
ugly dichotomy reflects the Guyanese people's awareness that they exist
outside these glossy transnational representations of Caribbean beauty
and global capitalism. With the tourist-friendly image of Rihanna re-
cruited to promote Barbados's beauty, Guyana is relegated to ugliness
and erasure—the underbelly of sand loss and the gendered landscape of
some of the most vulnerable casualties of the Anthropocene.

## Finding Guyana in Sand

I was not alone in my initial myopia regarding Guyana's sand. In 2018,
perched high within the Guyana Marriott Hotel, where I had gone in
hopes of witnessing ExxonMobil's presence (the company's executives
flocked to the new hotel), I snapped a photo of the coastline view from

my window, replete with a white, sandy strip of beach, and, beyond it, the murky waters of the Atlantic Ocean.[9] I captioned the photo provocatively "#Guyana is beautiful" and shared it via social media. It was not long before the image prompted responses from members of the Guyanese diaspora who surmised that the white sand had to have been "imported." Their suspicions were only partially correct—yes, the strip along Georgetown's coast was not originally blanketed in white sand. But rather than being "imported," the sand was most likely trucked in from local East Bank Demerara sand pits. Both the nine-story Marriott hotel and the stretch of beach alongside it are products of Guyanese sand. Four years later, the white sand strip alongside the Marriott hotel was still there. The scientist Neville Trotz bristled when I mentioned the transplanted white sand belt: "I hope that's the last time it happens in Guyana. It's really stupid. You don't tamper with coastlines like that, there are coastal dynamics with the way sand is deposited and the way it's removed. Intervening even in that limited area can have impacts along the coast" (Trotz 2022b).

Right around the time when I shared the photograph from the Marriott hotel, I visited what had been Mr. R.'s sand mining company. Mr. R. had died and his widow, Mrs. R., had taken over as head of the operation. Through a mutual acquaintance, I came to meet Mrs. R. Her security-conscious office, tucked away behind a guarded gate and on the top floor of what looked from the outside like a regular house, featured a large portrait of her husband. Save for the looming photograph of Mr. R., in contrast to the male-dominated public space of the sand mines, I found Mrs. R. and two other women, apparently administrative staff, running the business. When I explained that I was writing a book about Guyanese sand, with a focus on the ways in which it shapes Caribbean beach destinations, Mrs. R. did not miss a beat. She knew exactly what I meant, and in polished, quantifiable terms, she proceeded to enumerate some of her company's export successes. Quickly locating a website on her computer and turning the monitor to face me, she shared an image of a gorgeous, sprawling beachfront hotel located in one of the Caribbean islands known for five-star resorts. I marveled at the beautiful expanse of stark, white sand and the unbelievable turquoise hue of the water. "That's our sand," she said. I took "our" to mean both Mrs. R.'s company and Guyana. "The sand affects the tint of the water," she explained. "That water looks like that because of the reflection from the sand." Of course, I thought, sand, along with sediment, silt, and algae, does affect how we view the color of water.

Sand is perhaps the ultimate example of the everywhere- and no-whereness of Guyana. At the time of this writing, the steady army of trucks marches on, hauling mounds of silica-quartz from East Bank Demerara to all parts of the country, their loads routinely spilling a thin, white, powdery trail along the thoroughfare. The grains are evidence that one can follow, like a trail of breadcrumbs, to track where the sand was extracted and where it lands. As sand extraction persists, will we eventually find no sand in Guyana? What will become of the ecosystems that sand supports? Will the coastlines of other Caribbean nations, the ever-expanding system of roads, and the Silica Cities of the future bear the inscrutable presence of Guyana's scattered bounty? The trail of sand grains reveals that they already do.

4

Recasting El Dorado

*Representing Oil, Politics, and Ethnic Conflict*

In present-day Georgetown, a mélange of foreigners, including American oil executives, oil workers, and investors from various countries, flock to the government-owned Marriott Hotel, which opened in 2015 to cater to international business travelers.[1] When I visited in 2018, the hotel's posh pool overlooking the transplanted white sand beach was desolate, but by August of 2022, it hosted a boisterous crowd of petroleum executives and employees, American military personnel, and a few well-heeled members of the Guyanese diaspora who were back home for business or pleasure.[2] The tall fence that separated the pool from the beach was now impassable (one could unlock the gate with a room key in 2018), and if guests wanted to join the locals who strolled along the seawall at sunset and played music from speakers in their cars on weekends, they had to ask hotel security to unlock a side gate leading out from the parking lot, rather than directly onto the beach. The locked gate was now the only tangible remnant of a conflict between the hotel and Georgetown's residents; in 2018 the Marriott had posted twenty signs on the sandy strip stating that it was "Private Property and . . . access without permission [was] prohibited" (Sohan 2018). However, since the Guyanese government had previously designated the beach as part of the Sea Defense Reserve, the hotel had no legal claim to the action it took to bar the public (Sohan 2018). The resolution of the dispute in favor of the public (in which the state's laws worked against the government-owned hotel) was in stark contrast to the private beachfronts at many hotels in Barbados and other parts of the Caribbean, where locals are banned from accessing beaches adjacent to resorts.

ExxonMobil's offshore oil rigs are not visible from Georgetown's coast. But the hotel has emerged as an emblem of the trappings of new oil. And from the beach alongside the Marriott, I could see one of two massive trailing suction hopper dredges (TSHDs), owned by the Belgian company, Jan De Nul, dredging sand just off the shore—its floating pipeline funneling the wet, murky sand towards a disposal area west of the channel at the mouth of the Demerara River. When I asked the owner of a sand equipment company about the purpose of the dredging, he informed me that because the waters leading to the river's mouth are too shallow to accommodate large vessels, the TSHDs were brought in to dredge channels, allowing trade ships to pass. This dredging never ceases; it must be a perpetual operation because sand continuously resettles in such shallow waters. The nonstop dredging is an eerie, automated, modern-day incarnation of the monumental human labor expended when enslaved Guyanese moved one hundred million tons of clay to "humanize" the coastal landscape.

Not surprisingly, in the nation's papers a battle unfolded over the impacts of dredging sand close to the mouth of the river, with environmentalists and fishermen on one side, and the dredging operation and the Environmental Protection Agency (EPA) on the other. The environmentalist Janette Bulkan penned a letter to the editor of *Stabroek News*, asking if the EPA had called for an Environmental Impact Assessment in advance of the operations. "By its nature, dredging disturbs the natural environment," Bulkan wrote. "And here, affects the livelihoods of fishermen" (Bulkan 2022). Bulkan's letter elicited a "nothing to see here, folks" response from NRG Holdings (the local consortium formed to oversee the shore base dredging facility) in which they assured the public that they had held "extensive consultations" with the fisherfolk prior to commencing dredging and had submitted an Environmental Management Plan to the EPA, resulting in a judgment that the project would have "no significant impacts" on the fisherfolk (*Stabroek News* 2022b). Less than a month later, the same paper published the fishermen's side of the story—dozens of them said "their fish pens have been fouled by the mud and refuse thrown up by dredging off the Demerara River mouth" (Sutherland 2022). They recounted that their catch was now mostly trash: "The dredging raising up all these things (trash and seaweed) on the ocean floor and that's what we find in our fish pens and just a little bit of fish" (Sutherland 2022).

As we have seen, although oil fuels Guyana's development dreams, the country's future will be built on sand. Sand, transported on trucks across the East Bank and dredged up off Georgetown's shores, is at once a foundational resource for modernization and a symbol of impending environmental catastrophe and pernicious social inequalities. The traffic jams that ensue from the constant, large-scale movement of sand have further marginalized the villagers of the East Bank from the capital, and sand dredging has threatened the livelihoods of fisherfolk who rely on the Demerara River. In the images one finds of the soil dredged up by TSHDs off Georgetown's shores, the wet sand looks a lot like thick, dark liquid—to the naked eye it is almost indistinguishable from oil. Although the murky sand dredged up in this area does not contain oil, it evokes the twinned enterprises of sand and oil extraction. And the complaints that environmentalists and fisherfolk voiced in response to the sand dredging echo the outcries over ultra-deepwater oil drilling at Liza 1, the first site of ExxonMobil's extraction operation in the Stabroek Block. Experts aver that ExxonMobil has disregarded proper safety measures and has failed to sufficiently prepare for the possibility of an oil spill (Juhasz 2021). Describing Exxon's safety measures as "superficial," analysts note that even the oil company itself estimates that a spill "could send oil throughout the Caribbean Sea, across Trinidad and Venezuela, and as far as Jamaica" (Juhasz 2021).

Critics charge that the oil company is taking advantage of the Guyanese government's desire for rapid development, and is "cutting corners" in terms of safety in its own rush to produce eight hundred thousand barrels of oil per day (Juhasz 2021). If that projection is met, Exxon's operation in Guyana would be "the largest single source of fossil fuel production in the world" (Juhasz 2021). Environmental watchdogs, including Vincent Adams, Guyana's former environment chief, worry that the company "has no respect for the people's health, safety and environment" (Juhasz 2021). Adams returned to Guyana in 2018, after having worked at the US Department of Energy for thirty years, to take on the role of executive director of the EPA. He was let go in August of 2020 when President Irfaan Ali's administration took over, a fact that, coupled with critiques that the agency was putting the oil company's interests ahead of those of the people and the environment, casts the EPA in a corruptive light.[3] With no significant fossil fuel production before Exxon arrived on the scene, Guyana was "a carbon sink that absorbs far more of the planet-heating greenhouse gas than it emits" (Juhasz 2021). Now, experts fear that the company's drilling and gas flaring will turn the country into one of the world's biggest "carbon bombs" (McGreal 2022).

While sand trucks and hopper dredges move voluminous mounds of sand, and oil drilling causes monumental destruction to the sea floor and to the environment, the pointer broom methodically attends to small piles and single grains. It brooms into the light how communities on the ground make sense of these upheavals, allowing us to witness what the oil discovery means for everyday people. The critiques voiced in the previous paragraph, published in two articles in the *Guardian* (US edition), are divergences from the forms of erasure that channel through most of the international press coverage of Exxon's oil discovery in Guyana. This chapter sweeps across international representations of the oil boom—which have been steadfastly focused on presenting the nation as on the brink of the "resource curse"—juxtaposing them with the way Guyanese interpret the interplay between Exxon's efforts to turn Guyana into a "cash cow" (Juhasz 2021) and their own government's prioritizing of oil wealth over social and environmental concerns. When I asked friends and family if they saw any signs that the government was passing on the oil riches to regular folks, I heard a common response: "Dem thiefin' the money!"[4] What will the oil bonanza mean for the villagers in Sarah Johanna and the fishermen at the mouth of the Demerara? This chapter traces the legacies of El Dorado to situate the oil discovery within Guyana's long history of global racial capitalism and its present-day quest for development. I argue that the single-minded focus on managing petroleum profits, especially when it is filtered through the deficient trope of ethnic conflict, simplifies Guyanese politics and co-opts spectacular examples of violence while obscuring local understandings and more everyday violence against women and children.

## The Lost City of Gold and the Resource Curse

Guyana is clearly one of the most interesting oil and gas production scenarios in the world today. Between its frontier quarrel with Venezuela, political tensions, lack of infrastructure and internal uncertainties, whoever follows what is happening in that country cannot ignore the huge opportunities that are opening in South America.
—Luis Fernando Panelli, "Is Guyana a New Oil El Dorado?"

"Is Guyana a New Oil El Dorado?" This was the titular query of a 2019 article in the *Journal of World Energy Law and Business* (Panelli 2019). One of many articles about Guyana published since the 2015 oil discovery—both in trade journals and in popular outlets—in what one journalist dubbed a new "cottage industry of international press about the potential 'resource curse' that oil could bring" (Calder 2020), the piece recasts my homeland as the place to watch in terms of oil and gas extraction.[5] The pivot from an international press that had for so long ignored Guyana to a steady stream of coverage starting in 2015 felt like representational whiplash. And, as I perused the numerous offerings by writers with Guyana now squarely in their sights, I pondered the relationship between the historical legacies of El Dorado—the mythic lost city of gold that induced sixteenth-century European explorers to trek across the northern region of South America—and the contemporary realities of the resource curse. Alternatively known as the "paradox of plenty," the resource curse is the idea that countries rich in natural resources tend to fail in terms of maintaining democracy, peaceful conflict resolution, economic stability, and public welfare. That the resource curse is often situated alongside the concept of *Dutch disease*—a theory about the causal relationship between an overemphasis on natural resources and the decline in other sections, derived from the discovery of a profitable natural gas field in the Netherlands in 1959—seemed like bitter irony to me, as the Dutch were the first Europeans to establish colonies in the country we now call Guyana. As noted earlier, the Dutch imprint on Guyana remains, not only in its system of dykes and dams but also in a myriad of names, from its iconic market and one of its mostly widely circulated daily newspapers—Stabroek—to towns and estates such as New Amsterdam, Nooten Zuil, and Ruimveldt.

The connection to Dutch disease prompted me to explore how Guyana's (in)ability to manage new oil was being understood in the international press, not only as a window into a linked path to present-day ramifications of Guyana's colonial legacy but also as a way of deconstructing shifting, contemporary conceptions of global Guyana. Anthropologist Ryan Cecil Jobson analyzes those very correlations with the past, particularly with regard to colonial capitalism's influence on Guyanese racial formations, in his article, "Black Gold in El Dorado: Frontiers of Race and Oil in Guyana" (2019). Jobson offers a thoughtful account of racialized alliances and divisions among Guyanese workers and an erudite analysis of past extractive commodities alongside the vast reshaping of Guyana's landscape that I will not retell here (originally historicized, as he notes, in Walter Rodney's *History of the Guyanese Working People*). Like Jobson, I argue that recent representations of Guyana traffic in a neoliberal discourse that does not account for how colonial legacies are implicated in the nation's chances for economic and political success. Here, I focus on the actual international *representations*, putting them in conversation with Guyanese accounts. I take up the proliferation of reporting in both the international press and Guyana's press that offers journalistic, editorial, and layperson understandings of oil and politics. While in these portrayals, oil "triggers the resource curse" (Cummings 2018), I aver that the international coverage fails to recognize how the persistent imprints of colonialism have set Guyana up for said curse, instead recasting the nation and, most importantly, the Guyanese people as lacking in the sophistication and technological/global economic know-how to manage petroleum extraction and its concomitant finances.

I rely on local daily newspapers as entry points into Guyanese contestations of state corruption as well as into their acute awareness of the nettlesome dynamics between "ethnic conflict" and the struggle over the 2020 Guyanese elections. Guyana has several widely circulated daily newspapers and a rich tradition of utilizing the press to voice political resistance, perhaps best illustrated in the visionary political activism of Albert Raymond Forbes Webber, who formed the West Indian Press Association (Cudjoe 2011). Guyanese of all stripes are avid newspaper readers. While many rural homes lack televisions and the Internet, one can always find the daily newspaper on kitchen tables and on rum shop counters.[6] Newspapers connect Guyanese to happenings in Georgetown and beyond. That global interface, as I have underscored throughout this book, is a constitutive element of society—Guyanese people read the papers to keep abreast not only of national politics but also of the greater world. Guyanese are especially in tune with American politics, and in addition to newspapers, those with access to televised news and the Internet are keenly aware of the ways in which they are rendered or ignored, particularly in the US press. So, when the oil discovery sparked a fresh international focus on Guyana, the representational whiplash that I felt as a Guyanese living abroad resonated with people at home, too, who knew that the myth of El Dorado was once again on our shores.

## Striking Oil

On May 20, 2015, an ExxonMobil-led consortium announced that it had found commercial quantities of oil in the Stabroek Block, 190 kilometers off the Guyanese coastline. The announcement sent shock waves through the international oil-industry community and cast a new, stark light on long-ignored Guyana. The petroleum conglomerates revealed that the sea floor beneath Guyana's coast holds one of the most valuable oil and natural gas discoveries in decades (Krauss 2017). With ongoing exploration discovering more than six million barrels of oil by 2019, "equivalent to what the industry calls a 'supergiant' oilfield," there were production estimates of over one million barrels per day within ten years (Tamboli 2019). At the time of the initial announcement, the recoverable oil was estimated to be worth over $200 billion. By 2020, even with the already troubled industry sent into a deeper tailspin in the wake of the global financial crisis stemming from the COVID-19 pandemic, Guyana was still expected to be the site of Exxon's largest-capacity FPSO (floating production storage and offloading unit) ever (Panelli 2019). ExxonMobil, and the industry more broadly, were already in precarious financial standing even before the COVID-19 crisis: "The growing Guyana exploration [was] part of a slow global recovery of the oil industry, which was hobbled by a collapse in oil prices," business reporter Clifford Krauss noted in the *New York Times* (Krauss 2017). And the discoveries kept coming. Seven years in, and after twenty-five more discoveries, the amount of oil found in Guyana's offshore waters is unmatched across the world. Estimates placed the oil and gas potential at nearly eleven billion barrels—about a tenth of the world's conventional discoveries. With the stakes so high in Guyana, a country consistently ranked as one of the poorest in the hemisphere, it was no surprise that the international business press began churning out story after story about what the oil bounty would mean for the world's newest petrostate. Guyana stood to triple its GDP if the oil extraction unfolded as planned, setting the nation up to become the richest in the region (Calder 2020). Observers evoked the quest for El Dorado, not as a way of characterizing the frenetic discovery efforts of a troubled oil industry that desperately needed Guyanese oil but instead as a descriptor for a country on the verge of dramatic transformation.

## The Ghosts of El Dorado

Today, the legend of El Dorado figures into popular understandings of the presumptive pitfalls of black gold. The lost city of gold is the stuff of contemporary action-adventure and animated films, including, but by no means limited to, *El Dorado* (1988); *The Mask of Zorro* (1998); *The Road to El Dorado* (2000); *National Treasure: Book of Secrets* (2007); *Indiana Jones and the Kingdom of the Crystal Skull* (2008); *Black Panther* (2018); *Dora and the Lost City of Gold* (2019); and *Uncharted* (2022). While the myth of El Dorado (*Black Panther* relocating it to Africa, aside) can be traced to the Muisca people of Colombia and to Spanish conquests in Latin America, it encompasses a capacious terrain—across Guiana, Venezuela, Brazil, Suriname, and French Guiana—that was in the crosshairs of conflicts among British, Spanish, and Dutch empires. And while some may be quick to point out that Ciudad Guayana, the site of the mythical El Dorado, is in contemporary Venezuela, not neighboring Guyana, border disputes in this area date back to the 1400s.[7] Before Europeans arrived, these countries were far less discrete territories, characterized by power struggles between Indigenous Arawak and Carib peoples who populated the region. Even today, land disputes between Guyana and Venezuela continue to blur the borders between these two nations, with Venezuela claiming ownership of an area that represents nearly three-quarters of Guyana's territory. Not surprisingly, Venezuela's recent decree asserting ownership of the Guyana-Essequibo territory, which includes the recent offshore oil discovery, came immediately after Guyana announced finding oil.[8]

And it is the exploratory missions of British Elizabethan hero Sir Walter Raleigh, author of *The Discoverie of Guiana* (1596), that perhaps best illustrate how the region figured into early British imaginings even before Great Britain gained colonial control in Guiana. Raleigh's story, like a number of the films I have referenced, recounts a relentless pursuit of treasure, an attempt to exploit South American territories in order to enrich outsiders, and the dastardly demise that often befalls cinematic bad guys. But Raleigh, although beheaded in 1618 after failing to make good on two promises to British royalty—that he would find a gold mine on the Orinoco River, home of the famed city of gold, and that he could do so without bringing violence to Spanish subjects settled there—is actually remembered as a hero of the British empire. Far from being relegated to the annals of British history, only to find currency in the stuff of action-adventure films, the legacy of El Dorado continues to haunt understandings of "discovery" and natural resources in Guyana, and even the vestiges of Raleigh as hero/antihero still color contemporary imaginings of England's history and its present-day male Anglo explorers. I discussed one such vestige earlier, embodied in celebrity chef Gordon Ramsay, who approached contemporary Guyana's culinary frontiers with the romanticized zeal of an explorer uncovering treasures buried deep in the rainforest.

British historian Paul Sellin revisits Raleigh's legacy as a "cold case" in his book *Treasure, Treason, and the Tower: El Dorado and the Murder of Sir Walter Raleigh* (2011). Sellin surmises that George Villiers (Duke of Buckingham and presumed ally) betrayed Raleigh by withholding documents that could have substantiated the explorer's claims of having found evidence of gold along the Orinoco River. At least one reviewer agreed that Sellin's book vindicates "Raleigh's efforts to secure mineral wealth for his monarch and his nation" (Fleck 2013). More critical readers argued that Sellin depicted Raleigh's historical legacy as that of an antihero—when in fact he has "usually been portrayed as one of the great heroes of British history"—and that Sellin's work is tainted by hyperbolic praise for Raleigh and lacking in actual archival research (Cross 2014, 266). Yet, even his critic, Robert Cross, concludes that Sellin (and perhaps by extension Raleigh?) provides some "useful insight on El Dorado" (Cross 2014, 267). But what constitutes useful information on El Dorado, especially if the analysis eclipses the ways in which the search for gold plundered Guiana, positioned British marauders as heroes, and contributed to our continued myopia about the nation and its people? Thankfully, Joyce Lorimer offers a postcolonial-informed reading in her review of Sellin's work: "Ralegh [*sic*] was unfairly convicted of treason in 1603 and unjustly put to death in 1618, but the failure to take up his Guiana ventures reflects his contemporaries' assessment of personal risk versus certain profit. The 'last-chance' expedition of 1617 cannot be inflated into a tragic loss of opportunity to establish the colonial basis of an English empire in Latin America which, according to Sellin's extraordinary concluding peroration, would have introduced common law, religious toleration and intellectual enlightenment in place of the *'plague'* of authoritarian military rule inherited from Spain" (Lorimer 2013, 284, emphasis added). Cutting to the heart of Sellin's positioning of Raleigh as potential White savior of Latin America, Lorimer signals that the contemporary neoliberal logic I address in this chapter has its origins in centuries-old attitudes towards the region.

## The Coming Plague in a Vast, Watery Wilderness

In place of the plague of authoritarian rule from Spain from which Sellin suggests Raleigh might have saved the region, we find a newly imagined "plague" hobbling contemporary Guyana's chances for success. I am not referring to COVID-19, but rather to the plague of underdevelopment and ethnic politics, perhaps most acutely illustrated in the *New York Times*: "A plague of ethnic tribal politics has produced a fragile state with an economy propelled by drug trafficking, money-laundering, and gold and diamond smuggling" (Krauss 2018a).

Almost every sentence of Clifford Krauss's lengthy, front-page July 2018 article (with accompanying photo spread) oozes with "evidence" that Guyana is a backwards, "forgotten by time" wasteland destined to mismanage its oil bounty. Its landscape: vast, watery, and wild. Its roads: dirt. Its houses: on stilts. Its children: naked. Its climate: muggy. Krauss uses the word "plague" to describe Guyana's politics and its power grid ("blackouts [are] a regular plague in the cities"). Guyana's government is inexperienced in international business ventures and in the ways of regulating big oil. Its college-educated youth have largely fled to the United States and Canada to escape "H.I.V. infection, crime, and suicide." The article recalled Donald Trump's famous "shithole countries" description, which the former US president used to describe Haiti and African nations in January of 2018. Both characterizations rehash tired victim-blaming Global North stereotypes of "underdeveloped" nations that smack of neocolonial paternalism. In the context of *Times* coverage of Guyana's petroleum discovery, the devastating portrayal denies Guyana's complexity, a distortion that augurs a perilous trajectory for its oil boom. Perhaps more pointedly, the dialogues I uncover from the local press demonstrate that the Guyanese people interpret their government's handling of the oil money not as indicative of inexperience but rather as revealing a savvy form of corruption. As people in Guyana see it, quick-and-dirty deals with the oil conglomerate put fast money into the hands of those in power.

The narrative in the *Times* glosses over how managing the oil wealth is read within the country and by much of its population (who are indeed poor but will readily tell you that they are not backwards). It also deemphasizes the ways in which ExxonMobil and other international big-business investors prioritize petroleum extraction over environmental oversight. The article pivots, dangerously, from considering Exxon's hollow promise of preparedness to handle the possibility of an environmental catastrophe in the form of an oil spill to intimating that Guyanese workers, not the petroleum conglomerate, are obstacles to environmental precautions due to their "lackadaisical attitude toward safety" (Krauss 2018a). Although only six hundred Guyanese were employed in mostly low-level roles at drill rigs, shore bases, and offices at the time of the article's publication, Krauss infers that a major environmental threat will come in the form of backwoods, careless Guyanese workers who, at best, are described as prone to excessive smiling (read: stupid). Never mind that the United States has experienced at least forty-four major oil spills since 1969, including the catastrophic Exxon Valdez spill in 1989, which until the 2010 Deepwater Horizon well blowout, was the worst release of liquid petroleum hydrocarbon in US waters. Still, Krauss advances a neoliberal logic that portrays American businesspeople and Exxon experts as capable, knowledgeable, and intrepid, while, like the "warped wood" staircase that leads to the office of Guyana's understaffed senior oil regulator (it "could sorely use a coat of paint"), Guyana's people, its democracy, and its landscape are all in need of a gut remodel to bring them up to speed with Exxon's discovery.

Guyanese responded to Krauss's article with the hashtag "#LifeInThe-WateryWilderness," in which they deployed acerbic wit to criticize the journalist: "So fortunate to have an entitled, privileged, & disconnected foreign white man speak for the people of Guyana. Thank you @ckrauss massa, we are lost without you. @nytimes we could do without the neo-colonial undertones next time, ok? Find local writers" (Rodrigues 2018).

The tweets in the hashtag also called out the inaccuracies in Krauss's reporting, with several noting that the country has more than three paved highways, and one relating that seeing children playing naked is not a regular occurrence: "Cliff @ckrauss Can you believe @spbj28 had the audacity to show up to our play date with clothes on?" (Kinah K 2018).

Read closely, even Krauss's take inadvertently reveals that some Guyanese are savvy regarding international business and the pitfalls of the resource curse: he shares the example of Dawn Chung Layne, owner of a sewing business, who was attending workshops on business development financed by Exxon. Krauss quotes Chung Layne: "Check out the Trinidad economy. They thought oil was the best thing since sliced bread, and they spent Sunday to Sunday. They stopped producing and imported everything with oil money. It could happen here" (Krauss 2018a). Far from an outlier, Chung Layne's comparative analysis of the potential failures of overreliance on petroleum earnings is repeatedly echoed in Guyanese citizens' discourse in the nation's press. But the *Times* article saddles Guyana alone with the task of escaping the resource curse, while fueling the narrative that fosters a self-fulfilling prophecy of the country's impending failure. How could such an uncivilized, ill-prepared, and "forgotten by time" place successfully transform into one of the wealthiest nations in the region?

## State Corruption Here and There

Undoubtedly, state corruption, an issue only hinted at in the piece but a focal point of some of Krauss's other *Times* articles on Guyana's oil boom, has played a significant role in its chances for economic success from the very moment of the discovery announcement. However, like so much of the Global North discourse on Guyana, Guyanese political corruption was construed as a by-product of ethnic conflict, even while fraud ran rampant in America's own "musty" and outdated White House. Replete with double standards and paradoxical logic, the article evokes Walter Rodney's most famous theoretical framework in *How Europe Underdeveloped Africa*: given that corporations based in the United States, Spain, the UK, China, and Canada hold petroleum blocks in Guyana, and a Belgian company owns the two massive trailing suction hopper dredges that continuously clear the path for large vessels entering its waters, a number of the very countries that underdeveloped Guyana in the first place now stand to profit once again from its resources while blaming Guyanese for any mismanagement (Rodney 2018/1972). And while the Guyanese state's hand in putting the nation on a direct path to the resource curse should not be underemphasized, I follow anthropologist Deborah A. Thomas in noting that "predatory, violent, and illegal forms of rule are legacies of colonial state formation and plantation-based extraction" (Thomas 2011, 13).

As the *Times'* lead reporter on Guyana's oil discovery, a role he sometimes shares with Anatoly Kurmanaev, Krauss has dominated Guyana's representation in one of America's most widely read and respected news outlets. The *New York Times* shapes contemporary American understandings of Guyana. The culturally biased reporting exhibited in the article I have analyzed here is also evidenced across numerous pieces on Guyana, in which beauty and order are only present in the form of vestiges of British colonial rule. Guyana's national assembly is described as "a British colonial relic with a regal dome and window balconies," and these remnants of colonialism stand in contrast to what Guyanese have done with the place: the national assembly, "paneled in mahogany, is a hotbed of division" (Krauss 2018b).

The hotbed to which Krauss refers is evidenced in a vote of no confidence, which the handling of the oil discovery sparked against Guyana's then president, David Granger. Granger's opposition accused him of signing a deal that was grossly advantageous to Exxon. Even when the petroleum giant and Guyana renegotiated the initial contract in 2016, Guyanese and outside industry analysts understood the agreement as highly favorable to Exxon, with Guyana receiving a below-average share of oil production (Kurmanaev and Krauss 2020). Exxon acknowledged finding another major reserve only three days after the second deal was signed. In 2018, confidence in Granger declined further when he shut down unprofitable state-owned cane processing plants, which provided employment to seven thousand sugar workers, most of whom were Indo-Guyanese. The sugar workers accused the Afro-Guyanese president of targeted economic repression. When Guyana held national elections on March 2, 2020, the world was watching to see who would govern this so-long-overlooked country now that it had morphed into the world's newest petrostate. Granger claimed victory amid objections from the High Court, CARICOM, and other international observers, and the opposing party. Opposition supporters staged protests, blocking roads and setting fires. International observers and Guyanese of all political alliances deplored the police killing of one teenage protester, Devon Hansraj, and the proliferation of racist social media posts, a number of which were anti-Black (Calder 2020; *Kaieteur News* 2020a). By the culmination of the electoral process and in the weeks following the swearing-in of the new Guyanese president, Irfaan Ali, three more teenage boys were killed—their murders linked to the election conflict.

The election results were mired in a five-month standoff between Granger and the opposition leader, Irfaan Ali.[9] Observers were quick to point out the marked racial divide in Guyana's electoral system—while Granger's largely Afro-Guyanese PNC (People's National Congress) dominates the APNU+AFC coalition (A Partnership for National Unity–Alliance for Change), Ali's oppositional PPP (People's Progressive Party) is primarily Indo-Guyanese.[10] Commentators also emphasized that the racially defined two-party system had resulted in a winner-take-all framework with whichever group was represented by the party in power having greater, unevenly distributed access to resources—hence the fear that the petroleum jackpot would disproportionately benefit the ethnic group whose party held control.

Long in the making, this ethnic divide formed out of the British colonial system that set Afro- and Indo-Guyanese at odds with one another. It was later solidified with US/CIA intervention in Guyana's nascent democracy in the mid-1960s. Foreign meddling dashed the hopes of multiethnic coalition building that independent Guyana's founders, Cheddi Jagan and Forbes Burnham, initially attempted to create. In 2020, with the vote count close, but clearly in favor of Ali, Granger claimed victory on the basis of one contested Georgetown district. With Granger's self-appointed chief elections officer, Keith Lowenfield, charging fraud in the form of hundreds of deceased or emigrated people recorded as voting, and alleging that ballot boxes were stuffed with votes for Ali's party, Granger used tactics reminiscent of those of the Forbes Burnham administration in an attempt to secure his victory. However, the opposition party disputed his efforts, leading to foreign oversight from CARICOM, the Organization of American States, and the US Senate Foreign Relations Committee, with each entity debunking Granger's claims of election fraud and imploring him to concede power peacefully. Michael Pompeo's US State Department followed up by imposing sanctions on Guyana. Months after the March 2, 2020, presidential elections, recounts confirmed Ali's victory, and he assumed office on August 2 of that year.

It stands to reason that both Granger and Ali were motivated by the promise of oil wealth. But the same might be said for the US State Department. It was just a few years prior that Rex Tillerson, former ExxonMobil chief executive, served as then president Donald Trump's secretary of state. Krauss wrote with balanced objectivity about Tillerson, who had been scheduled to meet with Guyana's President Granger in 2017, but the visit was canceled when Tillerson was nominated to take over as US Secretary of State (Krauss 2017). Krauss gives Tillerson the benefit of the doubt, noting at the time, "If he is confirmed, Mr. Tillerson has pledged to recuse himself from any decision that might affect ExxonMobil for one year, and to consult with ethics officers at the State Department after that" (Krauss 2017). We subsequently learned that Tillerson was only one of many Trump appointees with conflicts of interest stemming from their big business connections.[11]

Although the malfeasance around the 2020 Guyana elections fits neatly into Western notions of poor countries' culpability in ensuring the resource curse, US discourse, in which the press largely ignored the intricacies of local dynamics while promoting the El Dorado–derived Western hero narrative, furthered the interests of the Western oil conglomerates. Meanwhile, the United States began to lose its own grasp on democracy. The parallels between Guyana's electoral fraud and Trump and his followers' election meddling in the United States were not lost on everyone; one op-ed argued that the United States was on the verge of a contested election in 2020, much like Guyana's, and similarly shaped by racialized divisions and identity politics (Gest 2020). However, the article's deeply flawed lede read as follows: "A country has reached a constitutional crisis. The validity of its national election is in dispute. The party in power is almost entirely supported by native-born people with centuries-long heritage in the country. Official results point to their defeat at the polls by an opposition party predominated by people of immigrant origin" (Gest 2020). The scenario is meant to represent Guyana's election quagmire, while simultaneously and surprisingly describing the political climate leading up to the 2020 US presidential election. While the author is correct in asserting that the United States has something to learn from Guyana about the threat of a president falsely claiming that an election that does not result in his victory is rigged—an untruth former President Trump has voiced repeatedly since 2020—its dichotomous delineation of a political system divided between "native-born people" (read: Republicans in the United States, PNC in Guyana) and an "opposition party dominated by people of immigrant origin" (read: US Democrats and Guyanese PPP) is problematic to say the least. This logic is faulty in relation to the United States, and equally defective in relation to Guyana, even though it is commonly applied in discussions of the latter. Suffice it to say that although, as Gest avers, the two major American political parties are increasingly divided along racial lines, with immigrants and people of color voting for Democrats while non-college-educated Whites typically vote Republican, these White voters are no more "native-born people with centuries-long heritage in the country" than are African Americans, Latinx, Asian Americans, and other minority groups. To suggest that racialized minorities are not native born, while Italian Americans, Irish Americans, and Americans with ancestry from other European countries are native born, denies racialized people's centuries-long presence in the country they played a primary role in building, while completely erasing Indigenous peoples.

In the context of Guyana, the statement is equally inaccurate, but regurgitates a political simplification used internationally and locally to separate Afro- and Indo-Guyanese, namely, that Black people are Guyanese natives, while Indians are immigrants. Although over 170 years separated their inception on Guyanese soil, of course, both Afro- and Indo-Guyanese are transplanted peoples, brought to Guyana to support colonial capitalism. Still, as noted earlier, I saw this very misconception reflected at Guyana's National Archives, which housed only records of "foreign births," meaning Indian indentured laborers. Moreover, Gest's analysis also misses the boat in terms of the more consequential gaps and fissures in the Guyanese electoral system. With Indo-Guyanese comprising about 40 percent of the population and Afro-Guyanese making up 30 percent, only a multiethnic coalition and/or election tampering could ensure a Granger/PNC electoral victory. The binary party system ignores the interests not only of Indigenous Guyanese, who comprise almost 10 percent of the population, but also of mixed-race Guyanese, who represent close to 18 percent and straddle the ethnic divides of the nation. And with Guyana's most recent census indicating that both Indo- and Afro-Guyanese populations are declining, while the Amerindian and mixed-raced populations are increasing, the ethnically divided two-party system clearly marginalizes a significant and growing segment (*Stabroek News* 2016).

The contested election on the heels of new oil once again distinguished Guyana as a site of violent ethnic strife, fueling an international press already prone to portraying its people and its government through a damaging Global North perspective. During the five months between the election and when Ali was officially sworn in, international coverage focused on how the electoral conflict jeopardized both ExxonMobil's investment and Guyana's big break. When Granger seemed bent on standing by a falsified victory, the coverage highlighted how US, Canadian, British, and European Union officials insisted that they would not consider a president sworn in under contested results to be legitimate (Kurmanaev 2020a). The reporting on Guyana's elections linked the contested presidential vote to ExxonMobil's now-imperiled plans to dramatically increase the number of barrels of oil it would produce per day. And the *Times* reported that former Guyanese president Bharrat Jagdeo said his party would lobby for international sanctions against Guyana if the Granger-controlled electoral board refused to implement a recount (Kurmanaev 2020a). The coverage foregrounded an ethnically divided Guyana and violent clashes with police (Kurmanaev 2020b, 2020c). Even allowing that foreign analysis is oftentimes not as detailed as local reporting, the international news wedded Guyana's ethnic divide and its mishandling of the oil money as a fait accompli with little to no attention to the complexities of Guyana's political scene. Mirroring the coverage of almost every crisis in the Caribbean, international discourse was far more preoccupied with the potential losses for the oil conglomerate than with on-the-ground realities in Guyana.

## "Nobody Wins an Election in Guyana"

It behooves us to examine the oil discovery and the political stalemate it triggered as interpreted by the Guyanese people and narrated in the local press. While US reporting emphasized the unpreparedness of the state to manage its oil riches, concomitantly typecasting the Guyanese people as unskilled and naïve in matters technological and environmental, and in regard to global finance, Guyanese contradicted those characterizations. Yes, Guyanese underscored a deep sense of cynicism about the initial deal their government struck with the oil conglomerates (they worried that it favored the petroleum companies and sold Guyana short), about the lack of proper environmental protections in the agreement, and about who would reap the benefits. Although their concerns correspond with US criticism of the Guyanese government, importantly for our purposes, they also contested the negative depiction of the Guyanese people. We can consider the international representation of the elections and the oil discovery as part of the political economy of erasure that has constricted understandings of global Guyana. Attention to Guyanese interpretations, then, provides an illuminating counterbalance.

In numerous letters to the editor in Guyana's *Stabroek News*, commencing with the initial discovery announcement and continuing even after the contested presidential election was resolved, Guyanese voiced exacting critiques that demonstrated a keen awareness of how colonial legacies had set the nation up for the dreaded resource curse. They also took state officials to task and revealed finespun analyses of the potential hazards and benefits of the discovery and the agreements attached to it. Concerned that Guyana was at risk for transitioning from being labeled "Booker's Guiana" (referring to the stronghold of Booker McConnell, one of the most powerful companies in the British empire) to being called "ExxonMobil's Guyana," one letter pointed out that the government already had a National Competitiveness Strategy, a 125-page document that outlined a clear plan for advancing local interests in relation to foreign companies (Northe 2019).[12] Questioning the APNU+AFC government's decision to allow ExxonMobil to produce a plan for how Guyana's share of oil and gas revenues would be spent, the letter insisted, "The only thing that appears to be clear is that the caretaker APNU+AFC Government is promoting neo-colonialism in our country. In so doing, they have allowed a small group free reign to move around duping our people" (Northe 2019). Sometimes penned by industry insiders and government advisors, many of these letters were decidedly partisan, faulting either the then-presiding Granger APNU+AFC administration or the opposing PPP. The latter was the case in a letter submitted by one of Granger's advisors, which shirked blame for an early, undisclosed agreement signed with ExxonMobil when it was later revealed that the agreement disproportionately favored the oil conglomerate (Mangal 2019). The general tenor of letters submitted by Guyanese not employed by either party voiced fear that the petroleum profits would not improve their living conditions. Such missives often displayed an international awareness: "Ask the citizens of Iraq, Libya, Syria, Nigeria, Uganda, Sudan, Venezuela, Brazil and Trinidad, how well the oil trickle-down theory is working for them so far" (Dudhnath 2019).

Across various press outlets, and irrespective of partisan debates, Guyanese commentators adeptly critiqued not only the failure of the Granger administration to negotiate a more equitable contract with ExxonMobil but also the unfulfilled promises of Ali's opposing camp. Ali campaigned on the platform that his administration would renegotiate the problematic ExxonMobil deal, but by August of 2020, after he had taken office and appointed former President Bharrat Jagdeo as his vice president, the administration stated that the deal would not be renegotiated. Guyanese responded by calling out the administration's backpedaling: "The government is squandering goodwill over the misappointments, missteps, and exclusion of people of perceived competence, credibility, and integrity and including those who stood with it in dark times. Guyanese will not forget its refusal to review the biased Exxon contract" (Philadelphia 2020). And although the US narrative resorted to a paternalistic logic, suggesting that the only recourse for a Guyanese populace that was lacking in both oil industry expertise and technological knowledge was to rely on outside aid, locals countered by calling on the government to seek assistance from experts among the Guyanese diaspora (*Kaieteur News* 2020b).

Guyanese were shrewd in proclaiming President Granger's corruption in the form of closed-door dealings with ExxonMobil and in terms of election malfeasance. But they also cast a critical eye on Irfaan Ali's corruption, after the former housing minister was brought up on nineteen fraud charges for selling government-owned land at undervalued prices to a number of state officials, including Jagdeo (Craig 2019). Nicknamed "Irfraud Ali" in the state-owned *Guyana Chronicle*, the politician also drew outrage from APNU+AFC supporters when it was uncovered that he claimed to have earned a degree from a nonexistent business college (*Guyana Chronicle* 2020).

In a column entitled "Our Racial Hypocrisy: The Post-Election Protests," published shortly after the elections and amidst PPP-led protests, David Hinds underscored how the two-party system destined Guyana to an endless racial tug-of-war in which the losers were bound to demonstrate because their interests would certainly be tabled. Hinds pointed out that the March 2020 post-election protests defied the local bromide that Afro-Guyanese were more prone to aggressive uprising, as Indo-Guyanese took to the streets and clashed with police. Hinds, an Afro-Guyanese, called for a more balanced view that took into account the all too real marginalization that the losing group, whether Black or Indian, was certain to feel: "African-Guyanese who denounce the protests are hypocritical. I am very sure that had the elections results [*sic*] gone the other way, African-Guyanese would have been on the streets burning tyres and blocking traffic. . . . Indian-Guyanese are also hypocritical. Those very protestors at Lusignan, Better Hope, Bath, and other areas, were only yesterday calling African-Guyanese hooligans for what they themselves are now doing. . . . No side would allow the other to govern Guyana. We always knew this, but we persist with the winner-loser paradigm. In the end, nobody wins an election in Guyana" (Hinds 2020). Hinds echoed the sentiments I heard from Guyanese at home and across the diaspora, the woeful acknowledgment that the system was deeply flawed and that the people, no matter their ethnicity, would always suffer.

In keeping with this book's focus on Guyana's global circulations, I would be remiss not to consider how the nation's oversized diaspora made sense of these issues and events. A nuanced analysis of Guyana's electoral crisis appeared in the form of a *Stabroek News* "From the Diaspora" column written by D. Alissa Trotz and Arif Bulkan. Calling for a dismantling of the winner-take-all dual-party system, Trotz and Bulkan noted that many Guyanese recognize rampant corruption on both sides. The authors trace Guyana's contemporary election mayhem to the collapse of the multiracial anticolonial movement—a movement in which Walter Rodney played an instrumental role—and "the intervention of the joined imperialist forces of the UK and the US and the convulsive coastal racial disturbances of the 1960s that delivered almost unshakable constituencies of African and Indian Guyanese to two major political parties" (Trotz and Bulkan 2020). Voicing deep concerns that the latest form of resource extractivism would lead to the destruction of the seabed, and arguing that it "has drastically raised the stakes for this miserable election," the authors make a compelling case for interpreting foreign intervention not as a democratic move in support of the Guyanese electorate but rather as the latest example of a long and well-documented practice of securing Western economic interests in the region (Trotz and Bulkan 2020).

An insightful observation offered in Trotz and Bulkan's column, one that disrupts the notion that the majority of Guyanese themselves are on board with the hard ethnic lines of the two-party system, is that, at varying moments, leaders of both parties have promised national unity, only to continually fail to curb the very authoritarian elements they claimed to eschew. Trotz and Bulkan paint a picture less of an electorate that is loyal to ethnic divisions and more of a state that is well practiced in stoking ethnic divides, falsifying elections, and paying lip service to "unity." In stressing the resistant voices of activists such as Walter Rodney and Andaiye, the Guyanese feminist and early member of the WPA, Trotz and Bulkan point to a tradition that contests the divisiveness of a destructive political system predicated on maintaining the suffering of the Guyanese masses.

The very international business press I have deconstructed here inadvertently bolsters Trotz and Bulkan's insistence that economic interests motivate intervention from Global North countries. As Luis Fernando Panelli posits in his answer to the titular query I referenced at the start of this chapter—"Is Guyana the New Oil El Dorado?"—"The good news is that Ali is a market-friendly politician and he is very concerned about the growth of his country, although there are serious corruption charges against him" (Panelli 2019, 368). The "good news," then, for the oil conglomerates and the countries in which they are based is that Ali is "market-friendly" first, and "concerned about the growth of his country" second. When outsiders discussed ethnic conflict during the election stalemate, they fell back on tired, simplified characterizations of Guyana as a state besieged by ethnic violence. Yet, as we have seen, Guyanese of various ethnic backgrounds were keenly aware that they were caught between a rock and a hard place, not only in terms of their deeply marred binary political system but also in relation to Western conglomerates, now once again searching for El Dorado within Guyana's waters.

## Death at the Dawn of Development

By the time the dust finally settled after the months-long elections stand-off, four murdered teenage boys and a seriously injured teenage girl were just the highest-profile casualties linked to violent election protests (although the girl's story received less coverage than that of the boys). In March of 2020, in the early protests by opposition PPP supporters (who objected when Granger claimed victory over Ali), police fatally shot Devon Hansraj, an Indo-Guyanese teenager from Cotton Tree in West Coast Berbice. According to police, the eighteen-year-old had chopped officers with a cutlass during a clash between law enforcement and the crowd of protesters—one officer reportedly sustained lacerations to his head and two fractured arms (*Kaieteur News* 2020d).[13] But Hansraj's father contested the police account that his son initiated the violence, instead explaining the boy's death as the result of a dispute he had with police and complaining that he was prohibited from viewing Devon's body (*Kaieteur News* 2020b). During the same protest, Anurada Sukra, an Indo-Guyanese teenage girl, was struck several times by stray police gunshots as she photographed the events from the sidelines (*Kaieteur News* 2020d). Then, on September 6, just five weeks after Ali had been sworn in, the mutilated bodies of two Afro-Guyanese teenage cousins, Isaiah Henry and Joel Henry, were found in coconut fields, also at Cotton Tree. With the area known to be primarily Indo-Guyanese, Afro-Guyanese residents from Number Five Village, where the boys had lived, saw the gruesome murders as racially motivated and took to the streets, setting more than a dozen tires ablaze and blocking a main road (*Guyana Times* 2020). Because of the impasse on the road, Anurada Sukra's family was unable to transfer her to another hospital better equipped to address her injuries (*Kaieteur News* 2020c).[14] And three days after the Henry boys' bodies were found, Haresh Singh, a seventeen-year-old Indo-Guyanese boy, whose relatives had been questioned in connection with the Henry boys' deaths, was brutally murdered.

In the days following these horrible acts of violence, the public assessment of the murders—in the Henry boys' case as hate crimes and in Haresh Singh's case as racialized retaliation—dominated the local press and even appeared in the *New York Times* (Yahya-Sakur and Kurmanaev 2020). In the *Times*, the murders fit neatly into the international repre-

sentation of Guyana as a nation wracked by ethnic conflict and a place
where the petroleum jackpot had exacerbated the political divides between Indo- and Afro-Guyanese (Yahya-Sakur and Kurmanaev 2020).[15]
But in the weeks and months ahead, in the local press, the murders of
the Henry boys and of Haresh Singh were not so facilely reconciled.
The police had written off Singh's relatives as suspects in the death of
the Henry boys, arraigning three other persons for the crime—a development that did not sit well with those who blamed Singh's family for
the murders. In their investigation of Haresh Singh's murder, the police
concluded that one of the suspects had confessed that "he was part of
an initial plot to murder Singh as revenge for Isaiah [Henry's] murder"
(*Guyana Times* 2021). The suspect, Phillip Anderson, said that one of
the Henry boys' relatives had enlisted him in the revenge killing. As for
the Henry boys' murder, forensic analysis of the crime scene cast doubt
on the characterization of the killings as hate crimes; it appeared that
the boys' bodies had been dumped in the coconut fields of Cotton Tree
after the fact (*News Room* 2020). These new details offered up by police
dominated the local press. The murder of the Henry cousins was also
resolved in the minds of police when they elicited a confession from
one of three suspects in the homicides (Bacchus 2021). Contrary to the
narrative that situated the boys' death as racially motivated, the suspect
confessed that they murdered the boys because they had interfered with
the three men's marijuana-growing operation (Bacchus 2021). The case
had finally come to a close after international authorities, including the
FBI and the CARICOM's Implementation Agency of Crime and Security, lent the Guyanese authorities technical assistance (Bacchus 2021).

 In the months leading up to and in the weeks following this resolution of the Henry boys' murder, a cloud of accusations and questioning
of police tactics and responses swirled. There were competing narratives
about the guilt and innocence of the victims and suspects, and what
provoked the crimes, as many Guyanese of both African and Indian ancestry were reluctant to accept police accounts of all three crimes (*Kaieteur News* 2021). The disconnect between the way these murders were
understood in the international press and the way they were addressed
in the local discourses is marked. Internationally, the spectacle of the
contested election and the spotlight of the oil discovery were deemed as
emblematic of the nation's fragmented ethnic landscape. On the ground,

however, the ethnic-conflict narrative was only part of a more complex set of discourses illustrating that both Afro- and Indo-Guyanese deeply distrusted the police and saw politicians as stoking the flames of the ethnic divide. One editorial in *Kaieteur News* summed up some of these local narratives: "One of those narratives was that since the boys bodies [*sic*] were found in a predominantly East Indian area that the deaths were a result of race-hate. Some disgraced politicians capitalized on this narrative, going so far as urging villagers to defend themselves. . . . It was even alleged during the police investigation that a politically-exposed person had told the family to say the deaths were race-based. This allegation, if true, would suggest that there were forces seeking to keep the race-based narrative alive" (*Kaieteur News* 2021). From the perspective of local discourses, the tragic murders of all the boys were co-opted by powerful, politically motivated "forces." These competing local narratives unsettle the simplistically demarcated international coverage that was bent on characterizing Guyana's electoral process as torn apart by politically motivated ethnic violence. With the world watching Guyana's transformation into a petrostate, four dead boys and an injured girl were arguably relegated to the sidelines: mere flash points that signified the political turmoil that had beset Guyana at a critical turning point.

While the murders of these youth made international headlines, the everyday forms of violence that Guyanese people experience, especially women and children, go unnoticed in the political economy of erasure that engulfs this country. Walking along the transplanted beach adjacent to the Marriott Hotel, overlooking the tenebrous waters of the Demerara River and the Atlantic Ocean beyond it, I was overcome by the feeling that this white sand beach marked the precipice of both modernization and catastrophe. My mother tells me that when I was an infant and had trouble sleeping, she would drive me to the seawall that juts alongside this beach, and that the sound of crashing waves and the cool breeze off the sea would lull me to sleep. Strolls along the seawall are a welcome respite for many of Georgetown's residents. But, for the anthropologist Shanya Cordis "The seawall is also a space of death, the killing fields where the disposed bodies of other Guyanese women and men have been similarly discovered and scrutinized in political discourse as indicative of the country's collective social decay and psyche of violence, viewed as impediments to social and economic advancement" (Cordis 2019, 18).

I recalled Cordis's writing when, in March of 2022, the body of a mixed-race Guyanese woman was found lying face down in the sand behind the Marriott (*Kaieteur News* 2022). Cordis recounts that another Guyanese woman, whose body had washed up on the shore in 2015, had been murdered and dismembered (Cordis 2019, 19).[16] That woman, Samantha Benjamin, had been working to expand her boutique and save money to purchase a vehicle. She did not live to see the fruits of her labor or the advancement of her country. Jennifer Sweetnam, the woman found in the sand behind the Marriott in 2022, had died of an apparent drowning, and had no "visible marks of violence on her body" (*Stabroek News* 2022c). Police said Sweetnam's relatives told them she suffered from depression (*Stabroek News* 2022c). The newspaper story implies that Sweetnam, who had worked as an information technology manager at Guyana's Mercy Hospital, had committed suicide (recall that Guyana has one of the world's highest suicide rates). Upon reading the story, I couldn't help but think about the juxtaposition of the luxury hotel and the contested beach just beyond its very tall gates—if the gates were not so high, the hotel crowd not so separated, or the hum of the sand dredges not so loud, might someone have seen or heard Sweetnam before it was too late? But perhaps she had drowned further down the shore only to be dredged up by the sea onto the Marriott's beach. If so, how can we make sense of the face-down lifeless body of a mixed-race Guyanese woman washed up at the brink of the sea and on the precipice of the country's transformation into a petrostate? Fragile ecologies are being dredged up in the waters where the sea swells delivered Jennifer Sweetnam's body. Guyana's most vulnerable citizens have always been casualties within the currents of global capitalism. My pointer broom strokes past the tumultuous beach and onto the road in the coda.

# Coda

## *The Road Ahead*

My great-grandmother, Tily Mackania Abinsetts, the daughter of an indentured laborer from India and an Afro-Guyanese man, outlived her Indian husband, Robert Ranjit Jaisingh. According to the oral history passed down in my family, Robert died of natural causes in his late sixties or early seventies. As my Aunt Gene tells the story, every day for about three weeks following Robert's death, Tily crossed the East Bank Public Road and walked to the family cemetery, where she sat and cried at Robert's grave. On her way back home from the cemetery one afternoon, she was struck by a motorcyclist who lost control when he hit a pothole in the road. The cyclist survived, but Tily died shortly after in the hospital. The motorcyclist was a man known to the family who was on his way to his job at the Atkinson Airfield (which would later become Timehri International Airport and then, Cheddi Jagan International Airport). The airfield, which had opened in 1941, was initially used as a US military base to protect the region against possible attacks from German forces during World War II. Ivan O. Carew, who worked at the airfield, remembered its transformation from what had been a hilly and forested terrain into the airstrip: "I remember it was the Elmhurst Contracting Co. that started the ball rolling; work went on practically non-stop, 24/7, cutting down trees, laying out sites for roads; huge Mac trucks transporting sand of which there was an abundance in the hills" (Carew 2011). Although Aunt Gene is unable to recall the year in which Tily died, her recollection of it being soon after the air force base opened places my great-grandmother's death in the mid-1940s. And Carew's account reveals that at this pivotal moment in Guyana's development, the nation's infrastructure depended on the transportation of an "abundance" of sand. Aunt Gene's and Carew's recollections underscore that the East

Bank Public Road was a busy throughway shuttling the workmen who toiled "24/7" at the airstrip.

Tily was not the only woman in my family who was the victim of an accident on the Public Road. A few years earlier, when my mother was between two and three years old, she was struck by a vehicle. Aunt Gene has told me this story many times. In one version, my mother was hit by a gigantic truck. "She was playing with your uncle near *the road*. He throw the ball and she run to catch it. And that big truck *hit your mother*. Just a little slip of a girl. And it send she flyin' into the air. It fractured she skull, nearly kill she. Months in hospital." In another telling, Aunt Gene says my mother was struck by a large Pan American Airlines wagon, which resembled a contemporary station wagon. At eighty-four years old, her mind is sharp and her propensity for story telling is unfiltered, but her details sometimes shift. In my mother's rendition, although she does not remember the accident itself, adults later told her that both she and her older brother had run into the road to retrieve the ball. After the accident, the truck driver said that in his split-second attempt to avoid hitting both children, he "saved the boy" and crashed into my mother. By all accounts, my mother was severely injured—her skull was fractured—and she spent months in the hospital.

My mother's body still bears scars from the accident, and it is difficult for me to gauge how much of her reticence in terms of providing details should be chalked up to the young age at which it occurred or to lasting trauma. These are understandably dark corners for my mom, and I am reluctant to rustle them with my pointer broom. For two generations of women in my family, the Public Road has been a site of death and grave injury. Still, while the road took my great-grandmother, it did not take my mother. Others have not been as fortunate. Fatalities are all too common along the country's primary avenue, which has a long history as a lawless, poorly maintained, and violent thoroughfare. The vehicular deaths of residents whose villages hug the road continue to this day, and in the present moment, Guyana's campaign for development has coincided with renewed calls for more safety measures as trucks hauling sand and other materials dominate the inadequate street.

I wrote about the ways in which the boulevard ravaged my maternal line in an op-ed published in *Stabroek News* entitled "Danger Ahead: A Crisis of Roads and Sand" (LaBennett 2022). Having visited Guyana just weeks before penning the piece, I had heard story after story about how the relentless traffic was leaving commuters stranded as the avenue was beset by commercial vehicles and materials being transported for trade and construction. While this was a nuisance for the businesspeople and taxi drivers zooming between the airport and the capital, for the villagers who lived along the route there was a constant struggle to maintain their own and their children's safety. Deadly accidents abounded, and complaints about the motorway unfolded in the newspapers in vividly frightening imagery: "Many drivers are compelled to navigate on the other side in cat-and-mouse dodges with oncoming traffic; this is neither recommended nor safe. It can be tests of nerve, skill, and vehicular and internal fortitude. To those congested pictures one can add the constant passage of loaded sand trucks and other machined beasts of burden; all loaded, all racing to some destination, all ignoring danger areas and rushing pell-mell forward" (*Kaieteur News* 2019). The government responded with promises and plans for new and expanded roads (*Guyana Chronicle* 2021). I saw many of these new avenues already in use in August of 2022. But the Public Road remains congested and overrun—it is both the literal pathway to development and the symbol of all that torments Guyana (LaBennett 2022).

In the damaging *New York Times* representation that I deconstructed earlier, Guyana's lack of roads emerges as a sign of its unpreparedness to handle the oil boom; Clifford Krauss points to the country having "only three paved highways" as indicative of its severe underdevelopment (Krauss 2018a). We might contrast this with the anthropologist Julie Livingston's depiction of the insatiable quest to build more and more roads as exemplifying what she calls self-devouring growth (Livingston 2019). Roads play a prominent role in Livingston's analysis of Botswana as a parable for humans consuming themselves in the relentless global push for urbanization. She writes that at independence Botswana had only twelve roads, but by 2019 it had constructed over seven thousand (Livingston 2019, 86; LaBennett 2022). The building of telecommunications, roads, hospitals, and schools, supported by diamond mining, solidified Botswana's identity as a successful upper-middle-income country, but also situated it at the confluence of significant forms of climate and environmental destruction, including ever-rising temperatures, a sinking water table, and endangered wildlife (Livingston 2019, 3). Along with this troubling picture of Botswana's ecological future, Livingston details the tragic social impacts of self-devouring growth: among many heart-wrenching examples is her recounting of an incident when a five-ton truck collided with a bus carrying fifty passengers. Six people died and sixteen others sustained serious injuries (Livingston 2019, 88).

As new roads, malls, hotels, and office buildings are constructed throughout Guyana, the sand pits multiply, deepen, and widen, and the trucks hauling the vital resource across the country ceaselessly speed along the nation's main artery. The acceleration of road works projects is displacing people and animals, clearing trees, and ransacking sand deposits. There is a deeply foreboding sense that resonates within the small East Bank villages that flank the Public Road. At an inflection point in which the country is racing to modernize its infrastructure, the road ahead is rife with uncertainty and danger for its rural citizens. Although signs of growth appear everywhere, thus far the oil wealth has only exacerbated the social and geographic divide between these rural communities and the capital. My cousins in Sarah Johanna complain that the noise from the never-ending stampede of trucks and heavy machinery rattles them in their beds as they try to sleep at night. Self-devouring growth is already choking the nation with noise pollution, overworked roadways ill equipped to support commutes to work, school, and medical treatment, and mounting vehicular deaths. While some might counter that road deaths are the unfortunate side effect of the social improvements that additional roadways and hospitals will bring, we must also weigh the catastrophic environmental consequences of such forms of "growth" (Livingston 2019; LaBennett 2022).

We must consider the accidents that ended my great-grandmother's life and marred my mother's as haunting signposts along the road to development. As an indentured laborer, Tily's mother, Poragia Shewdesi, laid the earlier groundwork that brought Guyana to the crossroads of capitalist expansion. In the *longue durée* of this nation, through Indigenous dispossession, African enslavement, and Asian indenture, the upheaval of Guyanese women's lives, and their reproductive and physical labor, have propelled global capitalism, but their stories have been erased. These stories, along with the example of the woman who washed up on the beach alongside the Marriott Hotel, and the framing of the murders of four teenagers killed during the violence surrounding the national election, illustrate the centrality and the precarity of Guyana's women and children in the face of the nation's continuing quest for advancement and engagement with the global economy.

\* \* \*

The Guyanese people I know are anxiously observing the quickly unfolding tides of change lapping up on our shores. ExxonMobil's presence has been accompanied by a steady influx of multinational corporations with ties to the United States, China, Syria, Brazil, and Venezuela, among other countries. In some respects, the tides appear to be turning, and where once Guyanese looking for better lives found themselves excluded in places like Barbados and Venezuela, since 2016, up to sixty thousand Venezuelans have taken up residence in Guyana.[1] Resource extraction also transplants self-devouring growth across borders. Gold and oil extraction along the Venezuela-Guyana border evinces this: "In these borderlands and coastal waters between Guyana and Venezuela, a quiet regional war for resources is beginning to emerge, one in which the capitalist extraction of petroleum and gold veil even deeper forms of subjugation that trap the present in a long history of violence" (Tamboli 2019, 422). Those forms of subjugation include the devastating destruction/contamination of forest land and waterways that sustain life for Indigenous Guyanese, and the trafficking of Guyanese and Venezuelan women who supply miners and smugglers with sex (Tamboli 2019, 431). Just as African enslaved women and Indian indentured women were brought to sustain global capitalism in colonial Guiana, today the poorest Guyanese and Venezuelan women are trafficked as part of the infrastructure of violent extraction.

The activism of Andaiye, the Guyanese feminist who worked alongside Walter Rodney, underscores not only the Guyanese people's strident contestation of the state's role in fomenting the interethnic antagonisms that have occupied both local and foreign reporting but also their incisive understanding of how global capitalism stokes violence against women and maintains structures of inequality. In a speech delivered in 2002, she outlined a sweeping vision of the stakes of a feminist campaign attuned to how economic growth in places like Guyana masks gendered inequalities, relegates the majority of Indigenous peoples to abject poverty, and kowtows to foreign investors "always poised for flight" to the next country where they can find cheap labor (Andaiye in Trotz 2020, 18).[2] Andaiye spotlights these hierarchies and power dynamics as she lays out an inclusive vision of global feminist activism: "What would follow from this is that the campaign must be global; that different sectors with different levels of power must organize autonomously so they can cross their divides on the basis of equality; and that for the campaign to serve the interests of all who are exploited, it must be led and waged in the interests of the poorest women, who bear the greatest burden of unwaged and low-waged caring labour, which is the foundation of all economies" (Andaiye in Trotz 2020, 18). Such a vision for a global feminism that looks out from Guyana must equally account for the positionalities of all women, including African, Indian, Dougla, Chinese, and Indigenous women. It must take into consideration the opaque corners of the political economy of erasure that exploits women who cross borders into Barbados and into the Amazonian-Caribbean borderlands, but also within national borders in centrally located coastal towns. It must prioritize the most vulnerable people whose labor supports capitalist expansion. And it must preserve the fragile ecologies that sustain life for all of us.

How can we position the attention to extractivist expansion, read through the specter of "ethnic conflict," alongside the insights of the previous chapters? Ultimately, this book has illustrated that oil may fuel the transformation of this nation's presence on the world stage, but its global outreach and its pertinence to transnational processes have been constituted not only in its resources but also in the inscrutable, but deeply meaningful and complex cultural negotiations of its ethnic groups, and its women in particular. In the previous chapter, my reading of local and international coverage of Guyana's presidential election revealed how the drive for capitalist extraction contorts the narratives around ethnic conflict—considered by many to be Guyana's distinguishing feature. However, the chapters of this book have cast the reductive rubric of "ethnic conflict" into sharper relief. Chapter 1 repositioned Guyanese women's self-identifications within cross-racial intimacies and kinship formations to untangle the knotty contours of a political economy of erasure. Themes of marriage and family resurfaced in chapter 2, as I countered the stereotype of the Guyanese woman as homewrecker with a historical analysis of migration and intermarriage that conjoins Guyana and Barbados. Contradictory gendered racializations of Guyanese women as at once promiscuous troublemakers and subservient homemakers channel across the globe, from India to the Caribbean, and from Guyana to Barbados and back again. Taking a pointer broom to the interstitial spaces of Afro-Asian intimacies and transnational kinship ties, this book's first two chapters unsettled gendered racializations embodied at the autoethnographic level in my Dougla great-grandmother, and at the mass-mediated level in the persona of Rihanna. Although Barbadian anxieties over competition for scarce resources have pigeonholed the Guyanese woman as a foreign threat, Rihanna's Guyanese ancestry is erased in a wave of Bajan nationalism. Global superstar RiRi reemerges as the symbol of Bajan tourism in chapter 3, with beach sand clinging to her bare knees—erosion and erasure are the by-products of the ecological calamities that are concretized in the inextricable linking of Caribbean women's bodies to conceptualizations of environmental beauty.

Sleek images like that of a bikini-clad Rihanna have come to occupy global popular representations of women and shorelines in the region, but violent extractive industries devastate the environment and sustain the unseen trafficking of women and girls. Guyana is on the threshold of economic transformation, but its impending environmental disasters, whether in the form of disappearing sand deposits or a looming oil catastrophe, will have malignant repercussions for all of us. Looking at and looking out from Guyana affords a shift in perspective from narratives—in the news and entertainment media—that muddle these undercurrents, just as they position the nation as everywhere and nowhere. The cyclical refrain of this coda is intentional; like the *sssweeep, sweep, sweep* of the pointer broom and the back-and-forth flow of the tides, pernicious global race-gender formations and the very resources that shape the Caribbean and fuel the world traverse Guyana's shores, and are swept out across space and time, and back again. Writing against the ways in which this country has been depicted as isolated and backwards, this book has traced the intercontinental patterns of movement that connect Guyana's women and its ecology to larger processes charted over vast landscapes and temporalities—like ephemeral broom strokes on a sandy beach in the morning light.

# ACKNOWLEDGMENTS

Even though looking at the world from the vantage points of life in Guyana and Brooklyn has marked my scholarship from the start, this project necessitated a recalibration of my approach to academic work. Writing during the COVID-19 pandemic, just after moving away from family and friends in New York, compounded the solitary work of completing this manuscript, but also impressed upon me an urgent sense of purpose. This project forced me to identify and strengthen new muscles, balance love and respect for family alongside scholarly pursuits, and confront with fresh eyes the social and environmental challenges people in Guyana, the Caribbean, and across the diaspora face. My hard work alone would not have realized this book. I relied on many people to whom I am immensely grateful—colleagues, mentors, friends, and family who have supported me throughout the years and whose encouragement enlivened the pages of this text.

This book would not exist if it were not for the fortitude, humor, humility, and love that extends from my family across the Guyanese diaspora. The sisterhood between my mother, Iris LaBennett, and my aunt, Gene King, has always been a source of inspiration. Their pointer broom strokes swept us to new shores, sifted through painful obstacles along the way, and uncovered more solid ground for me to stand on. Stories passed down from our ancestors and shared with eloquence, wit, and searing insight from Aunt Gene animated the autoethnographic and oral history portions of this work. My mother's tenacity, coupled with her uncompromising insistence on speaking her own truth, has made me a more courageous scholar. Although my mom and Aunt Gene provided the family history that anchors this book, I am thankful to all my aunts, uncles, and cousins for grounding my awareness of what it means to be Guyanese.

In Guyana, members of my extended family, especially Barney and Wayne Jaisingh, were expert guides who set me on paths that unlocked key components of the book's chapters. Everyone in Sarah Johanna welcomed me warmly every time I went home. Anne Jaisingh's friendly face was often the first I saw on our little road. I also want to acknowledge the Guyanese folks of all stripes whose stories I encountered in the local press and share in this book: women and children whose lives were upended by political turmoil; and feminists and environmental activists who speak back to the extractivist violence that shapes the nation's future. I am sincerely appreciative, too, for the assistance and expertise of the archivists at the Walter Rodney Archives.

When I began the research for this book, a fellowship from Cornell University's Atkinson Center for a Sustainable Future propelled me to advance my understanding of climate catastrophe, while funding from the Vice Provost for Research and Advanced Study and from the Society for the Humanities provided crucial travel support. I thank Kevin C. Quin for the research assistance he provided at the start of this project. I am grateful for the network of colleagues that stems from my time at Cornell: two preeminent Caribbeanists, Gerard Aching and Viranjini Munasinghe, listened with warmth and enthusiasm, and offered valuable feedback while I laid the project's foundations; Kevin Gaines and Penny Von Eschen served as mentors whose approach to life and work were shining examples; Judith Byfield, Renate Ferro, Renee Milligan, Tim Murray, Carina Ray, Samantha Sheppard, and Dagmawi Woubshet were kindred spirits who shared meals, sparked ideas, and made Ithaca feel like home. And I will forever hold dear my bond with Lyrae Van Clief-Stefanon, whose radiance, creativity, and friendship have given me strength.

I found an invigorating new home at the University of Southern California, where I completed this work. I am thankful for funding for a book workshop provided by Dean Sherry Velasco and the Dana and David Dornsife College of Letters, Arts, and Sciences. And I was fortunate to have landed in the Department of American Studies and Ethnicity (ASE), where I joined dedicated colleagues: Alicia Chavez, Juan De Lara, Adrian De Leon, Chris Finley, Sonia Flores, Stanley Huey, Lanita Jacobs, Kara Keeling, Dorinne Kondo, Kitty Lai, Lydie Moudileno, Viet Nguyen, Jujuana Preston, Leland Saito, George Sánchez, and Jackie Wang. I am especially indebted to colleagues whose boundless spirit of collegiality helped smooth my transition to Los Angeles: with consummate camaraderie, Evelyn Alsultany helped me navigate a new place while finishing this book; conversations with Sarah Gualtieri boosted my will power; Edwin Hill's positive vibes set a refreshing tone for this chapter of my career; Natalia Molina's warm welcome eased the sense of disorientation that accompanied my relocation; John Carlos Rowe performed miraculous acts of administrative support; Nayan Shah's wise council, scholarly example, and conviviality were beacons guiding my path; Karen Tongson's collaborative spirit prompted me to cultivate fruitful exchanges; and Francille Rusan Wilson's devotion to Black studies along with her warm-heartedness made a world of difference. I am also thankful for the network that extended from these colleagues and beyond ASE, including Ange-Marie Hancock Alfaro, Kenneth Foster, Jane Junn, Jessica Ng, and Peter Redfield.

I had truly remarkable early mentors who nurtured my academic trajectory and transformed a first-generation college student into a scholar; Ann duCille set a singular example of excellence and continues to motivate me to write with passion; Elizabeth Traube cultivated my interest in popular youth culture and anthropology; and the late Steven Gregory instilled a profound love of ethnography that energizes me to this day.

A compassionate circle of colleagues and friends, new and old, has modeled innovative, rigorous scholarship coupled with good-heartedness. My gratitude to Vanessa Agard-Jones, A. Lynn Bolles, Jacqueline Nassy Brown, Arnaldo Cruz-Malavé, Arlene Dávila, James Davis, Nicole Fleetwood, Farah Jasmine Griffin, Beverly Guy-Sheftall, Loren Kajikawa, Joe Lowndes, Irma McClaurin, Michael Omi, Laura Pulido, Gina Athena Ulysse, and Howard Winant. Special thanks to Dána-Ain Davis for listening and advising thoughtfully during long phone calls; Glenn Hendler for initially welcoming me into American studies; and John L. Jackson Jr. for always supporting my work. Elizabeth Chin offered a ready ear, artful, razor-sharp comments, and a much-needed vote of confidence that permeates the pages of this book. Her scholarship has always galvanized me, and her visionary leadership is a gift to contemporary ethnographers. And, since our undergraduate days, it has been a privilege to collaborate with Daniel Martinez HoSang and to call him my friend.

An earlier draft of this book benefited immeasurably from Deborah A. Thomas's discerning eye and Alissa Trotz's generative suggestions. I am incredibly appreciative for their deeply constructive feedback, which urged me to clarify my argument and my intentions.

One particularly rewarding outcome of this project was the ways in which it connected me with scholars, scientists, artists, and activists working on and in Guyana, throughout the Caribbean, and across its diaspora. At every turn, colleagues introduced me to their friends and associates, expanding my support network. A cluster of panels that Kamala Kempadoo and Alissa Trotz organized for the annual meeting of the Caribbean Studies Association made me realize that I was not working alone. Ulric (Neville) O'D Trotz and Andre Mann generously shared their vast knowledge and expertise at a key juncture. Aliyah Khan's willingness to help me solve an archival mystery was a true example of scholarly goodwill. I thank her and the group of experts she enlisted: Gaiutra Bahadur, Najnin Islam, Rajiv Mohabir, Lisa Outar, and Kaneesha Parsard. Grace Aneiza Ali was an essential interlocutor who fortified my resolve to realize this work and encouraged me to write about art elsewhere—sparking new collaborations and scholarly avenues. Thanks to Grace, I connected with the artist Deborah Jack, who graciously allowed me to write about her work. Yonette Alleyne's delicious cuisine brought Guyana to Southern California. Earlier collaborations with Shelley Worrell and Janluk Stanislas fostered connections with key cultural sites in Brooklyn and supported my commitment to community-engaged pedagogy. A special shout-out to Mohamed Q. Amin and the Caribbean Equality Project for sharing their stories with my students and for tirelessly supporting Caribbean LGBTQ+ immigrants in Queens, New York.

I am thankful for the care with which Jennifer Hammer and the editorial board at New York University Press have guided this, my second project with the press. And I am extremely grateful to the anonymous reviewers whose judicious attention to the manuscript and wonderfully constructive suggestions led me to improve the finished product in a myriad of ways.

I am deeply grateful to the artist Keisha Scarville for contributing the beautiful photograph that graces this book's cover and for rendering Guyana and its diaspora with such intentionality throughout her brilliant work.

Through The OpEd Project, Katie Orenstein empowered me to amplify my voice as a public-facing scholar and connected me with the genius that is Harriet A. Washington, and an amazing sisterhood of change makers, including Christina Greer, Zeba Khan, Kirsten Swinth, and Christiana Zenner. Katie and Harriet offered support that extended well beyond my Public Voices Fellowship, and Christina Greer has been particularly generous in making introductions and sharing contacts.

Decades-long friendships with a core group of close confidants, including Nicole Davis, David Drogin, and Melissa Woods, have gotten me through hard times and made celebratory moments even better. Distance and a global pandemic could not sever a steadfast bond with Oscar Montero and Johnny Loflin, who have demonstrated what a lifetime with a loving partner looks like and have taught me how to appreciate what really matters—looking out for each other, creating space for what feeds your soul, and knowing when to say, "I'll catch the next one."

My dog, Bagel, was my constant companion when I began this project, and his spirit continues to comfort me through all that I do. I hit the jackpot when I met my partner, Shawn McDaniel. This would not have happened without your love, devotion, and unwavering understanding. No one has uplifted me more. For keeping me afloat, for being the best sounding board, for always believing in me, for meeting every challenge we have faced with astonishing reserves of patience, humor, and thoughtfulness, I thank you. Until the end of time, I truly adore you. You're my favorite.

# NOTES

PREFACE

1 I am grateful to Alissa Trotz for encouraging me to engage Brathwaite's conceptualization of *tidalectics*.

2 Because much of Guyana is below sea level, houses are built on tall stilts. The area below the house, the Bottom House, serves as shelter for domesticated animals such as chickens, as a place to hang hammocks, as a play area for children, and to house family-owned storefronts like Rum Shops and small convenience stores. The Bottom House and the yard, which is often cultivated as a kitchen garden, are extensions of the home.

3 For a thoughtful analysis of gendered violence and the cutlass, see Kaneesha Cherelle Parsard's "Cutlass: Objects toward a Theory of Representation" (Parsard 2016). Although I am emphasizing the cutlass and the pointer broom as gendered instruments, I do not mean to suggest that they are the exclusive domain of their respective gendered users. For example, a female broom maker (today these are skilled artisans; most women purchase ready-made brooms) may wield a cutlass to cut down the coconut leaves necessary to make brooms. Moreover, I have observed male gardeners simultaneously using the cutlass *and* the pointer broom to groom yards and clear debris. But both examples involve skilled artisans/workers. In common, daily use, the pointer broom is most often used by women, while the cutlass is used by men.

4 This book utilizes the multiple and inconstant racial categorizations employed in Guyana historically and in the present day. The descendants of enslaved Africans are alternatively referred to as "African," "Afro-Guyanese," and "Black" in contemporary everyday conversation, and "Negro" in colonial-era documents. People use the terms "Indo-Guyanese," "Indian," and "East Indian" to denote descendants of Indian indentured laborers. "Coolie" was used in the colonial era and is still used conversationally today. And the country's national census lists East Indian, African/Black, Amerindian, Chinese, Mixed, Portuguese, White, and Others as its racial categories. To this list of racial categories this book adds "Dougla," a local designation describing individuals of African and Indian parentage.

INTRODUCTION

1 See Idrovo, Grant, and Yanoff regarding brain drain (2022). For data on poverty, see Sekhani 2017. For statistics on alcoholism, see World Health Organization

2018. US data on sex trafficking in Guyana can be found in US Department of State 2020. For data on suicide and domestic partner violence, see Henry 2020. For a thoughtful analysis of relational gendered violence as it pertains to Black and Amerindian women, see Cordis 2019.

2 Here, my argument is related to but diverges from the case Ulysse makes about Haiti: "Throughout its history, Haiti, like its women, has been both hyper-visible and invisible" (Ulysse 2015, 54). I contend that Guyana has been central to global processes but overwhelmingly elided in geopolitical and popular discourses, while its women have also been instrumental but obscured actors.

3 While English is Guyana's official language, Guyanese Creole or "Creolese," which blends English with African, Indian, and Amerindian languages, is widely spoken, in addition to other languages including Hindustani among older Indians, and Amerindian languages such as Arawak, Wapishana, Macusi, Akawaio, and Wai-Wai.

4 Throughout this text, I use the name of the British colony, "Guiana," to connote colonial British Guiana, and the contemporary spelling, "Guyana" to refer to the independent nation.

5 Jagan was elected chief minister in 1953 when Britain granted Guiana home rule. However, the British reversed course because Jagan's Marxist leanings alarmed foreign investors who had lucrative gold and oil projects in the country (Bahadur 2020). Focused on protecting those interests, Britain overthrew the nation's popularly elected government. Although the British governor suspended Guiana's constitution and removed Jagan from office in 1953, he later served as premier of British Guiana between 1961 and 1964, and was elected president in 1992. For a concise analysis of Britain's role in ousting Jagan and how grabs for oil and other resources sparked these processes, see Bahadur 2020. The ways in which the CIA furthered US and British interests by branding Jagan a Communist and delegitimizing his 1953 election demonstrate that the nation's politics have always been intricately connected to broader geopolitical, resource-driven power struggles. And transnational kinship ties have been a critical element of these dynamics: Janet Rosenberg Jagan, a White, Jewish woman from Chicago who married Jagan in 1953, became the secretary of the early PPP coalition led by Cheddi Jagan and Burnham. Janet's political affiliations, including her membership in the Young Communist League, were held up as evidence of her and her husband's Communist affiliations. Janet Jagan would go on to serve as the first female prime minister and the first female president of Guyana, when she succeeded her husband after his death, also making her the first American-born woman to be elected president of any country. Supporters of the Jagans affectionately referred to her as "Comrade Janet" and as "the blue-eyed *bhowgie*" (borrowing the Hindi term for sister-in-law). In light of this book's arguments around the racialized and gendered erasure of Guyanese women, Janet Jagan's political ascendance to the top echelons of government begs future scholarship.

6 I joined the outcries on Twitter: "Misrepresenting Guyana as a place 'forgotten by time' where children play 'naked in the muggy heat' denies its complexity.

Dangerous distortions like this inform the perilous trajectory of my homeland's oil boom. Do better @nytimes" (LaBennett 2018b).

7 Of course, both articles' narratives, alternately portraying Guyanese as indolent and as industrious, are equally reductive and flawed.

8 It is fitting that the Windrush generation was named after a ship, the *Empire Windrush*, which brought immigrants from Jamaica to Tilbury in 1948. It is also significant that many of the Windrush immigrants arrived as children and had resided in the UK for decades before having their legality for citizenship questioned, while "losing the right to work, to rent property, to receive pensions, to access their bank accounts or even to access vital healthcare—a particularly cruel twist of fate as so many of those affected have spent their lives in the service of [the British] National Health Service" (quoted in Gentleman 2018).

9 Grant's delineation of ringbang resonates with this book's application of *tidalectics*. The musician conceived of ringbang as a fusion of Caribbean musical genres, and as an aesthetic and a philosophy (Rollins 2000). In defining it, Grant said, "Ringbang is the thing that makes the soul quiet. That in a musical concept is rhythm. A child is given ringbang when a mother rocks it in her arms. Ringbang allowed the slaves to communicate. Ringbang is a bridge that allows us to stop being so insular; it is a concept predicated on our being able to communicate with one another" (quoted in Rollins 2000).

10 And Guyanese culinary delights and spirits, once siloed in Caribbean neighborhoods, now seem to be transcending these immigrant food hubs. Faye Gomes, a Guyanese chef, received accolades from food critics for "one of London's best street food trucks" anchored to the street near the Elephant and Castle Station, a twenty-minute car ride from Brixton (Nunn 2019). These examples, along with the story of Guyanese establishing an enclave in Schenectady, a three-hour drive from New York City, are part of a new chapter in the broadening reach of the Guyanese diaspora. These new enclaves, also emerging in relatively remote places like Lake County, Florida, are rich but for the most part understudied sites of Caribbean migration. Until the oil discovery, this widening presence was largely ignored in popular discourses, but with increasing frequency, I have begun to see Guyana materialize across multiple US and global cultural registers. And this channeling of Guyanese people and culture is a quiet trend across world cities and even in suburban areas. In both urban and rural New York, on bar menus in toney gentrified Brooklyn, and in remote, intellectual Ithaca, I found El Dorado, one of Guyana's deep, dark rums, to be the central ingredient in of-the-moment cocktails. In New York's Soho, far from "outer borough" neighborhoods in Caribbean Brooklyn and Queens, I ate Guyanese-style chow mein at Miss Lily's, a trendy restaurant with additional outposts in Manhattan's East Village, Negril, and Dubai. In Los Angeles, I ordered goat curry and *salara* (a sweet, red coconut bread) prepared by Yonette Alleyne, a Guyanese chef. I also ate pepper pot seasoned with Guyanese *cassareep* served in pricey touristy restaurants in Barbados.

11 *Stabroek News* covered the opening, and the accompanying images of audiences at Caribbean Cinemas in Giftland Mall reveal a modern shopping center that shares many similarities with US malls. However, we should resist simplistically pointing to the mall as proof that Georgetown is modern. The anthropologist Arlene Dávila has written insightfully about the boom of shopping malls across Latin America, complicating the assumption that malls signify a "coming of age" for these countries (Dávila 2016). She suggests that the development of the mall in Latin America "is best understood in relation to the speculative processes it unleashes around land and space and especially in terms of its marketing of flashy, modern, organized spaces for leisure and consumption anchored in the illusion of accessibility to a middle-class world" (Dávila 2016, 3).

12 Rénee Alexander Craft has argued that forms of symbolic identification with Africa and Wakanda like those that Guyanese at Giftland Mall enacted are part of a "Wakanda Diaspora carnival," embodied performances that connected an imagined community across the African diaspora (Craft 2018, 386).

13 But Wright was subsequently cast to play "a real-life Black Panther," the Trinidadian physician/activist Altheia Jones-LeCointe, in Steve McQueen's *Mangrove*, part of an acclaimed Amazon Prime anthology called *Small Axe* that explored London's Caribbean community between the late 1960s and mid-1980s.

14 The Guyanese roots of famous women such as the groundbreaking politician Shirley Chisholm and global superstar Rihanna have not translated into the way these personae are understood in the American popular culture. As a researcher who has studied Caribbean girls' interactions with US popular culture and looking back on my shared sense of identity with Eddy Grant, I can only imagine how much it would have meant to me as a young girl to have been able to identify with a political trailblazer like Chisholm at a time when representations of Guyanese people were so few and far between. Chisholm's father was born in Guyana and moved to Barbados, where he met her mother. Although Chisholm referred to her father as "a native of" Guyana in her memoir, *Unbought and Unbossed*, historian Anastasia Curwood notes that he was born in Guyana to Barbadian parents (Curwood 2023, 9). Still, the family's migratory process mirrors the long history of kinship ties between the two countries.

15 Yahima self-identifies as "Woman, man, two-spirit." Critics noted that "two spirit" is an Indigenous American term that can refer to both intersex and trans people, but doesn't always indicate those identities (Hill 2020).

16 Fans of the show would be quick to point out that the character who murders Yahima, Montrose Freeman, subsequently comes out as gay. In flashbacks *Lovecraft* reveals that Montrose's queer identity provoked his own father to beat him violently. In this way, the show suggests that his annihilation of Yahima is perhaps a twisted attempt to silence their queerness, and his own, during a historical moment (the 1950s) when coming out would subject him to violent discrimination. For me, Yahima's murder echoed historian Marjoleine Kars's account of the brutal killing of an unnamed Indigenous Guyanese woman, which sparked the 1763

Berbice slave rebellion (Kars 2016). Kars documents how a Dutch colonial over-seer ordered three enslaved men to string up and beat an enslaved woman named Charmante along with the Indigenous woman. Although Charmante survived, the brutal beating set a year-long rebellion in motion (Kars 2016, 39–40). Kars presents the violence which the enslaved men enacted as part and parcel of the struggle for emancipation under a brutal colonial system of gender inequalities in which "controlling women . . . became an integral part of power among male rebels" (44).

17  Needless to say, Yahima does not get to voice their preferred pronouns during the episode, but I am using "they/them" to connote the character's intersex identity.

18  Guyanese cuisine was also featured, around the same time, in another "eater series," PBS's *No Passport Required*, hosted by the New York–based, globally recognized celebrity chef, Marcus Samuelsson. Whereas, in my view, Ramsay's program channeled in tired colonial tropes, Samuelsson's visit to the Indo-Guyanese community in Queens, New York, presented a more sophisticated overview of the Indian, African, Chinese, Portuguese, and Amerindian elements of Guyanese cuisine.

19  Also notable is Shona N. Jackson's book, *Creole Indigeneity: Between Myth and Nation in the Caribbean* (2012). Jackson relies on "Creole" rather than "Dougla" to connote people of African and Indian descent. I would argue that "Dougla" is a more salient emic term. What Jackson more explicitly terms "Creole indigeneity" represents an original framing that differs from the one I advance in this book, even though we begin from the somewhat mutual starting point of being racially mixed Guyanese.

20  But while the important studies outlined in this paragraph have begun to fill gaping holes to advance fresh understandings of Guyana and Guyanese, the words "Guyana" and/or "Guyanese" remain conspicuously absent from the covers of all but two of these texts. This omission of the country's name perhaps signals an anxiety on the part of publishers, who may fear that Guyana lacks name recognition, which of course ironically contributes to its invisibility.

21  I thank James Davis for initially encouraging me to explore the mudhead stereotype.

22  Among the many indicators of the flood's devastation, Vaughn notes that when over fifty-two inches of rain fell within an eight-day period in early January 2005, Leptospirosis, "a zoonotic waterborne disease, knew no boundaries, wreaking havoc across rural and urban environs alike," and disaster shelters housed more than five thousand people, over half of whom were children (Vaughn 2022, 4, 35). Vaughn posits that although the disaster in Guyana differed from New Orleans's Hurricane Katrina in terms of "infrastructural origins, needs, and environments, race emerged in both locales as a condition of vulnerability" (Vaughn 2022, 7).

23  Although Rodney's points about Africans molding the land are critical, this framing of Guyana as a swampland that was humanized only after the arrival of Africans can be read as reproducing the logic of the settler-colonial project

that dispossessed Indigenous peoples. Shanya Cordis astutely troubles this logic: "By mobilizing a discourse of having labored the land as slaves and indentured servants, creoles assert their claims of belonging, in turn displacing indigenous ontological being in Guyana and the Caribbean more broadly" (Cordis 2019, 29).

24  Among the examples the *Oxford English Dictionary* uses are "shut up, you Milesian mudhead, and listen to me," from Hay's *Brighter Britain!* and "not in those many words, but plainly enough for one who is not altogether a mud-head" from *Kim*.

25  Following Prashad, I have chosen not to put the word "coolie" in scare quotes even though I acknowledge the extremely negative history of the term. Prashad offers a useful genealogy of the word (Prashad 2001).

26  In "Autoethnographies of a Pandemic from Brooklyn's Epicenter," Theoharis et al. illustrate how, especially during the isolation and curb in travel stemming from COVID-19, autoethnography was privileged over more traditional ethnographic methods. Their collection of autoethnographies written by students at Brooklyn College, scholars who were at once at the epicenter of the battle against the coronavirus in the United States, and situated in the heart of West Indian Brooklyn, offers a compelling case for the efficacy of autoethnography as a methodology uniquely suited to a moment in which researchers were, due to social-distancing guidelines and travel restrictions, quite literally prohibited from engaging in traditional forms of participant observation and ethnographic interviewing, while also acutely focused on the poignancy and potentiality of centering family relations.

27  Here, I am also borrowing from Michael Omi and Howard Winant's influential theorization of racial formation and their notion of "racial projects" (Omi and Winant 1994/1986).

28  Audra Simpson advances a related notion of "ethnographic refusal" in her treatment of the asymmetrical power relations that inform research on Indigenous peoples (Simpson 2007).

29  This rate of outmigration has remained the highest in the world but has been in decline. By 2020, the UN Population Division estimated that 36.4 percent of Guyana's native-born population was living aboard (Buchholz 2022).

## CHAPTER 1. FROM FULL NEGRO TO DOUGLA GIRL

1  My goal here is related to Saidiya Hartman's endeavors, particularly in "Venus in Two Acts," in which she argues that her aim is "not to give voice to the slave but rather to imagine what cannot be verified" (Hartman 2008, 12). Although my treatment is not "a history written with and against the archive" in quite the same way as Hartman's (2008, 12), I want to acknowledge how archival research, oral histories, and autoethnography, my primary methods, even when combined, continue to construct incomplete histories, leaving gaps, fissures, and unexplained dark areas.

2  Here, I follow Gates and Appiah in interpreting Hurston's autobiography as an "anthropology of the self" (Gates and Appiah 1993, 242), due to its reliance on the

anthropological gaze situated alongside hyperbolic folk songs and other elements that resisted truthful self-representation (Gates and Appiah 1993, 244).

3  My nod to Jamaica Kincaid's scathing testimonial on the ugliness of Caribbean tourism, *A Small Place*, is intentional. And although much greater in land mass than Kincaid's Antigua, Guyana is the site of far less tourism.

4  This quotation appears in the tagline for the column "The World beyond George-town," a weekly series in *Stabroek News*.

5  Oral history interviews with my aunt, Gene, corroborate this account. According-ing to Gene, Robert was a land surveyor employed to oversee the East Bank Demerara Water Conservancy, a shallow water storage area adjacent to the larger estate of Land of Canaan (which previously encompassed Sarah Johanna). The reservoir was a catchment area to mediate floods and provide irrigation for agricultural lands (rice and sugar), and drinking water for the region. Robert happened upon the abandoned estate while surveying the area and purchased it for "a few thousand dollars," according to my aunt. I was unable to find histori-cal records to pinpoint the date of this purchase, but my aunt's account places it circa the early 1910s.

6  British plantation owners devised complex and convoluted laws aimed at limiting freed Africans' abilities to own land in the post-emancipation era. These laws developed in concert with preferential ownership laws that par-celed out land to Indian indentured laborers in order to keep them bound to plantations. My grandmother's pride in owning both her land and her house stems in part from communal land ownership laws under which individuals could own a structure, but not necessarily the land on which it stood. For details on colonial-era land tenure see Smith 1956; for more on formerly en-slaved Africans' efforts to farm and buy land in Guiana, see Brown 2016; and for an in-depth analysis of gender and land tenure in British colonial law, see Clarke 1999.

7  Housing insecurity has proliferated in Guyana since the ethnic conflicts of the 1960s, when racially segregated squatting settlements formed. For a discussion of the politics around squatting, including raids and seizures that squatters continue to face in the contemporary period, see Vaughn 2022, 183–85. For a more detailed overview of housing insecurity, land allocation, land titling, and squatting, see Johnson-Bhola 2018. Based on my interactions with members of the community who used the term "Somalia" to refer to the squatting area, the term connoted the squalor of the area rather than the racial demographics of its inhabitants, who, from my observations, were racially diverse, including Venezuelan immigrants, Indigenous Guyanese, and some Indo- and Afro-Guyanese. Still, the "Somalia" label of course evokes the African continent and Blackness, thus juxtaposing Blackness with poverty.

8  The piece does very briefly paraphrase one unnamed female resident as "promptly repl[ying] that the crime rate is very low, and that she could not recall" complaints about unlawful activities in the village (Clarke 2011).

9 Guyana's global circulations and exchanges are evident in the diversity of religious belief systems practiced there. For a thoughtful analysis of global Guyanese interactions with Islam, see Khan 2020.

10 I was born in Georgetown. The first year of my life was divided between Georgetown and the Caribbean island of St. Lucia.

11 Within this configuration, Portuguese, who came as indentured workers from Madeira, the Azores, and Cape Verde, were not designated as Europeans.

12 Du Bois relates a story about how, when he was a young schoolboy, a White female classmate refused his calling card. Wright notes that Du Bois uses this anecdote to symbolize the rejection of the Negro man in America (Wright 2004, 126). Wright homes in on this story to argue that it illustrates the complex interplay between gender discourses and nationhood (Wright 2004, 126). Upon his sexual maturity, the nation rejects Du Bois, and he relies on a heteropatriarchal metaphor to describe this moment when he realized he was Other (Wright 2004, 11).

13 Guyana's 2012 Census marks its East Indian population at 43.45 percent and African/Black population at 30.20 percent. Other ethnic groups comprise much smaller percentages, with Amerindians at 9.16 percent, Chinese at 0.19 percent, Portuguese at 0.20 percent, Whites at 0.06 percent, and "Other" at 0.01 percent. Although Guyana's census does not specify the ethnic compositions of its "Mixed" category, the 2012 Census numerates this group at 16.73 percent. We can compare this with Trinidad, where, according to the 2011 Census, East Indians comprise 35.43 percent of the population and Africans comprise 34.22 percent, and where there is a census category for "Mixed-African and East Indian" numbering 7.66 percent. In Trinidad, the "Mixed-Other" group comprises 15.6 percent. The fact that in Trinidad "Mixed-African and East Indian" is the only specified mixed-race group (with all other mixed people falling into the "Mixed-Other" group) suggests that mixed African-Indians are the single largest mixed-race group. Since Guyana is home to an even larger Indian population than Trinidad, and because Indians and Africans are the nation's largest ethnic groups, I suspect that Guyana is home to more Douglas than Trinidad is.

14 There are various spellings of the term, including "douglas," "doogla," and "dogla." While most of the scholars writing on the subject have opted not to capitalize the term and often place it in quotation marks, I have followed Gabriella J. Hosein (2016) in capitalizing the term and rescuing it from scare quotes as a step towards finally and more fully acknowledging Dougla as a legitimate identity.

15 Dougla can also refer to other Indian mixed-race persons, such as those who are Chinese and Indian. In these cases, however, the term is often qualified as in "Chinni-dougla."

16 I am encompassing Dougla feminism and Dougla poetics under the same umbrella due to their shared agendas. Shalini Puri coined the term "dougla poetics" and mobilized it as a critique of the ways in which creolization privileges African elements over Indian cultural processes and to highlight interracial exchanges between Indo- and Afro-Caribbeans (Puri 2004).

17 Hosein also identifies this singular quality of K. Kempadoo's essay (Hosein 2016, 207).

18 Some scholars such as Shibata have maintained that Douglas are more negatively regarded by Indo-Guyanese than by Afro-Guyanese and that the very fact that the term originates in India suggests that such mixture was more taboo for Indians than for Blacks (Shibata 2002).

19 Here, we might consider Barratt and Ranjitsingh's insistence that "embodied Indianness, Africanness, and Blackness, as the measures used to determine if a Dougla is mixed enough, are all inevitably complicated when interpreted beyond simple stereotypes" (2021, 52). Respondents in Barratt and Ranjitsingh's study sometimes reified stereotypes such as what they term the myth of the Dougla "fire"—the notion that Douglas embody hypersexuality— but even in such cases, the authors' inclusion of actual Dougla voices upsets these tropes (2021, 161).

20 Of course, Deborah A. Thomas has complicated Jamaica's similar motto, "Out of Many, One People," contending that this form of multiracial creole nationalism gave way to what she terms "modern blackness," an African American popular culture–influenced form of urban blackness (Thomas 2004).

21 Although Rodney is writing about an earlier period in Guyanese history, his conclusions are applicable to understanding the paralleled interests of the Guyanese working people, both Black and Indian. He writes, "It has been argued in this study that racial conflict was far less pronounced than might have been expected from the manner in which the two main races were thrown into economic competition; but I am not seeking to minimize a crucial aspect of the historical reality. Indentureship and racial competition held back the development of a plantation workers' movement until long after the period in question" (Rodney 1981, 219). Rodney recognizes the reality of ethnic rifts between Indo- and Afro-Guyanese, but he does not see violent conflict as indicative of the relationship between the two. Still, Sidney Mintz articulated the following critique of Rodney's position: "But in his desire to depict the working class as ideologically undivided, Rodney tends to play down the significance of the peasantry (in contrast to the plantation workers) in recent Guyanese history. His hopes for Guyana's future have interfered with his understanding of Guyana's past" (Mintz 1982).

22 Wynter delineated her theory of humanness in essays such as "1492: A New World View" (1995) and "Unsettling the Coloniality of Being/Power/Truth/Freedom: Towards the Human, after Man, Its Overrepresentation—An Argument" (2003).

23 Although my mother's oldest sibling, Gene, was the first of my grandmother's children to emigrate to the United States, Gene's children lived with her husband in Georgetown. When our mother departed for America, my brother and I became the first set of grandchildren that Victorine raised. And because Victorine's daughters were among the first to leave the village, my brother and I held an unusual social status.

24 Stephanie Black's documentary, *Life and Debt*, chronicles how international policies that favored European milk farmers and eliminated subsidies for

Jamaican farmers led to the collapse of that nation's local dairy farming industry (Black 2001). This process, which largely substituted powdered milk for fresh milk in Jamaica and in Guyana, contributed to the lack of vitamin D in children's diets.

25 On a subsequent research trip to Guyana in 2018, I once again attempted to locate genealogical documents on my father's family, but the trail ran cold. Without knowing my paternal grandmother's name, I was unable to locate my father's birth certificate, which would have been the initial document necessary for tracing his ancestry.

26 Walter Rodney notes, for example, that in 1881 Immigration Agent-General Crosby was lobbying for the importation of Madras Indians over others, a difference he articulated "as one of 'race,'" and he further contended that the 'natural' antipathy of the races concerned would stand in the way of 'combination'" (Rodney 1981, 185). Planters racialized indentured laborers by these differences and manipulated cultural distinctions between Indians by purposefully mixing immigrants from different backgrounds within one plantation to obstruct worker unity (Rodney 1981, 185).

27 Here, Shepherd is concerned with summarizing treatments that position neoslavery frameworks against material-benefits analyses. For Shepherd, that emigration and indentureship were not as brutal as slavery is beside the point (Shepherd 2002, xvii–xviii).

28 I thank Aliyah Khan and the group of experts she enlisted in my pursuit of solving this mystery: Gaiutra Bahadur, Najnin Islam, Rajiv Mohabir, Lisa Outar, and Kaneesha Parsard. The fact that the "wC" notation stumped these scholars focused on indenture and racial identity in Guyana underscores the singularity of Tily's records.

29 We might interpret Poragia's small stature as evidence of her young age (especially with the knowledge that the adult women in my maternal line tend to be significantly taller than four feet, nine inches), suggesting that she could have been considerably younger than twenty-one. However, her documented height might also reflect the more diminutive stature of women from the time and location in which she was born or indicate the cursory nature of medical examinations of indentured women.

30 We know from Shepherd's historical research that the *Lightning*, the ship on which Poragia traveled, was a sailing ship that in 1878 had made the trip from India to Jamaica in 112 days—this gives us an idea of the length of her journey to Guiana. Shepherd notes that although some steam ships were in use after 1884, the *Lightning* was a sailing ship (Shepherd 2002, 18).

31 Shepherd records the female-to-male indentured ratio in Guyana at 11:100 in 1851, 62:100 in 1858, 58:100 in 1891, and 73:100 in 1914 (Shepherd 2002, 11). While she does not provide the ratio for 1881, the year Poragia arrived, it can be surmised that men still outnumbered women at that point but perhaps not as much as at the start of indentureship.

32 Paul Joseph López Oro has made a compelling case for understanding Blackness as indigenous to the region (López Oro 2021).

33 Rodney notes that planters' exploitation of and abuses against indentured laborers continued after their time expired and that upon expiration of their contracts, they were actively discouraged from seeking repatriation (Rodney 1981, 155–56).

34 Rodney documents the legal minimum wage for indentured laborers at the time to be twenty-four cents per day, or between fifty and eighty-eight dollars per year (Rodney 1981, 34).

35 We can note the double death here—"killed and murdered"—and might consider this alongside the double murder of the intersex Indigenous character on *Lovecraft* (discussed in the introduction).

36 Jackson offers a thoughtful discussion of anthropologists as "good secret-keepers about certain things" (Jackson 2013, 91). For more on "public secrets" see Taussig 1999. For a discussion on disclosing secrets in anthropology, see Manderson et al. 2015.

37 The oral history of that region includes stories about Makanya, who, in the early eighteenth century, was one of two sons of the chiefdom ruler, Simamane (Eldredge 2015, 173).

38 Respondents in Barratt and Ranjitsingh's study of Dougla subjectivity also noted the significance hair holds in parsing Dougla identity, pointing to "hair privilege, hair prejudice, and hair struggles" (Barratt and Ranjitsingh 2021, 157).

39 I subsequently decided that creating a genealogy based on the archival findings and providing copies for my mother to disperse might have stoked her aims of putting our Indian relatives "in their place," but would divorce the family tree from the richer, more complicated account I have crafted in this book.

40 I have altered the details of our relative's identity and her relatedness to my grandmother in order to protect her anonymity.

41 Victorine's documented race of "Calcutta," which deemed her as Indian, is in keeping with Dougla scholars' conclusions that Dougla identity is subsumed into either African or Indian racial categorization after one generation.

42 While we can ponder the possibility of an intersex embodiment in relation to this crossing out of "M" for "male" and replacing it with "F" for "female," it is impossible to know, based on the materials I found, whether this was a meaningless mistake, or perhaps indicative of a records official who was so flummoxed by Tily's interracial identity that it also cast her gender into uncertainty, or something more.

43 Barratt and Ranjitsingh provide interesting firsthand accounts of how "surnames mediate the experience of Douglaness significantly" (2021, 141).

44 Obeah is an Afro-Caribbean syncretic religious belief system practiced in Anglophone Caribbean nations including Guyana, Suriname, Belize, Jamaica, Trinidad and Tobago, Barbados, and the Bahamas. For a thoughtful analysis of obeah in relation to other syncretic religions of the Caribbean, see Aisha Khan's *Callaloo Nation: Metaphors of Race and Religious Identity among South Asians in Trinidad,*

in which she notes the negative assumption among Indo-Caribbean people that "to practice obeah is to engage, more or less, in evil" (Khan 2004, 116). Still, importantly, Khan also emphasizes mixing and slippages that complicate hard and fast distinctions between Indo-Trinidadian culture and "Negro culture," quoting Niehoff and Niehoff to underscore that "Indo-Trinidadians 'borrowed heavily from their Negro neighbors. Almost all the traditional spirits derived from Negro culture'" (Niehoff and Niehoff 1960, 168, 182, quoted in Khan 2004, 108). "Mixing," Khan argues, "begins on the subcontinent with ambiguous distinctions between Muslim and Hindu practice, and continues in the New World with ambiguous distinctions between 'coolie' and 'creole' grassroots traditions" (Khan 2004, 108).

45 For more on the sociopolitical meanings attached to the Afro-Creole jingle, "Coolie Water Rice," see Rohlehr 1988.

46 I found no evidence suggesting that Sarah Johanna was ever an African village. However, up to 1841, formerly enslaved Africans purchased property in nearby Craig Village (Farley 1964). A list of plantations and Negro villages from 1860, transcribed by Sharon Anderson, as part of the Guyana/British Guiana Genealogical Society, indicates that in 1860, Sarah Johanna was an abandoned estate (Anderson 2007). A British Directorate of Colonial Surveys map of operating sugar estates drawn in 1949 shows that Sarah Johanna and Land of Canaan were not under cultivation at the time, but that active sugar plantations continued to abound in the surrounding region. Various historical accounts suggest that abandoned plantation estates such as Sarah Johanna would have been eyed by ex-slaves as potential sites for either purchasing land or squatting (Farley 1964; Josiah 1997).

47 The Regional Refugee and Migrant Response Plan (RMRP) estimated that 24,500 Venezuelans were resident in Guyana as of May 2022 (Idrovo, Grant, and Yanoff 2022).

## CHAPTER 2. RIHANNA'S GUYANESE PATTACAKE AND THE HOMEWRECKING STATE IN BARBADOS

1 I have changed the name of the store and am using pseudonyms for its owner and employees to protect their anonymity.

2 Examples of the harassment Guyanese immigrants faced ranged from having officials demand their proof of legal status in public settings, delaying the renewal of work permits, and late-night immigration raids to round up undocumented immigrants. These charges of harassment were covered in various press outlets (COHA 2009; *Stabroek News* 2009; *Guyana Chronicle* 2017).

3 The most popular of the island's festivals, Crop Over dates back to the 1780s, when it marked enslaved Africans celebrating and taking over the streets—the culmination of hard labor when the harvesting of sugar cane was completed. While much can be said about the context in which the song was released and performed during the Crop Over festival, my aim here is not to contextualize "GT Advice" within Crop Over and the myriad social and historical meanings that are attached to the festival. And although it is significant to note, for example, that the

Bajan entertainment website, Bajantube, ranked "GT Advice" as the number one Crop Over song of 2009, I am more concerned with how the song frames Guyanese femininity and Guyana's cultural influence than with its place in Crop Over.

4 These include Benjie's, a sore muscle balm; citronella, a mosquito repellant; "candle grease," most likely a reference to "soft candle," which has been used throughout the Caribbean as a homeopathic treatment for diabetic foot wounds; and "Alcolada" or Alcolado, a mentholated splash lotion used to treat everything from headaches to the common cold and insect bites.

5 For a thoughtful critique of Wilson's reputation/respectability framework see Thomas (2011, 143–45).

6 Soon after the track's release, a Bajan calypso singer, Shantelle Cummins, released a response record, "Keep Yuh Guyanese Wine," aimed at "represent[ing] Bajan women" (*Guyana Chronicle* 2009).

7 Limacol is a mentholated lotion (which also is bottled as an astringent liquid) manufactured in Guyana. It is marketed as having "the freshness of a breeze in a bottle," but as a child I associated its strong odor with illness because my grandmother always doused me with it when I had a fever. In this way, it functions much like Alcolado in the "GT Advice" song.

8 I am referring here to the working people's uprisings, which Walter Rodney meticulously documented (Rodney 1981).

9 In each of the accounts from police magistrates that Harris details in 1840, the police documented having granted more emigration certificates to men than to women (all three to men in St. James, seven to men and five to females in St. Lucy, three to men and one to a woman in St. Thomas, and fifty-six to men and twenty-five to women in St. Michael) (Harris 2010, 243–44).

10 Contrary to the popular notion of the Bajan man going to Guyana to "get a wife," Brathwaite met Doris in Barbados: "takes one look at this irie dahta of Guyana then visiting Barbados April 1960 and married her by May" (Brathwaite 1993, 191, quoted in Walmsley 1994, 748).

11 For a thoughtful and detailed account of the development of his typeset and of Doris's influence, see Jenny Sharpe's *Immaterial Archives: An African Diasporic Poetics of Loss*, in which she analyzes how, after Doris's death, Brathwaite was unable to access his work on her computer. Sharpe writes, "Brathwaite was filled with the sense of contradiction between word fragments and their cadence in song when he began experimenting on Doris's computer after her death. As his fingers moved across the letters on the keyboard of what was previously a cold and dead machine, he felt a silent and unseen spirit move him" (Sharpe 2020, 128).

12 The estimate of Rihanna's fortune is reported in Berg 2021.

13 More recently, in 2021, Rihanna was named a national hero of Barbados by Prime Minister Mia Mottley. The singer was only the second woman to receive this honorific, which allows her to use the title "Right Honorable."

14 LVMH stands for Moët Hennessy Louis Vuitton, a Paris-based multinational conglomerate that produces luxury goods.

15 As Beckles and Russell also note, Rihanna's upbringing in the hard-knocks Westbury section of Bridgetown gives her a local, girl-next-door credibility (Beckles
and Russell 2015).

16 According to the editorial, "The fact is that Barbadians have been referring to
Guyanese and Guyanese immigration in much the same language in which
Americans have been referring to Mexican illegal immigrants in the past few
years" (*Guyana Chronicle* 2006).

17 Sex trafficking is notoriously difficult to quantify. The US State Department
reports that while "human traffickers exploit both domestic and foreign victims
in Barbados," "documented and undocumented migrants from Guyana, Haiti,
Jamaica, and Venezuela are at high risk for trafficking" (US Department of State
2020, 99).

18 The singer also released an extended version of "Birthday Cake" that featured
Chris Brown, from whom she had split after he assaulted her, but with whom she
briefly reconciled around the time of the song's release.

19 Rihanna is not generally known for writing her own songs. It is, therefore, noteworthy that she is listed as writer for "Birthday Cake," credit that she shares in
this instance with only three other writers. On the other tracks for which she has
a songwriting credit, she often shares that recognition with as many as five or six
others. This suggests that "Birthday Cake" bears significant input from Rihanna.
While I do not focus on the song's meaning as a representation of her conflicted
relationship with Chris Brown, Esther Jones offers a cogent deconstruction of this
element (Jones 2015).

20 Although the restaurant's original name was "Miss Lily's Favorite Cakes," it
became commonly known in short as "Miss Lily's." While I observed the playing of Rihanna's "Birthday Cake" as part of birthday celebrations at the two
locations in New York City, in Soho and in the East Village, I was not able to
visit the other two outposts in Dubai and Negril. In keeping with the double
entendres around "cake" that I have suggested here, the *New Yorker's* review of
Miss Lily's Favorite Cakes notes, "Miss Lily's is a little racy, too; the name plays
on cakes of both the carrot and the cannabis variety, and an enormous print
of a busty girl in a wet T-shirt hangs by the entrance" (Lester 2011). At the end
of their meals, patrons of Miss Lily's receive their bill clipped to a postcard of
this image. Interestingly, the "busty girl" print is actually the famous Jamaican
Tourist Board photograph of Indo-Trinidadian model Sintra Bronte, whose
skin-tight wet t-shirt with the word "Jamaica" printed on it first appeared in
1972 and has since resurfaced as an iconic global pop-culture artifact. Of course,
the fact that this iconic image of Jamaican femininity is actually a Trinidadian
model resonates with the forms of slippage and erasure that characterize the
Bajan government's deployment of Rihanna's image as quintessentially Bajan
even though she is part Guyanese.

21 The ship has held powerful imagery in African diasporic theorizations, as the potent symbol of the middle passage, the vehicle for return to the homeland, and the

transporter of ideas and cultural products (Gilroy 1993; Brown 2005). It is also the vessel of searing loss of life, lineage, and kin, and has been deconstructed on the basis of the ways in which it haunts the afterlives of slavery and for what it leaves in the wake (Hartman 2008; Sharpe 2016), to list but a few treatments.

## CHAPTER 3. TRANSPLANTED BEACHES AND SILICA CITIES

1 I have changed the name of the video and am using pseudonyms for the parties involved in order to protect anonymity.

2 I use Ulric (Neville) Trotz and Andre Mann's real names with their permission, and to credit them for their intellectual property. I withhold the names of or utilize pseudonyms for other industry insiders and experts to protect their anonymity.

3 Carbon sequestration stores carbon dioxide to prevent it from entering the atmosphere. Stabilizing carbon is a method of curbing the warming of the earth's atmosphere.

4 Here, Livingston's analysis is related to Sylvia Wynter and Katherine McKittrick's musings in "Unparalleled Catastrophe for Our Species?" in which they posit that "the ever-increasing ratios of economic growth, concomitantly with its also ever-increasing ratios of fossil fuel–driven capital accumulations, are themselves also law-likely equated with ever-increasing ratios of global warming, climate change, and environmental instability" (Wynter and McKittrick 2015, 65).

5 Mann wanted me to be clear on his qualifications: he obtained a degree in economics from Stanford University, but is considered an industrial engineer, having practiced in that field since his graduation from Stanford.

6 In *The Devil behind the Mirror: Globalization and Politics in the Dominican Republic*, Steven Gregory documents how many North American and European men "become aware of the [Caribbean's] sex tourism industry . . . through Internet web sites that catered to male travelers interested in prostitution" (Gregory 2014, 139). He argues that "the development and social uses of web sites . . . highlight the role of new technologies in mediating transnational social hierarchies and, more to the point, recapitulating and reiterating an imagined geography of difference, rooted in enduring imperial power relations and representational schema" (Gregory 2014, 139). Although Gregory's insights are specifically focused on sites dedicated to male sex tourism, mainstream search engines—Google primary among them—also do this work of curating accounts from previous travelers in order to represent Caribbean locations and peoples in forms digestible and attractive to Global North tourists (albeit in a less overtly pornographic manner).

7 According to CARIBSAVE's Climate Change Risk Profile for St. Vincent and the Grenadines, "Annual losses in tourism resulting from the reduced amenity value from beach loss is estimated to be between US $46 million by 2050 to US $174 million by 2080 for a mid-range SLR [sea level rise] scenario" (Simpson et al. 2012, xviii).

8  I am defining "medium- and large-scale" sand mining as mining carried out by the ton. Experts told me that because sand is a relatively inexpensive resource, it is only profitable to mine and sell it by the hundreds of tons.

9  The first Marriott property in the country, the hotel opened in 2015.

## CHAPTER 4. RECASTING EL DORADO

1  Atlantic Hotel Inc., an agency of the government of Guyana, owns the hotel.

2  The military personnel I saw at the hotel were affiliated with the US Southern Command (SOUTHCOM), which oversees joint security operations in Central America, South America, and the Caribbean. Well-to-do locals also celebrate special occasions by dining and staying at the Marriott.

3  In March of 2022, the EPA remained silent amid allegations that it "systematically and knowingly" violated the Environmental Protections Act in granting an environmental permit for Exxon's Yellowtail Development Project and allowing the issuing of a license within just a few days. The move violated a law whereby "members of the public shall have 28 days . . . to make written submissions to the agency setting out those questions and matters which they require to be answered or considered in the environmental impact assessment" (Parsram 2022).

4  The government has positioned the rollout of various one-time cash grants, including a Ministry of Human Services and Social Security initiative to grant $25,000 in cash to persons with disabilities, pensioners, and those on public assistance, as examples of how it is passing on oil profits to vulnerable citizens (*iNews Guyana* 2021). But the people to whom I spoke stressed that such grants are a drop in the bucket—in this case $25,000 GYD converts to less than $115 USD— and said that obtaining the grant money is mired in prohibitive red tape.

5  For a thoughtful analysis of gas extraction in Latin America, see Gustafson 2020.

6  Interior Ameriondian villages are less able to receive daily periodicals, but even in the interior fishermen, fuel runners, miners, and smugglers carry newspapers and communicate news and information across international borders.

7  The current border between Venezuela and Guyana is the product of an 1899 Paris arbitration agreement between the two countries. As Guyana was approaching independence, in 1962, Venezuela voiced disapproval of the arbitration agreement, notifying the United Nations that it could no longer accept the arbitration judgment (Cummings 2018, 184). Interestingly, for our purposes, migration between Venezuela and Guyana is the mirror opposite of the historical migratory routes between Barbados and Guyana. In the 1980s and 1990s, economic difficulties led Guyanese to migrate to Venezuela for a better life. In the past five years, however, political and economic crises in Venezuela have prompted Venezuelans to migrate to Guyana for food and healthcare (Cummings 2018, 187; *Stabroek News* 2018). When, before the oil discovery, Guyana and Venezuela were on better terms, in a 2013 state visit to Guyana, President Maduro said that the border controversy was "'a legacy of colonialism' that required diplomacy to be resolved" (*Guyana Chronicle* 2013, 1, quoted in Cummings 2018, 194).

8 For a detailed overview of how the oil discovery reignited the centuries-old border dispute, see Cummings 2018. For a journalistic account of how oil wealth has
rehashed the border dispute in the age of social media misinformation, including a historiography of how the disagreement over the territory formed the "last
major dispute" between Britain and the United States, see Westfall and Herrero
2023. Guyana has also had a century-old border dispute with Suriname, over an
oil basin to its east, which reemerged in the early 2000s (Kuipers and Khan 2007).

9 CARICOM brokered a recount of the initial electoral votes, with participation
from the Organization of American States (OAS), the Carter Center (TCC), and
the International Republican Institute (IRI). Officials from the latter two organizations were not permitted to return to Guyana to oversee the recount because of
COVID-19 travel restrictions (Mowla 2020).

10 The APNU+AFC is a coalition party that was formed in 2011. It consists of a number of smaller parties, including the Guyana Action Party, the Guyana National
Congress, the Justice for All Party, the National Democratic Front, the National
Front Alliance, the People's National Congress (PNC), and the Working People's
Alliance (WPA), the last of which was founded by Walter Rodney. While, for example, Rodney's WPA was originally conceived as a multiethnic party, Granger's
ascendance to the presidency repositioned the PNC, which has traditionally
reflected Afro-Guyanese interests, as the dominant force behind the APNU+AFC.

11 And the Trump administration's imperial efforts in Venezuela included secret
meetings with military "coup plotters" hoping to overthrow President Nicolás
Maduro—a story about which the *Times* also reported (Londoño and Casey 2018).
As Vikram Tamboli notes, while at the helm of ExxonMobil, Tillerson refused to
give Hugo Chávez a greater cut of the company's profits, prompting Chávez to
nationalize oil in Venezuela. Exxon's executives and the Trump administration
exercised considerable power in that country's politics: "One of Exxon's principal
executives in Venezuela in 2007, Carlos Veccio, later became one of the most
influential characters behind self-declared president Juan Guaidó and the Trump
administration's recent attempted coup against Maduro's regime" (Tamboli 2019,
423).

12 For a thoughtful analysis of the Booker family's hold on Guyana, see Natalie
Hopkinson's, "The Booker Prize's Bad History," which positioned "the hottest
new start-up industry" of the 1800s, sugar, alongside the staggering wealth the
family-owned British multinational corporation accumulated at the hands of en-
slaved labor (Hopkinson 2017). Published in the *New York Times* in October 2017,
Hopkinson's op-ed does not explicitly mention oil, but the implication is clear: the
United States is currently focused on this country because it is once again the site
of a resource destined to enrich outsiders at the expense of Guyana and its people.
An American of Guyanese descent, Hopkinson counters the vast majority of the
*Times'* coverage. Her treatment of competition between Africans and Indians in
Guyana acknowledges how colonial actors like the Booker family set the stage for
ethnic discord.

13 The convenience of the cutlass as a symbol of racialized and gendered violence should not be lost on us.

14 I could find no additional reporting on Anadura Sukra.

15 The story's lede read, "The South American country, already deeply split by a presidential election and an oil windfall, is tested again as three teenagers are slain" (Yahya-Sakur and Kurmanaev 2020).

16 Samantha Benjamin, the woman about whom Cordis wrote, was not discovered in the same spot behind the hotel. She was found on the northern coast between Annandale and Buxton (Cordis 2019, 19).

CODA

1 According to the United Nations refugee agency, cited in Tamboli 2019.

2 I have summarized Andaiye's insightful speech for the sake of brevity. She links the search for cheaper labor to some of the processes I discussed in chapter 2: "Capital can move freely," she argues, "but not labor, except when the developed world needs our skills" (Andaiye in Trotz 2020, 18).

# BIBLIOGRAPHY

Agard-Jones, Vanessa. 2012. "What the Sands Remember." *GLQ: A Journal of Lesbian and Gay Studies* 18.2–3: 325–46.

Aksich, Caroline. 2019. "Where Chef Devan Rajkumar Eats Guyanese Food in Scarborough." *Toronto Life*, September 27. https://torontolife.com.

Ali, Grace Aneiza, ed. 2020. *Liminal Spaces: Migration and Women of the Guyanese Diaspora*. Cambridge, UK: Open Book Publishers.

Andaiye with D. Alissa Trotz. 2020. "1964: The Rupture of Neighborliness and Its Legacy for Indian/African Relations." In *The Point Is to Change the World: Selected Writings of Andaiye*, edited by Alissa Trotz, 58–76. London: Pluto Press.

Anderson, Sharon. 2007. "1860: Plantations and Negro Villages, British Guiana." *Guyana/British Guiana Genealogical Society*. www.gbggs.org/.

Ayed, Nahlah. 2022. "How Sand Shapes Our World." *CBCListen*, May 31. www.cbc.ca.

Bacchus, Sharda. 2021. "Three to Be Charged with Murdering Henry Cousins." *Stabroek News*, January 15. www.stabroeknews.com.

Bahadur, Gaiutra. 2013. *Coolie Woman: The Odyssey of Indenture*. Chicago: University of Chicago Press.

———. 2015. "Guyana's 'Dougla' Politics." Pulitzer Center, June 18. https://pulitzercenter.org.

———. 2020. "In 1953, Britain Openly Removed an Elected Government, with Tragic Consequences." *The Guardian*, October 30. https:/theguardian.com.

Barratt, Sue Ann. 2016. "What's in a Name? Nicki Minaj, Indian In/visibility, and the Paradox of Dougla Feminism." In *Indo-Caribbean Feminist Thought: Genealogies, Theories, Enactments*, edited by Gabrielle Jamela Hosein and Lisa Outar, 225–40. New York: Palgrave Macmillan.

Barratt, Sue Ann, and Aleah N. Ranjitsingh. 2021. *Dougla in the Twenty-First Century: Adding to the Mix*. Jackson: University Press of Mississippi.

Baver, Sherrie L., and Barbara Deutsch Lynch, eds. 2006. *Beyond Sun and Sand: Caribbean Environmentalisms*. New Brunswick, NJ: Rutgers University Press.

BBC News. 2020. "Indian Matchmaking: The 'Cringe-worthy' Netflix Show That Is a Huge Hit." July 28. www.bbc.com.

Beckles, Hilary McD. 2015. "Westbury Strikes Back: Rihanna Reclaimed." In *Rihanna: Barbados World-Gurl in Global Popular Culture*, edited by Hilary McD. Beckles and Heather D. Russell, 14–37. Kingston, Jamaica: University of the West Indies Press.

Beckles, Hilary McD., and Heather D. Russell, eds. 2015. *Rihanna: Barbados World-Gurl in Global Popular Culture*. Kingston, Jamaica: University of the West Indies Press.

Beiser, Vince. 2017. "Sand Mining: The Global Environmental Crisis You've Probably Never Heard Of." *The Guardian*, February 27. www.theguardian.com.

Berg, Madeline. 2021. "Fenty's Fortune: Rihanna Is Now Officially a Billionaire." *Forbes*, August 4. https://www.forbes.com.

Bethea, Dani. 2020. "Lovecraft Country Was Great until It Wasn't: From Sundown to a History of Violence." *Medium*, September 7. https://medium.com.

Black, Stephanie, dir. 2001. *Life and Debt*. New Yorker Films, Axiom Films.

Bolles, A. Lynn. 1985. "Of Mules and Yankee Gals: Struggling with Stereotypes in the Field." *Anthropology and Humanism Quarterly* 10 (December): 114–19.

———. 1996. *Sister Jamaica: A Study of Women, Work, and Households in Kingston*. Lanham, MD: University Press of America.

———. 2022. *Women and Tourist Work in Jamaica: Seven Miles of Sandy Beach*. London: Lexington Books.

Boylorn, Robin M. 2012. *Sweetwater: Black Women and Narratives of Resilience*. New York: Peter Lang.

Brathwaite, Kamau. 1993. *The Zea Mexican Diary: 7 Sept 1926–7 Sept 1986*. Madison: University of Wisconsin Press.

———. 1999. *ConVERSations with Nathanial Mackey*. Rhinebeck, NY: We Press.

Brennan, Denise. 2004. *What's Love Got to Do with It? Transnational Desires and Sex Tourism in the Dominican Republic*. Durham, NC: Duke University Press.

Brereton, Bridget. 1979. *Race Relations in Colonial Trinidad, 1870-1900*. Cambridge: Cambridge University Press.

Bronkhurst, Henry V. P. 1888. *Among the Hindus and Creoles of British Guiana*. London: T. Woolmer.

Brown, Alex. 2020. "Like Dragons Hoarding Gold: Lovecraft, 'A History of Violence.'" *Tor.com*, September 6. www.tor.com.

Brown, Eleanor Marie. 2016. "On the Evolution of Property Ownership among Former Slaves, Newly Freedmen." GWU Legal Studies Research Paper No. 2016.22. https://scholarship.law.gwu.edu.

Brown, Jacqueline Nassy. 2005. *Dropping Anchor, Setting Sail: Geographies of Race in Black Liverpool*. Princeton, NJ: Princeton University Press.

Buchholz, Katharina. 2022. "The World's Biggest Diasporas [Infographic]." *Forbes*, November 11. https://forbes.com.

Bulkan, Arif, and D. Alissa Trotz, eds. 2019. *Unmasking the State: Politics, Society, and Economy in Guyana, 1992–2015*. Kingston, Jamaica: Ian Randle Publishers.

Bulkan, Janette. 2022. "Why Is There No EIA for the Dredging of the Demerara Ship Channel?" *Stabroek News*, July 8. www.stabroeknews.com.

Calder, Jason S. 2020. "Ethnic Conflict Threatens Democracy in Guyana." *Foreign Policy*, March 26. https://foreignpolicy.com.

Carew, Ivan O. 2011. "Atkinson Field and World War II." *Stabroek News*, July 7. www.stabroeknews.com.

Caribbean Media Network. 2013. "Rihanna Dances with Her Grandfather." November 5. www.caribemedianetwork.com.

Cavanaugh, Ray. 2014. "Little Guyana, an Indo-Guyanese Enclave in Queens." *Washington Post*, October 9. www.washingtonpost.com.

Chisholm, Shirley. 1970. *Unbought and Unbossed*. Boston: Houghton Mifflin.

Chittal, Nisha. 2021. "The Kamala Harris Identity Debate Shows How America Still Struggles to Talk about Multiracial People." *Vox*, January 20. www.vox.com.

Chua, Charmaine. 2020. "'Sunny Island Set in the Sea': Singapore's Land Reclamation as Colonial Project." In *Digital Lives in the Global City: Contesting Infrastructures*, edited by Deborah Cowen, Alexis Mitchell, Emily Paradis, and Brett Story. Vancouver: University of British Columbia Press.

Clarke, Edith. 1999. *My Mother Who Fathered Me: A Study of the Families in Three Selected Communities of Jamaica*. Kingston, Jamaica: University of the West Indies Press.

Clarke, Roxanne. 2011. "The World beyond Georgetown: Sarah Johanna." *Stabroek News*, September 18. www.stabroeknews.com.

COHA (Council on Hemispheric Affairs). 2009. "'Barbadian First' Policy Flogs Guyanese in Barbados." August 5. www.coha.org.

Colchester, Marcus, and Jean La Rose. 2010. "Our Land, Our Future: Promoting Indigenous Participation and Rights in Mining, Climate Change, and Other Natural Resource Decision-Making in Guyana." *Final Report of the APA/FFP/NSI Project, Amerindian Peoples Association, Forest Peoples Programme and the North-South Institute*, May 31: i–37.

Cordis, Shanya. 2019. "Forging Relational Difference: Racial Gendered Violence and Dispossession in Guyana." *Small Axe* 23.3 (November): 18–33.

Craft, Renée Alexander. 2018. "Afrofuturism and the 2018 Wakanda Diaspora Carnival." In *The Routledge Companion to African American Theatre and Performance*, edited by Kathy A. Perkins, Sandra L. Richards, Renée Alexander Craft, and Thomas F. DeFrantz, 385–94. New York: Routledge.

Craig, Trishan. 2019. "19 Fraud Charges . . . Matter Adjourned as Ali Tries for Another Stay to Be Granted." *Kaieteur News*, August 27. www.kaieteurnewsonline.com.

Cross, Robert S. D. 2014. Review of *Treasure, Treason, and the Tower: El Dorado and the Murder of Sir Walter Raleigh*, by Paul R. Sellin. *Renaissance Quarterly* 67.1 (Spring): 265–66.

Cudjoe, Selwyn R. 2011. *Caribbean Visionary: A. R. F. Webber and the Making of the Guyanese Nation*. Jackson: University Press of Mississippi.

Cummings, Anthony R. 2018. "How Guyana's Oil Discovery Rekindled a Border Controversy." *Journal of Latin American Geography* 17.3 (October): 183–211.

Curwood, Anastasia C. 2023. *Shirley Chisholm: Champion of Black Feminist Power Politics*. Chapel Hill: University of North Carolina Press.

*Daily Chronicle* (Guyana). 1893. "Murder at Port Mourant." February 4.

*Daily Express*. 2011. "Hi-Tech Access to Paradise: How St. Vincent Is Changing the Way Tourism Works." April 19. www.trinidadexpress.com.

Danns, Ken. 2017. "Come-Back-fuh-Go-Back Guyanese: The Guyanese Diaspora as Strangers." *Guyana Chronicle*, July 23. https://guyanachronicle.com.

Dávila, Arlene. 2016. *El Mall: The Spatial and Class Politics of Shopping Malls in Latin America*. Berkeley: University of California Press, 2016.

Del Carmen Quintero Aguiló, María. 2019. "The Sands of Un-Certainty: Tidalectically Synthesizing Nature and Culture in Derek Walcott's *Omeros*." *CEA Critic* 81.1 (March): 1–10.

Derrida, Jacques. 1989. "How to Avoid Speaking: Denials." In *Languages of the Unsayable*, edited by Sandford Burdick and Wolfgang Iser, 3–70. New York: Columbia University Press.

Du Bois, W. E. B. 1969 (1903). *The Souls of Black Folk*. New York: New American Library.

Dudhnath, Rooplall. 2019. "Oil Wealth Trickling Down to the Masses Is a Pipe Dream." *Stabroek News*, August 20. www.stabroeknews.com.

Durham, Aisha. 2014. *Home with Hip Hop Feminism: Performances in Communication and Culture*. New York: Peter Lang.

Edmondson, Catie, and Emily Cochrane. 2020. "DeJoy Earned Millions from Company with Financial Ties to Postal Service." *New York Times*, August 24. www.nytimes.com.

Eldredge, Elizabeth A. 2015. *Kingdoms and Chiefdoms of Southeastern Africa: Oral Traditions and History, 1400–1830*. Rochester, NY: University of Rochester Press.

El-Hadi, Nehal. 2022. "Poetics, Politics, and Paradoxes of Sand." *Slow Factory*, February 16. https://slowfactory.earth.

England, Sarah. 2008. "Reading the Dougla Body: Mixed-Race, Post-Race, and Other Narratives of What It Means to Be Mixed in Trinidad." *Latin American and Caribbean Ethnic Studies* 3.1 (March): 1–31.

Farley, Rawle. 1954. "Rise of a Peasantry in British Guiana." *Social and Economic Studies* 2.4: 87–103.

———. 1964. "The Rise of Village Settlements in British Guiana." *Caribbean Quarterly* 10.1 (March): 52–61.

Fernandes, Andrea. 2018. "Traffickers Paying Guyanese Girls Airline Tickets to Come to Barbados." *Guyana Chronicle*, November 20. www.guyanachronicle.com.

Fleck, Andrew. 2013. Review of *Treasure, Treason, and the Tower: El Dorado and the Murder of Sir Walter Raleigh*, by Paul R. Sellin. *Journal of British Studies* 52.3 (July): 771–72.

Freeman, Carla. 2000. *High Tech and High Heels in the Global Economy: Women, Work, and Pink-Collar Identities in the Caribbean*. Durham, NC: Duke University Press.

Fritts, Rachel. 2019. "The World Needs to Get Serious about Managing Sand, U.N. Report Says." *Science*, May 10. www.science.org.

Gates, Henry Louis, Jr., and Kwame Anthony Appiah, eds. 1993. *Zora Neale Hurston: Critical Perspectives Past and Present*. New York: Amistad.

Gaunt, Kyra. 2006. *The Games Black Girls Play: Learning the Ropes from Double-Dutch to Hip-Hop*. New York: New York University Press.

Gentleman, Amelia. 2018. "MPs Urge May to Resolve Immigration Status of Windrush Children." *The Guardian*, April 16. www.theguardian.com.

Gest, Justin. 2020. "Does Guyana Foretell an American Future?" *Foreign Policy News*, July 29. https://foreignpolicy.com.

Gilroy, Paul. 1993. *The Black Atlantic: Modernity and Double Consciousness*. Cambridge, MA: Harvard University Press.

*The Gleaner*. 2016. "Beach Sand Policy Needed—Vaz." January 23. https://jamaica-gleaner.com.

Glissant, Édouard. 1997. *Poetics of Relation*. Translated by Betsy Wing. Ann Arbor: University of Michigan Press.

Gregory, Steven. 2014. *The Devil behind the Mirror: Globalization and Politics in the Dominican Republic*. Berkeley: University of California Press.

Grewal, Inderpal. 2005. *Transnational America: Feminisms, Diasporas, Neoliberalisms*. Durham, NC: Duke University Press.

Gustafson, Bret. 2020. *Bolivia in the Age of Gas*. Durham, NC: Duke University Press.

*Guyana Chronicle*. 2006. "Other Mexicans." November 23. https://guyanachronicle.com.

———. 2009. "'GT Girl' 'Crop Over' Song Has Bajan Women Up in Arms." July 5. https://guyanachronicle.com.

———. 2011. "Returning to Bread Basket Status." August 19. http://guyanachronicle.com.

———. 2013. "Venezuelan President Declares . . . : Border Dispute a Legacy of Colonialism, By-Product of Western Intervention; —as Guyana, Venezuela Agree to Renew UN Good Offices Process." September 1. https://guyanachronicle.com.

———. 2017. "Guyanese Continue to Be Harassed in Barbados." September 4. https://guyanachronicle.com.

———. 2020. "Irfaan Ali and His Qualifications." February 12. https://guyanachronicle.com.

———. 2021. "Eccles to Mandela Avenue Road Likely by November." January 24. https://guyanachronicle.com.

———. 2022. "Silica City." August 24. https://guyanachronicle.com.

Guyana Silica-Sand. 2019. "Guyana Shield Resources, Inc. New Silica Sand Mine on Demerara River, Guyana Ready to Load." November 28. www.facebook.com/guyana.silica.sand/.

*Guyana Times*. 2020. "Protests Erupt for Murders of Henry Cousins to Be Solved." October 5. https://guyanatimesgy.com.

———. 2021. "Haresh Singh Was Pulled off Motorcycle, Beaten to Head with Wood—Suspect Confesses." June 27. https://guyanatimesgy.com.

———. 2022. "Gov't in Talks with MIT on Developing Innovation Village in Silica City—Pres Ali." September 18. https://guyanatimesgy.com.

Haniff, Nesha. 1999. "My Grandmother Worked in the Field: Stereotypes Regarding East Indian Women in the Caribbean; Honorable Mention." In *Matikor: The Politics of Identity for Indo-Caribbean Women*, edited by Rosanne Kanhai, 18–31. St.

Augustine, Trinidad and Tobago: University of the West Indies, School of Continuing Studies.

Harris, Dawn. 2010. "Confined Spaces, Constrained Bodies: Land, Labour, and the 1836 Emigration Act of Barbados." *Journal of Caribbean History* 44.2: 237–54.

Harrison, Faye V., ed. 1997. *Decolonizing Anthropology: Moving Further toward an Anthropology for Liberation*. Arlington, VA: Association of Black Anthropologists, American Anthropological Association.

Hartman, Saidiya. 2007. *Lose Your Mother: A Journey along the Atlantic Slave Route*. New York: Farrar, Straus, and Giroux.

———. 2008. "Venus in Two Acts." *Small Axe* 12.2 (June): 1–14.

Hay, William Delisle. 2009 (1882). *Brighter Britain! Or Settler and Maori in Northern New Zealand*, vol. 1 of 2. London: Richard Bentley and Son. Available as an e-book from Project Gutenberg.

Henry, Daja E. 2020. "More Than 50 Years since Independence, Colonial Violence Plagues Guyana and Its Diaspora." Pulitzer Center, April 20. https://pulitzercenter.org.

Hernández-Ramdwar, Camille. 1997. "Multiracial Identities in Trinidad and Guyana: Exaltation and Ambiguity." *Latin American Issues* 13.4. https://mixedracestudies.org.

Hill, Nicole. 2020. "Lovecraft Country Episode 4 Review: A History of Violence." *Den of Geek*, September 6. www.denofgeek.com.

Hinds, David. 2020. "Our Racial Hypocrisy: Those Post-Election Protests." *Kaieteur News*, March 8. www.kaieteurnewsonline.com.

Hirsch, Afua. 2020. "Rihanna Talks New Music, Fenty Skincare, and Her Plans to Have '3 or 4 Kids.'" *Vogue*, March 30. www.vogue.co.uk.

Hopkinson, Natalie. 2017. "The Booker Prize's Bad History." *New York Times*, October 17. www.nytimes.com.

———. 2018. *A Mouth Is Always Muzzled: Six Dissidents, Five Continents, and the Art of Resistance*. New York: New Press.

Hosein, Gabrielle Jamela. 2016. "Douglas Poetics and Politics in Indo-Caribbean Feminist Thought: Reflection and Reconceptualization." In *Indo-Caribbean Feminist Thought: Genealogies, Theories, Enactments*, edited by Gabrielle Jamela Hosein and Lisa Outar, 205–23. New York: Palgrave Macmillan.

Hurston, Zora Neale. 1928. "How It Feels to Be Colored Me." *World Tomorrow* 11 (May): 664–67.

———. 1942. *Dust Tracks on a Road*. Philadelphia: J. B. Lippincott.

Idrovo, Camila, Jermaine Grant, and Julia Romani Yanoff. 2022. "Discovery of Oil Could Bring Migrant Labor Opportunities and Climate Displacement Challenge for Guyana." Migration Policy Institute, July 27. www.migrationpolicy.org.

*iNews Guyana*. 2021. "Distribution of $25,000 Cash Grants for Pensioners, Persons with Disabilities to Begin Oct 4." October 1. www.inewsguyana.com.

Jackson, John L. 2013. *Thin Description: Ethnography and the African Hebrew Israelites of Jerusalem*. Cambridge, MA: Harvard University Press.

Jackson, Shona N. 2012. *Creole Indigeneity: Between Myth and Nation in the Caribbean*. Minneapolis: University of Minnesota Press.

Jobson, Ryan Cecil. 2019. "Black Gold in El Dorado: Frontiers of Race and Oil in Guyana." Social Science Research Council, January 8. https://items.ssrc.org.

Johnson-Bhola, Linda. 2018. "Land Use Planning and Housing Development in Guyana: A Case Study of Two Housing Schemes." *International Journal of Interdisciplinary Social and Community Studies* 12.4: 7–21.

Jones, Adanna. 2016. "Can Rihanna Have Her Cake and Eat It Too? A Schizophrenic Search for Resistance within the Screened Spectacles of a Winin' Fatale." In *The Oxford Handbook of Screendance Studies*, edited by Douglas Rosenberg. *Oxford Handbooks Online*. doi:10.1093/oxfordhb/9780199981601.013.32.

Jones, Adanna, Oneka LaBennett, and Treva Lindsey. 2016. "Rihanna and Representations of Black Women." *The Oxford Comment*, Episode 39. October 6. https://blog.oup.com.

Jones, Esther L. 2015. "'What's My Name?': Reading Rihanna's Autobiographical Acts." In *Rihanna: Barbados World-Gurl in Global Popular Culture*, edited by Hilary McD. Beckles and Heather D. Russell, 96–118. Kingston, Jamaica: University of the West Indies Press.

Josiah, Barbara P. 1997. "After Emancipation: Aspects of Village Life in Guyana, 1869–1911." *Journal of Negro History* 82.1 (Winter): 105–21.

Juhasz, Antonia. 2021. "Exxon's Oil Drilling Gamble off Guyana Coast 'Poses Major Environmental Risk.'" *The Guardian*, August 17. www.theguardian.com.

*Kaieteur News*. 2014. "Sand Mining Must Be Done in Conformity with the Law." January 13. www.kaieteurnewsonline.com.

———. 2019. "The East Bank Demerara Carriageway." August 22. www.kaieteurnewsonline.com

———. 2020a. "Social Media Race Hate." September 17. www.kaieteurnewsonline.com.

———. 2020b. "Seek Diaspora Expertise in Oil Industry." August 20. www.kaieteurnewsonline.com.

———. 2020c. "Father of Teen Shot by Police during WCB Protest at Odds with Police." March 8. www.kaieteurnewsonline.com.

———. 2020d. "Teen Accidentally Shot At during Berbice Protests Left Stranded." March 8. www.kaieteurnewsonline.com.

———. 2021. "Why Are Some Persons Not Willing to Accept the Police Have Solved the Murders of the Henry Cousins?" January 18. www.kaieteurnewsonline.com.

———. 2022. "Body of Woman on Beach behind Marriott Hotel." March 4. www.kaieteurnewsonline.com.

Kars, Marjoleine. 2016. "Dodging Rebellion: Politics and Gender in the Berbice Slave Uprising of 1763." *American Historical Review* 121.1 (February): 39–69.

———. 2020. *Blood on the River: A Chronicle of Mutiny and Freedom on the Wild Coast*. New York: New Press.

Kempadoo, Kamala. 1999. "Negotiating Cultures: A 'Dogla' Perspective." In *Matikor: The Politics of Identity for Indo-Caribbean Women*, edited by Rosanne Kanhai, 103–13. Saint Augustine, Trinidad and Tobago: University of the West Indies, School of Continuing Studies.

Kempadoo, Oonya. 1998. *Buxton Spice*. Boston: Beacon Press.

Kershaw, Sarah. 2002. "For Schenectady, a Guyanese Strategy: Mayor Goes All Out to Encourage a Wave of Hardworking Immigrants." *New York Times*, July 26. www.nytimes.com.

Khan, Aisha. 2004. *Callaloo Nation: Metaphors of Race and Religious Identity among South Asians in Trinidad*. Durham, NC: Duke University Press.

Khan, Aliyah. 2020. *Far from Mecca: Globalizing the Muslim Caribbean*. New Brunswick, NJ: Rutgers University Press.

Kinah K (@justkinahiguess). 2018. "Cliff @ckrauss Can you believe @spbj28 had the audacity to show up to our play date with clothes on?" Twitter, July 21, 2018, 8:32 a.m. https://twitter.com/justkinahiguess/status/1020693054427148289.

Kincaid, Jamaica. 1978. "Girl." In *At the Bottom of the River*. New York: Farrar, Straus, and Giroux.

———. 2000. *A Small Place*. New York: Farrar, Straus, and Giroux.

King, Tiffany Lethabo. 2019. *The Black Shoals: Offshore Formations of Black and Native Studies*. Durham, NC: Duke University Press.

Kipling, Rudyard. 2014 (1901). *Kim*. Cambridge: Cambridge University Press.

Krauss, Clifford. 2017. "With a Major Oil Discovery, Guyana Is Poised to Become a Top Producer." *New York Times*, January 13. www.nytimes.com.

———. 2018a. "The $20 Billion Question for Guyana." *New York Times*, July 20. www.nytimes.com.

———. 2018b. "Oil and New Leadership Raised Hope in Guyana: But Political Rifts Are Resurfacing." *New York Times*, August 10. www.nytimes.com.

———. 2018c. "Venezuela Navy Interrupts Oil Exploration off Guyana." *New York Times*, December 23. www.nytimes.com.

Kuipers, Ank, and Sharief Khan. 2007. "U.N. Favors Guyana in Oil Border Spat with Suriname." *Reuters World News*, September 20. www.reuters.com.

Kurmanaev, Anatoly. 2020a. "Oil Bonanza Plunges Guyana into Political Crisis." *New York Times*, March 5. www.nytimes.com.

———. 2020b. "Crisis Deepens in Tiny Guyana, the World's Newest Petro State." *New York Times*, March 6. www.nytimes.com.

———. 2020c. "Guyana Leader Set to Take New Term after a Vote Denounced as Flawed." *New York Times*, March 14. www.nytimes.com.

Kurmanaev, Anatoly, and Clifford Krauss. 2020. "A Small Country, an Oil Giant, and Their Shared Fortune." *New York Times*, March 18. www.nytimes.com.

LaBennett, Oneka. 2018a. "'Beyoncé and Her Husband': Representing Infidelity and Kinship in a Black Marriage." *differences* 29.2 (September): 154–88.

——— (@onekalabennett). 2018b. "Misrepresenting #Guyana as a place 'forgotten by time' where children 'play naked in the muggy heat' denies its complexity. Dangerous distortions like this inform the perilous trajectory of my homeland's oil boom. Do better @nytimes." Twitter, July 20, 2018, 5:20 a.m. https://twitter.com/onekalabennett/status/1020282351392362504.

——. 2021. "Why We Should Take a Deeper Look at Rihanna's 'Savage X Fenty Show, Vol. 3.'" *The Grio*, October 5. https://thegrio.com.

——. 2022. "Danger Ahead: A Crisis of Roads and Sand." *Stabroek News*, August 21. www.stabroeknews.com.

Lamming, George. 1981. Foreword to *A History of the Guyanese Working People, 1881–1905*, by Walter Rodney, xvii–xxv. Baltimore, MD: Johns Hopkins University Press.

Lester, Amelia. 2011. "Miss Lily's Favorite Cakes." *New Yorker*, October 10. www.newyorker.com

Lewis, Linden. 2011. "Mudheads in Barbados: A Lived Experience." *Stabroek News*, August 1. www.stabroeknews.com.

Livingston, Julie. 2019. *Self-Devouring Growth: A Planetary Parable as Told from Southern Africa*. Durham, NC: Duke University Press.

Lomarsh, Roopnarine. 2016. "Dougla Identity." *Guyana Times*, October 25. https://guyanatimesgy.com.

Londoño, Ernesto, and Nicholas Casey. 2018. "Trump Administration Discussed Coup Plans with Rebel Venezuelan Officers." *New York Times*, September 8. www.nytimes.com.

Long, April. 2017. "The Totality: Rihanna." *Elle.com*, September 26. www.elle.com.

López Oro, Paul Joseph. 2016. "'Ni de aquí, ni de allá': Garífuna Subjectivities and the Politics of Diasporic Belonging." In *Afro-Latin@s in Movement: Critical Approaches to Blackness and Transnationalism in the Americas*, edited by Petra R. Rivera-Rideau, Jennifer A. Jones, and Tianna S. Paschel, 61–83. New York: Palgrave Macmillan.

——. 2021. "A Love Letter to Indigenous Blackness." *NACLA Report on the Americas* 53.3 (November): 248–54.

Lorimer, Joyce. 2013. Review of *Treasure, Treason, and the Tower: El Dorado and the Murder of Sir Walter Raleigh*, by Paul R. Sellin. *History: The Journal of the Historical Association* 98.330 (April): 283–84.

Lowe, Lisa. 2015. *The Intimacies of Four Continents*. Durham, NC: Duke University Press.

MacGregor, Sherilyn. 2006. *Beyond Mothering Earth: Ecological Citizenship and the Politics of Care*. Vancouver, Canada: University of British Columbia Press.

Mackey, Nathaniel. 1995. "An Interview with Kamau Brathwaite." In *The Art of Kamau Brathwaite*, edited by Stewart Brown, 13–32. Mid Glamorgan, Wales: Seren.

Madd feat. Guyanese Girl. 2009. "GT Advice." Nalini Sukhram, perf. by Eric Lewis. MADD Productions.

Mahabir, Kumar. 1996. "Whose Nation Is This? The Struggle over National and Ethnic Identity in Trinidad and Guyana." *Caribbean Studies* 29.2 (July–December): 283–302.

Manderson, Lenore, Mark Davis, Chip Colwell, and Tanja Ahlin, eds. 2015. "On Secrecy, Disclosure, the Public, and the Private in Anthropology: An Introduction to Supplement 12." *Current Anthropology* 56.12 (December): S183–90.

Mangal, Jan. 2019. "My Work Is to Highlight Grand Theft of the People's Wealth, Main Opposition Poses Biggest Threat to Oil Future." *Stabroek News*, June 22. www.stabroeknews.com.

Mangru, Basdeo. 1987. "The Sex Ratio Disparity and Its Consequences under the Indenture in British Guiana." In *India in the Caribbean*, edited by David Dabydeen and Brinsley Samaroo, 211–30. London: Hansib.

———. 2013. "An Overview of Indentureship in Guyana, 1838–1917." *Stabroek News*, May 4. www.stabroeknews.com.

Mann, Andre. 2022. Interview by author. Zoom, New York City and Los Angeles. November 25.

Márquez, John D. 2013. *Black-Brown Solidarity: Racial Politics in the New Gulf South*. Austin: University of Texas Press.

McArdle, Mairead. 2020. "CNN Suggests Harris Is 'Presumed Frontrunner' for 2024, Biden May Serve Only One Term." *National Review*, November 2. www.nationalreview.com.

McClaurin, Irma, ed. 2001. *Black Feminist Anthropology: Theory, Politics, Praxis, and Poetics*. New Brunswick, NJ: Rutgers University Press.

McGreal, Chris. 2022. "'We Can't Eat a New Road': Guyanese Voice Fears over True Cost of Exxon's Oil Bonanza." *The Guardian*, May 12. www.theguardian.com.

McKittrick, Katherine. 2013. "Plantation Futures." *Small Axe* 17.3 (November): 1–15.

Mehta, Brinda. 2004. *Diasporic (Dis)locations: Indo-Caribbean Women Writers Negotiate the Kala Pani*. Kingston, Jamaica: University of the West Indies Press.

Mies, Maria, and Vandana Shiva. 2014 (1993). *Ecofeminism*. London: Zed Books.

Mintz, Sidney. 1982. "Sugar and Slavery." *New York Times*, January 17. www.nytimes.com.

———. 1985. *Sweetness and Power: The Place of Sugar in Modern History*. New York: Penguin Books.

Mowla, Wazim. 2020. "Guyana's Recount: Patience, Not Sanctions." *Global Americans*, May 21. https://theglobalamericans.org.

Mullings, Leith. 1997. *On Our Own Terms: Race, Class, and Gender in the Lives of African American Women*. New York: Routledge.

Munasinghe, Viranjini P. 2006. "Dougla Logics, Miscegenation, and the National Imaginary in Trinidad." *South Asian Review* 27.1: 204–32.

Nettles, Kimberly D. 2008. *Guyana Diaries: Women's Lives across Difference*. Walnut Creek, CA: Left Coast Press.

New York City Department of Human Planning. 2013. "The Newest New Yorkers: Characteristics of the City's Foreign-born Population." www1.nyc.gov.

*News Room*. 2020. "Henry Boys Were Killed Elsewhere and Dumped: All Suspects Released." September 14. https://newsroom.gy.

Niehoff, Arthur, and Juanita Niehoff. 1960. *East Indians in the West Indies*. Publications in Anthropology, vol. 6. Milwaukee, WI: Milwaukee Public Museum.

Nnadi, Chioma. 2022. "Oh, Baby! Rihanna's Plus One." *Vogue*, April 12. www.vogue.com.

Northe, Erin. 2019. "ExxonMobil Should Not Be Allowed to Influence What Should Be Critical National Issues." *Stabroek News*, September 19. www.stabroeknews.com.

Nunn, Jonathan. 2019. "Find the Soul of Elephant and Castle in Faye Gomes' Guyanese Pepper Pot." *London Eater*, May 10. https://london.eater.com.

Omi, Michael, and Howard Winant. 1994 (1986). *Racial Formation in the United States: From the 1960s to the 1980s*. New York: Routledge.

Panelli, Luis Fernando. 2019. "Is Guyana a New Oil El Dorado?" *Journal of World Energy Law and Business* 12.5 (October): 365–68. doi:10.1093/jwelb/jwz022.

Papannah, David. 2020. "Sand Mining, Overweight Vehicles Causing Erosion along Linden Highway." *Stabroek News*, March 2. www.stabroeknews.com.

Parisi, Kassie. 2018. "Guyanese Culture in Spotlight in Annual Schenectady Celebration." *Daily Gazette*, September 2. https://dailygazette.com.

Parsard, Kaneesha Cherelle. 2016. "Cutlass: Objects toward a Theory of Representation." In *Indo-Caribbean Feminist Thought: Genealogies, Theories, Enactments*, edited by Jamela Gabrielle Hosein and Lisa Outar, 241–60. New York: Palgrave Macmillan.

Parsram, Kemraj. 2022. "EPA Remains Silent on Alleged Violations in Issuance of Yellowtail Permit." *Stabroek News*, May 4. www.stabroeknews.com.

Peake, Linda, and D. Alissa Trotz. 1999. *Gender, Ethnicity, and Place: Women and Identities in Guyana*. London: Routledge.

Peduzzi, Pascal. 2014. "Sand, Rarer Than One Thinks: UNEP Global Environmental Alert Service (GEAS)." *Environmental Development* 11 (July): 208–18. doi:10.1016/j.envdev.2014.04.001.

Philadelphia, Nigel. 2020. "Silence over Broken Oil Promise and Mis-appointments." *Kaieteur News*, August 19. www.kaieteurnewsonline.com.

Platts, John T. 1930 (1884). *A Dictionary of Urdu, Classical Hindi, and English*. London: W.H. Allen.

Prashad, Vijay. 2001. *Everybody Was Kung Fu Fighting: Afro-Asian Connections and the Myth of Cultural Purity*. Boston: Beacon Press.

Puri, Shalini. 2004. *The Caribbean Postcolonial: Social Equality, Post-nationalism, and Cultural Hybridity*. New York: Palgrave Macmillan.

Rahim, Jennifer. 2010. "Dougla, Half-Doogla, Travesao, and the Limits of Hybridity." *Anthurium: A Caribbean Studies Journal* 7.1: 1–14.

Raleigh, Sir Walter. 1905 (1596). *The Discovery of Guiana*. London: Blackie and Son.

Reckin, Anna. 2003. "Tidalectic Lectures: Kamau Brathwaite's Prose/Poetry as Sound-Space." *Anthurium: A Caribbean Studies Journal* 1.1 (December): 1–16.

Reddock, Rhoda. 1994. "'Douglarisation' and the Politics of Gender Relations in Contemporary Trinidad and Tobago: A Preliminary Exploration." *Contemporary Issues in Social Sciences: A Caribbean Perspective* 1: 98–124.

———. 2014. "'Split Me in Two': Gender Identity and 'Race Mixing' in the Trinidad and Tobago Nation." In *Global Mixed Race*, edited by Rebecca C. King-O'Riain, Stephen Small, Minelle Mahtani, Miri Song, and Paul Spickard, 44–67. New York: New York University Press.

———. 2016. "Indo-Caribbean Masculinities and Indo-Caribbean Feminisms: Where Are We Now?" In *Indo-Caribbean Feminist Thought: Genealogies, Theories, Enact-*

*ments*, edited by Gabrielle Jamela Hosein and Lisa Outar, 225–40. New York: Palgrave Macmillan.

Redfield, Peter. 2000. *Space in the Tropics: From Convicts to Rockets in French Guiana.* Berkeley: University of California Press.

Regis, Ferne Louanne. 2011. "The *Dougla* in Trinidad's Consciousness." *History in Action* 2.1: 1–7.

Reuters. 2020. "Exxon Could Delay Third Guyana Project as Government Review Drags On." April 7. www.reuters.com.

———. 2022. "Factbox: Offshore Discoveries Turn Tiny Guyana into Oil Hotspot." February 16. www.reuters.com.

Richardson, Ben. 2019. "Booker's Bitter Legacy: British Guiana after Empire." *The Disorder of Things*, February 11. https://thedisorderofthings.com.

Rihanna. 2011. "Birthday Cake." By Terius Nash, Robyn Fenty, Marcos Palacios, and Ernest Clark. Def Jam.

——— (@rihanna). 2012. "Big up to my Guyanese people!!!" Twitter, August 7, 2012, 7:39 a.m. https://twitter.com/rihanna/status/232848512235220992.

Rodney, Walter. 1981. *A History of the Guyanese Working People, 1881–1905.* Baltimore, MD: Johns Hopkins University Press.

———. 2018 (1972). *How Europe Underdeveloped Africa.* London: Verso.

Rodrigues, Tatianna (@R_Tatianna). 2018. "So fortunate to have an entitled, privileged, & disconnected foreign white man speak for the people of Guyana. Thank you @ krauss massa, we are lost without you. @nytimes we could do without the neocolonial undertones next time, ok? Find local writers." Twitter, July, 2018, 3:15 p.m. https://twitter.com/R_Tatianna/status/1022606388969779200.

Rohlehr, Gordon. 1988. "Images of Men and Women in 1930s Calypsos: The Sociology of Food Acquisition in a Context of Survivalism." In *Gender in Caribbean Development: Papers Presented at the Inaugural Seminar of the University of the West Indies Women and Development Studies Project*, edited by Patricia Mohamed and Catherine Shepherd, 223–89. Kingston, Jamaica: University of the West Indies Press.

Rollins, Scott. 2000. "Eddy Grant Talks about Ringbang." *Zeeburg Nieuws.* https://web.archive.org.

Salleh, Ariel. 2014. Forward to *Ecofeminism*, by Maria Mies and Vandana Shiva, ix–xii. London: Zed Books.

Scott, David. 2000. "The Re-Enchantment of Humanism: An Interview with Sylvia Wynter." *Small Axe* 8 (September): 119–207.

Scott, Sydney. 2020. "Rihanna Has a Message for Black Women at 2019 Diamond Ball: 'We Are Impeccable.'" *Essence*, December 6. www.essence.com.

Sekhani, Richa. 2017. "Poverty Facts: Almost 4 in 10 Guyanese Cannot Afford Basic Cost of Living." Guyana Budget & Policy Institute, August. https://gbpi.institute.

Sellin, Paul R. 2011. *Treasure, Treason, and the Tower: El Dorado and the Murder of Sir Walter Raleigh.* Burlington, VT: Ashgate.

Shah, Nayan. 2011. *Stranger Intimacy: Contesting Race, Sexuality, and the Law in the North American West.* Berkeley: University of California Press.

Sharpe, Christina. 2016. *In the Wake: On Blackness and Being*. Durham, NC: Duke University Press.

Sharpe, Jenny. 2020. *Immaterial Archives: An African Diaspora Poetics of Loss*. Evanston, IL: Northwestern University Press.

Sheller, Mimi. 2020. *Island Futures: Caribbean Survival in the Anthropocene*. Durham, NC: Duke University Press.

Shepherd, Verene A. 2002. *Maharani's Misery: Narratives of a Passage from India to the Caribbean*. Kingston, Jamaica: University of the West Indies Press.

Shibata, Yoshiko. 2002. "Intermarriage, 'Douglas,' Creolization of Indians in Contemporary Guyana: The Rocky Road of Ambiguity and Ambivalence." *JCAS Symposium Series* 13: 193–228.

Simmons, Kimberly. 2001. "A Passion for Sameness: Encountering a Black Feminist Self in Fieldwork in the Dominican Republic." In *Black Feminist Anthropology: Theory, Politics, Praxis, and Poetics*, edited by Irma McClaurin, 77–101. New Brunswick, NJ: Rutgers University Press.

Simpson, Audra. 2007. "On Ethnographic Refusal: Indigeneity, 'Voice,' and Colonial Citizenship." *Junctures* 9 (December): 67–80.

Simpson, M. C., et al. 2012. "CARIBSAVE Climate Change Risk Atlas (CCCRA)—St. Vincent and the Grenadines." Barbados: DFID, AusAID, and The CARIBSAVE Partnership.

Slocum, Karla. 2001. "Negotiating Identity and Black Feminist Politics in Caribbean Research." In *Black Feminist Anthropology: Theory, Politics, Praxis, and Poetics*, edited by Irma McClaurin, 126–49. New Brunswick, NJ: Rutgers University Press.

Smith, Raymond T. 1956. *The Negro Family in British Guiana*. New York: Humanities Press.

Smyth, Heather. 2014. "The Black Atlantic Meets the Black Pacific: Multimodality in Kamau Brathwaite and Wayde Compton." *Callaloo* 37.2 (Spring): 389–403.

Sohan, Charles. 2018. "Strip of Beach Could Not Be Classified as Private Property." *Stabroek News*, January 1. www.stabroeknews.com.

Solomon, Alva. 2019. "Venezuelans in Guyana Grapple with Wage Slavery." *Caribbean Investigative Journalism Network*, December 5. www.cijn.org.

Spillers, Hortense. 1987. "Mama's Baby, Papa's Maybe: An American Grammar Book." *Diacritics* 17.2 (Summer): 65–81.

Squire, Corinne. 2015. "Partial Secrets." *Current Anthropology* 56.S12 (December): S201–10.

*Stabroek News*. 2006. "The Dougla Identity." September 30. www.landofsixpeoples.com.

———. 2009. "Consulate Instructed to Follow-Up Reports of Barbados Raids." June 25. www.stabroeknews.com.

———. 2016. "Indian, African-Guyanese Numbers Continue to Decline, Census Finds: Mixed Race, Amerindian Populations Still Growing." July 19. www.stabroeknews.com.

———. 2018. "Guyanese 'Extra and Proud' at 'Black Panther' opening." February 24. www.stabroeknews.com.

———. 2022a. "Sand." May 2. www.stabroeknews.com.

———. 2022b. "'Extensive Consultations' Held with Fisherfolk prior to Demerara Dredging Activities—NRG Holdings." July 10. www.stabroeknews.com.

———. 2022c. "IT Manager Found behind Marriott Died of Drowning." March 10. www.stabroeknews.com.

Sutherland, Gaulbert. 2009. "Song about Guyanese Women Creating Uproar in Barbados." *Stabroek News*, June 22. www.stabroeknews.com.

Sutherland, Laurel. 2022. "Dozens of Fishers Said to Be Affected by Dredging of Demerara River Mouth." *Stabroek News*, August 5. www.stabroeknews.com.

Swan, Michael. 1957. *British Guiana: The Land of Six Peoples*. London: H.M. Stationery Office.

Tamboli, Vikram. 2019. "Hustling Fuel, Striking Gold: Smuggling in the Guyanese-Venezuelan Border." *NACLA Report on the Americas* 51.4: 422–32.

Taussig, Michael. 1999. *Defacement: Public Secrecy and the Labor of the Negative*. Stanford, CA: Stanford University Press.

Theoharis, Jeanne, Joseph Entin, and Dominick Braswell. 2020. "Autoethnographies of a Pandemic from Brooklyn's Epicenter." *Black Perspectives*, October 12. www.aaihs.org.

Thomas, Deborah A. 2004. *Modern Blackness: Nationalism, Globalization, and the Politics of Culture in Jamaica*. Durham, NC: Duke University Press.

———. 2011. *Exceptional Violence: Embodied Citizenship in Transnational Jamaica*. Durham, NC: Duke University Press.

Tripadvisor. 2016. "Top 10 Travelers' Choice Beaches in the World." February 17. Tripadvisor.com.

Trotz, D. Alissa. 2003. "Behind the Banner of Culture? Gender, Race, and Family in Guyana." *New West Indian Guide/Nieuwe West-Indische Gids* 77.1–2 (January): 5–29.

———, ed. 2020. *The Point Is to Change the World: Selected Writings of Andaiye*. London: Pluto Press.

Trotz, D. Alissa, and Arif Bulkan. 2020. "Guyana's Political Tragedy." *Stabroek News*, June 30. www.stabroeknews.com.

Trotz, Ulric (Neville). 2022a. "Guyana's Sand Deposits." *Stabroek News*, May 9. www.stabroeknews.com

———. 2022b. Interview by author. Zoom, Miami and Los Angeles. June 15, 2022.

Trouillot, Michel-Rolph. 1995. *Silencing the Past: Power and the Production of History*. Boston: Beacon Press.

Tsing, Anna Lowenhaupt. 2005. *Friction: An Ethnography of Global Connection*. Princeton, NJ: Princeton University Press.

Ulysse, Gina Athena. 2007. *Downtown Ladies: Informal Commercial Importers, a Haitian Anthropologist, and Self-Making in Jamaica*. Chicago: University of Chicago Press.

———. 2015. *Why Haiti Needs New Narratives: A Post-Quake Chronicle*. Middletown, CT: Wesleyan University Press.

UNEP (UN Environment Programme). 2022. "Sand and Sustainability: 10 Strategic Recommendations to Avert a Crisis." Geneva: GRID-Geneva, United Nations Environment Programme.

Urry, John. 2002. *The Tourist Gaze*. London: Sage.

US Department of State. 2020. "Trafficking in Persons Report, 20th Edition." June. www.state.gov.

*U.S. News & World Report*. 2017. "Best Caribbean Beaches." https://travel.usnews.com.

Valle, Sabrina. 2022. "Exxon Makes Three New Oil Discoveries in Guyana and Boosts Reserves." *Reuters*, April 26. www.reuters.com.

Vaughn, Sarah E. 2022. *Engineering Vulnerability: In Pursuit of Climate Adaptation*. Durham, NC: Duke University Press.

Wallace, Michele. 2008. *Invisibility Blues: From Pop to Theory*. London: Verso.

Walmsley, Anne. 1994. "Her Stem Singing: Kamau Brathwaite's *Zea Mexican Diary: 7 Sept 1926–7 Sept 1986*." *World Literature Today* 68.4 (Autumn): 747–49.

Watts, Jonathan. 2019. "Resource Extraction Responsible for Half of World's Carbon Emissions." *The Guardian*, March 12. www.theguardian.com.

Wekker, Gloria. 2016. *White Innocence: Paradoxes of Colonialism and Race*. Durham, NC: Duke University Press.

Welland, Michael. 2009. *Sand: The Never-Ending Story*. Berkeley: University of California Press.

Westfall, Sammy, and Ana Vanessa Herrero. 2023. "Oil Revives Bulk of Venezuelan Claim to Neighbor Guyana." *Washington Post*, February 15. www.washingtonpost.com.

Williams, Brackette F. 1991. *Stains on My Name, War in My Veins: Guyana and the Politics of Cultural Struggle*. Durham, NC: Duke University Press.

Wilson, Peter. 1973. *Crab Antics: The Social Anthropology of English-Speaking Negro Societies of the Caribbean*. New Haven, CT: Yale University Press.

World Health Organization. 2018. "Global Status Report on Alcohol and Health 2018." Geneva: World Health Organization.

Wright, Michelle M. 2004. *Becoming Black: Creating Identity in the African Diaspora*. Durham, NC: Duke University Press.

Wynter, Sylvia. 1995. "1492: A New World View." In *Race, Discourse, and the Origin of the Americas: A New World View*, edited by Vera Lawrence Hyatt and Rex Nettleford, 1–57. Washington, DC: Smithsonian Institution Press.

———. 2003. "Unsettling the Coloniality of Being/Power/Truth/Freedom: Towards the Human, after Man, Its Overrepresentation—An Argument." *CR: The New Centennial Review* 3.3 (Fall): 257–337.

Wynter, Sylvia, and Katherine McKittrick. 2015. "Unparalleled Catastrophe for Our Species?: or, To Give Humanness a Different Future: Conversations." In *Sylvia Wynter: On Being Human as Praxis*, edited by Katherine McKittrick, 9–89. Durham, NC: Duke University Press.

Yahya-Sakur, Nafeeza, and Anatoly Kurmanaev. 2020. "Killings Reignite Racial Tensions in Guyana." *New York Times*, September 10. www.nytimes.com.

# INDEX

Page numbers in italics refer to illustrations.

ecological erosion and, xv (*see also* erosion); ethnic conflict and, 180; gendered impacts, 32–33; impact on Amerindians, 136–37; race/gender constructions and, 87; sex trafficking in, xiv, 121, 137–39, 179. *See also* oil; sand mining

ExxonMobil: contract with Guyana, 161, 166–67; environmental safety and, 32, 151, 159; Guyana's election conflict and, 165; offshore oil rigs, 149, 151; oil discoveries in Guyana, 2, 6, 145, 155; Tillerson and, 163, 205n11; US State Department and, 163; Yellowtail Development Project, 204n3

Exxon Valdez oil spill, 159

family, 5, 28, 180; secrets, 29–30, 38, 73–74. *See also* autoethnographic kinship formation; interracial relationships; kinship formations; marriage

Farley, Rawle, 84

feminism: Black feminist anthropology, 26–28; ecofeminism, 33, 135; global, 179–80; Indo-Caribbean feminist literature, 47–48

Fenty, Ronald, 103

fishing, 150–51

floods, 21, 193n22

forestry, 66

French Guiana, 4, 34, 156

Gates, Henry Louis, Jr., 194n2

Gaunt, Kyra, 115

gender. *See* global race/gender constructs

gendered violence: capitalism and, 179; colonialism and, 193n16; cutlass as symbol of, 69–70, 206n12; erasure of, 172–73; extractive industries and, 32, 132, 135–39; intimate partner violence, 3, 69–70, 114, 117; kidnapping of Indian women and girls, 61, 63–64; race and, 12; transgressive relationships and, 73

Gene (author's aunt), xiii, 76, 77–78, 81–82, 175–76, 195n5

genealogy, 26–28, 38, 67, 101, 107, 117, 198n25, 199n39

Georgetown: academic representations of, 19–20; Afro-Guyanese population, 53; development in, 192n11; Dutch colonial architecture, 34–35, 141; international representations of, 13–14, 87; nicknamed "GT," 93; oil industry and, 149

Gest, Justin, 163–64

Ghatumphore (Ghatampur), 63

Gilroy, Paul, 115

Glissant, Édouard, 142

global race/gender constructs, viii–ix, 1–2, 5, 32, 38, 44–45; contestation of gender norms, 106; defined, 16–17; interracial relationships in colonial era, xv, 66–87; racialized misogyny, 103–4; sand and, 88, 120–21. *See also* Afro-Guyanese women; Bajan (Barbadian) women; Guyanese women; Indo-Guyanese women

global racial capitalism: Afro-Asian identity and, 39 (*see also* Dougla identity); classificatory systems, 28; environmental impacts of, 3, 15, 32; Guyanese social constructions and, ix; impact on women's lives, xiv, 138, 173, 178–79; labor and, 206n2; national development and, 123; race/gender constructions and, 87; sand exportation, 131–32. *See also* extractive industries

gold, 17, 66, 76, 128, 136, 139, 144, 157–58, 179, 190n5. *See also* El Dorado (lost city of gold)

Gomes, Faye, 191n10

*Gordon Ramsay: Uncharted* (National Geographic), 10, 13–16, 19, 20, 24, 157, 193n18

Granger, David, 161–67, 170, 205n10

# ABOUT THE AUTHOR

ONEKA LABENNETT is Associate Professor of American Studies and Ethnicity and Gender and Sexuality Studies at the University of Southern California. She is the author of *She's Mad Real: Popular Culture and West Indian Girls in Brooklyn* and coeditor of *Racial Formation in the Twenty-First Century*.